ultimateGuitar®
TAB TREASURE CHEST

ISBN 978-1-4584-1806-7

HAL•LEONARD®
CORPORATION
7777 W. BLUEMOUND RD. P.O. BOX 13819 MILWAUKEE, WI 53213

Visit Hal Leonard Online at
www.halleonard.com

CONTENTS

All the Small Things

Words and Music by Tom De Longe and Mark Hoppus

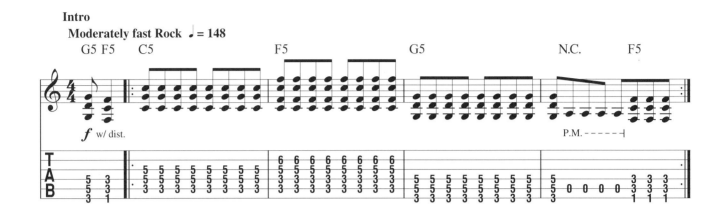

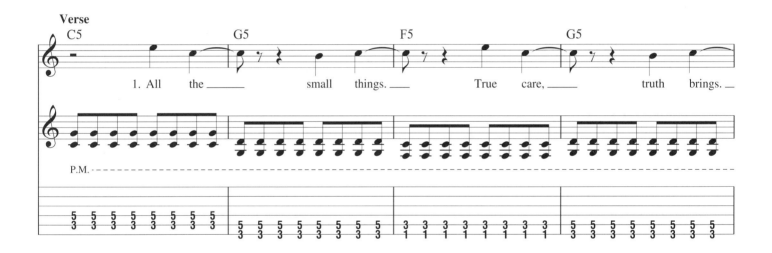

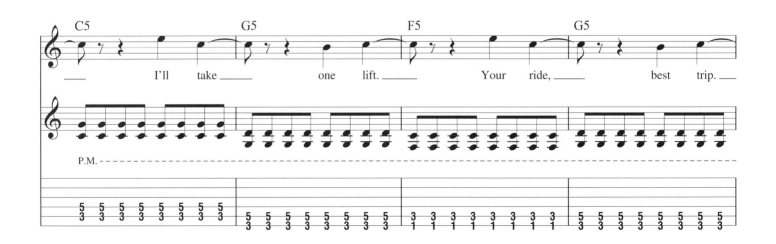

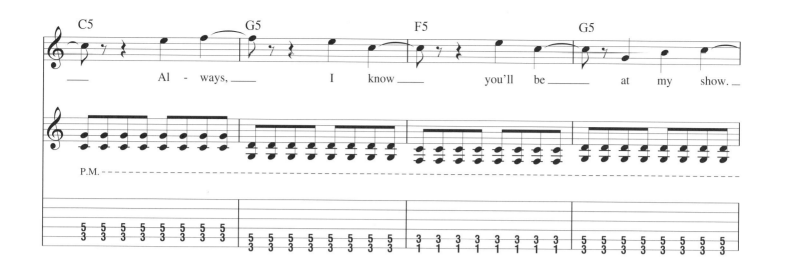

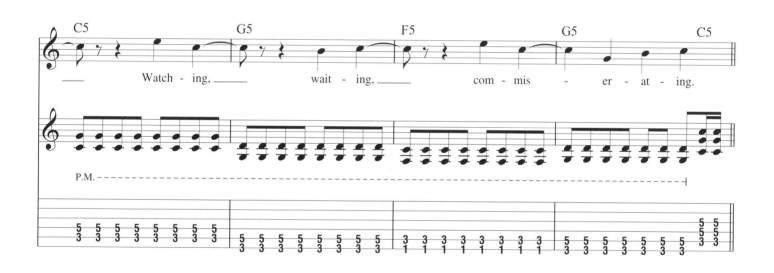

𝄋 Pre-Chorus

Chorus

To Coda ⊕

Interlude

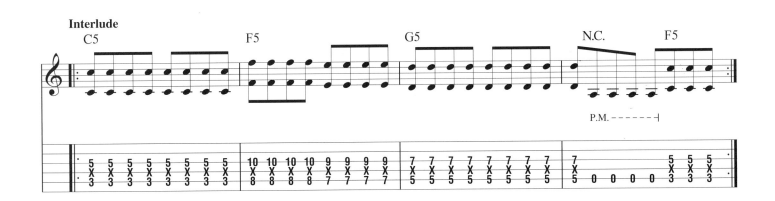

6

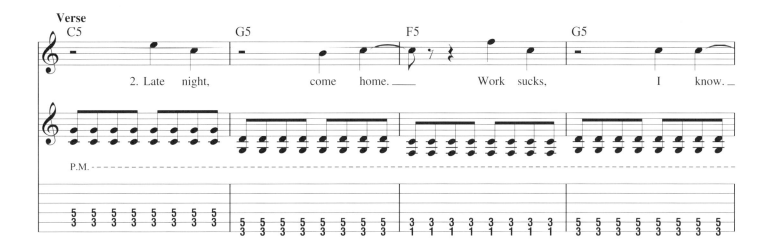

Verse

2. Late night, come home. ____ Work sucks, I know. _

D.S. al Coda

____ She left me ros - es by the stairs. _ Sur - pris - es let me know she cares. _

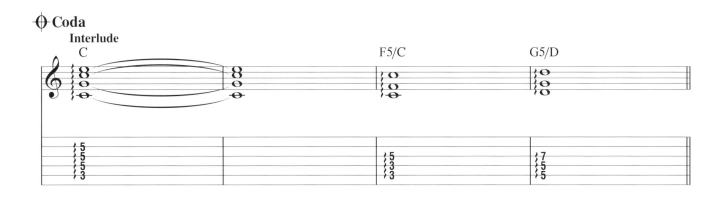

Coda

Interlude

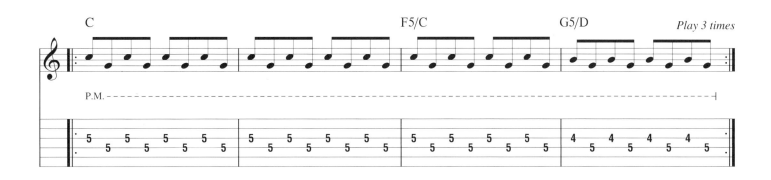

Play 3 times

Outro

Say it ain't so. I will not ___ go. Turn the lights ___

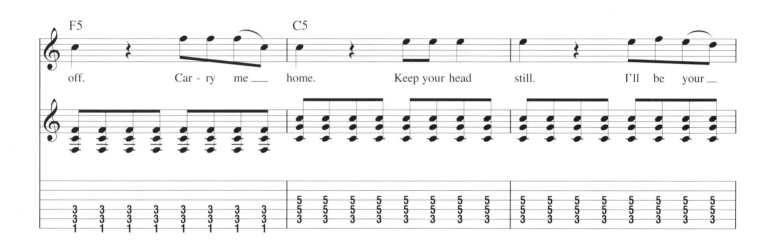

off. Car - ry me ___ home. Keep your head still. I'll be your ___

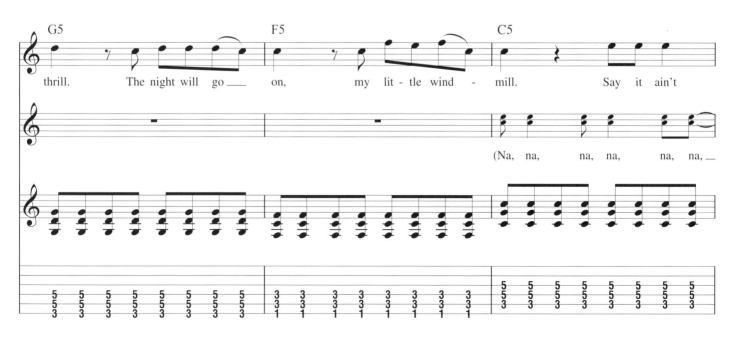

thrill. The night will go ___ on, my lit - tle wind - mill. Say it ain't

(Na, na, na, na, na, na, ___

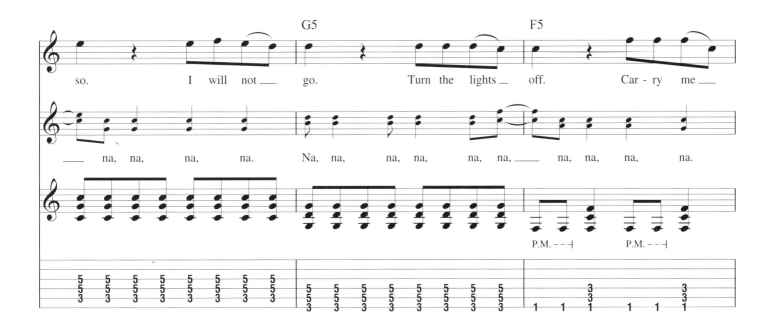

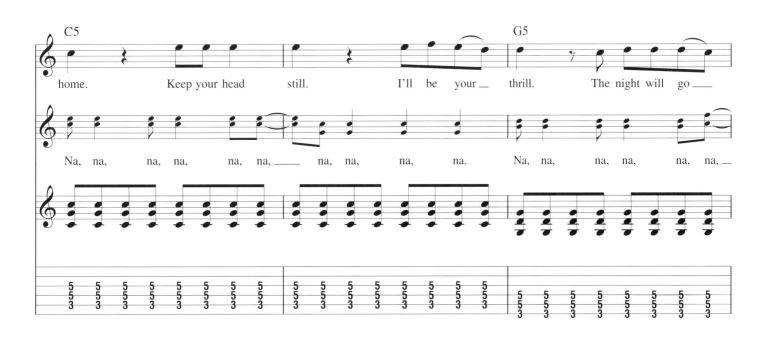

Blackbird

Words and Music by John Lennon and Paul McCartney

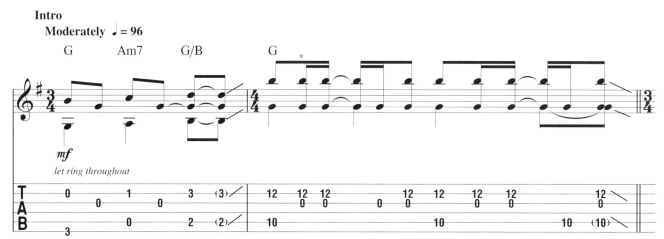

*Strum upstemmed notes w/ index finger of pick hand whenever more than one upstemmed note appears.

1., 2., 3. Black - bird sing - ing in the dead of night,

{ 1., 3. take _ these bro - ken wings _ and learn _ to fly. _ }
{ 2. take _ these sunk - en eyes _ and learn _ to see. _ }

All your life,

you were on - ly wait - ing for the mo - ment to a - rise.

- ment to be free. Black - bird fly,

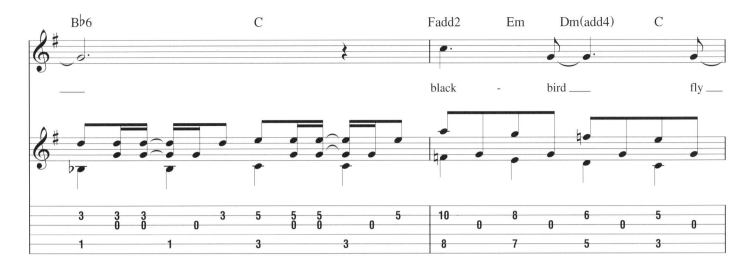

To Coda 1

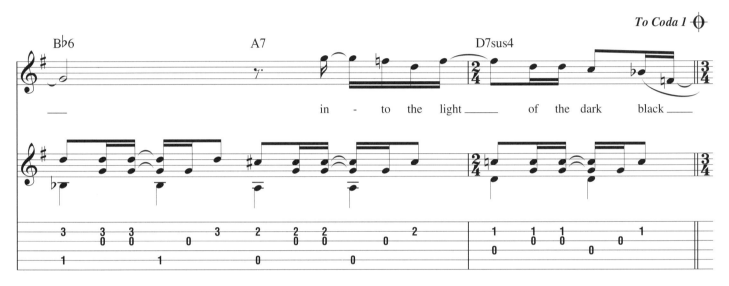

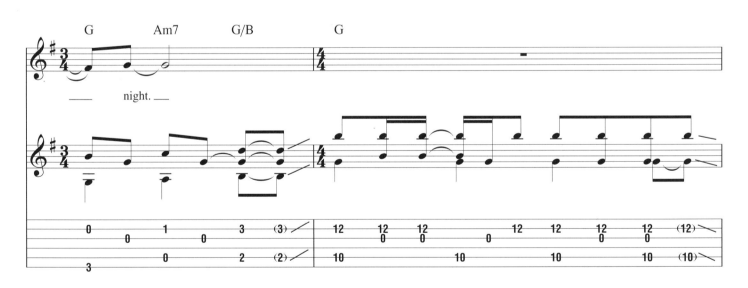

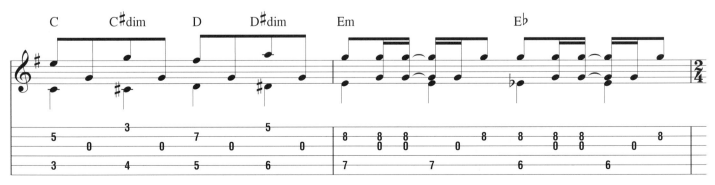

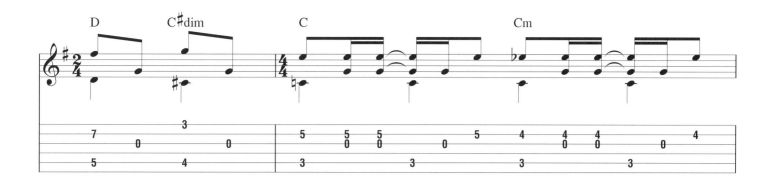

D.S. al Coda 1

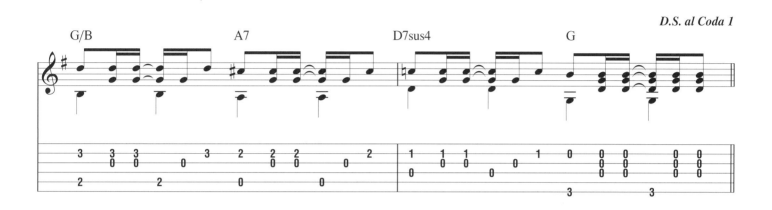

$\oplus$ **Coda 1**

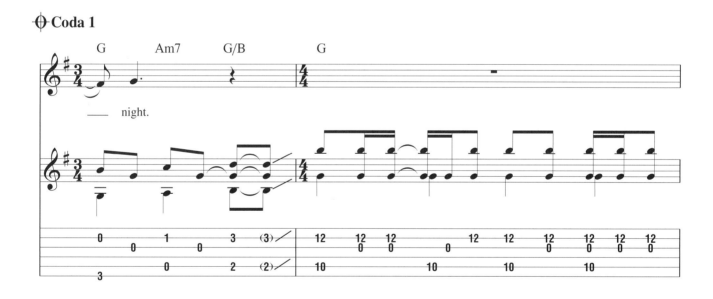

— night.

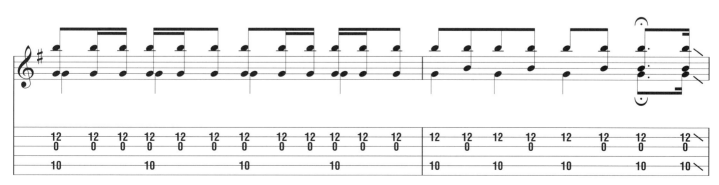

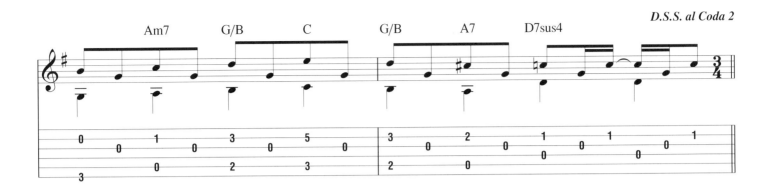

Coda 2

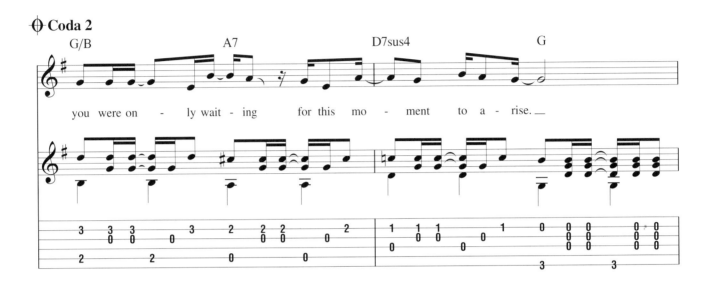

you were on - ly wait - ing   for this mo - ment to a - rise.__

You were on - ly __ wait - ing   for this mo - ment to a - rise._____

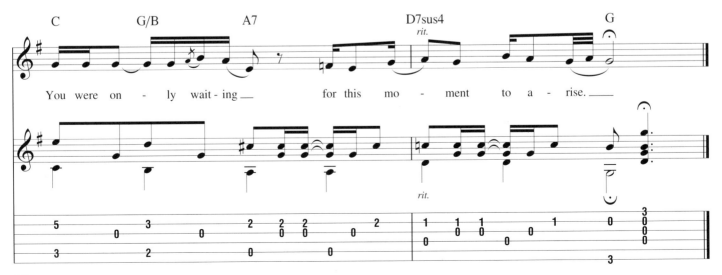

You were on - ly wait - ing __   for this mo - ment to a - rise._____

Bohemian Rhapsody

Words and Music by Freddie Mercury

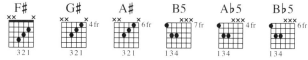

*Piano arr. for gtr.

*T = Thumb on ⑥

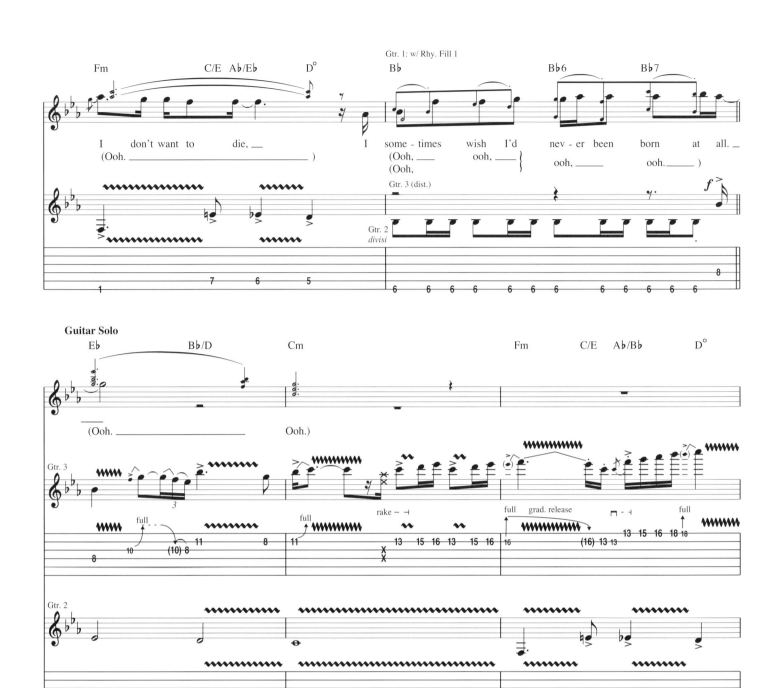

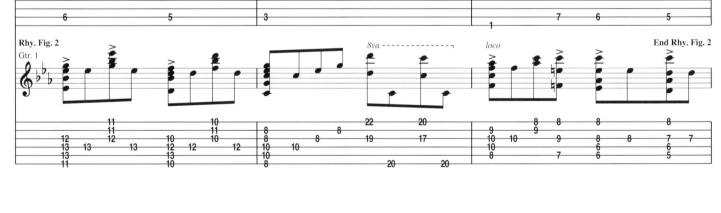

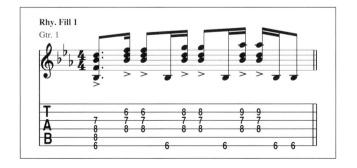

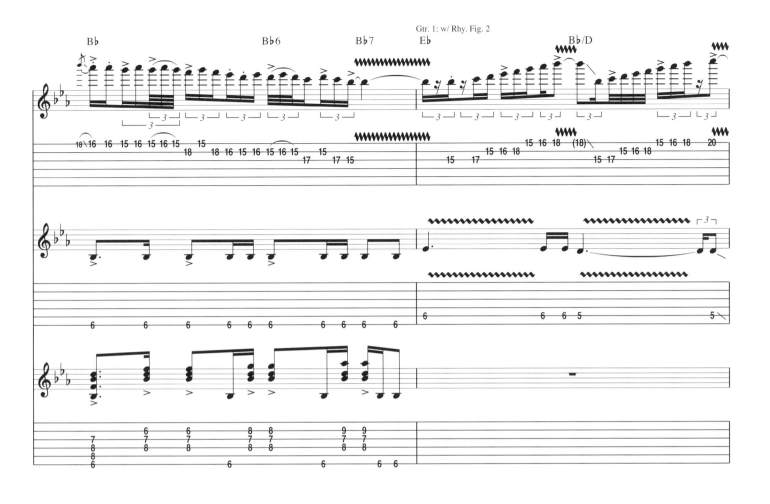

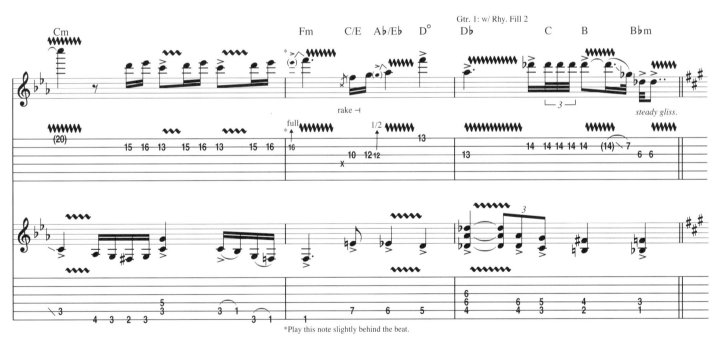

*Play this note slightly behind the beat.

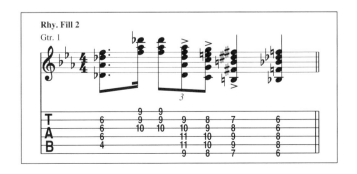

*Each of these notes is sung by a separate voice,
and each sustains into the next meas.

20

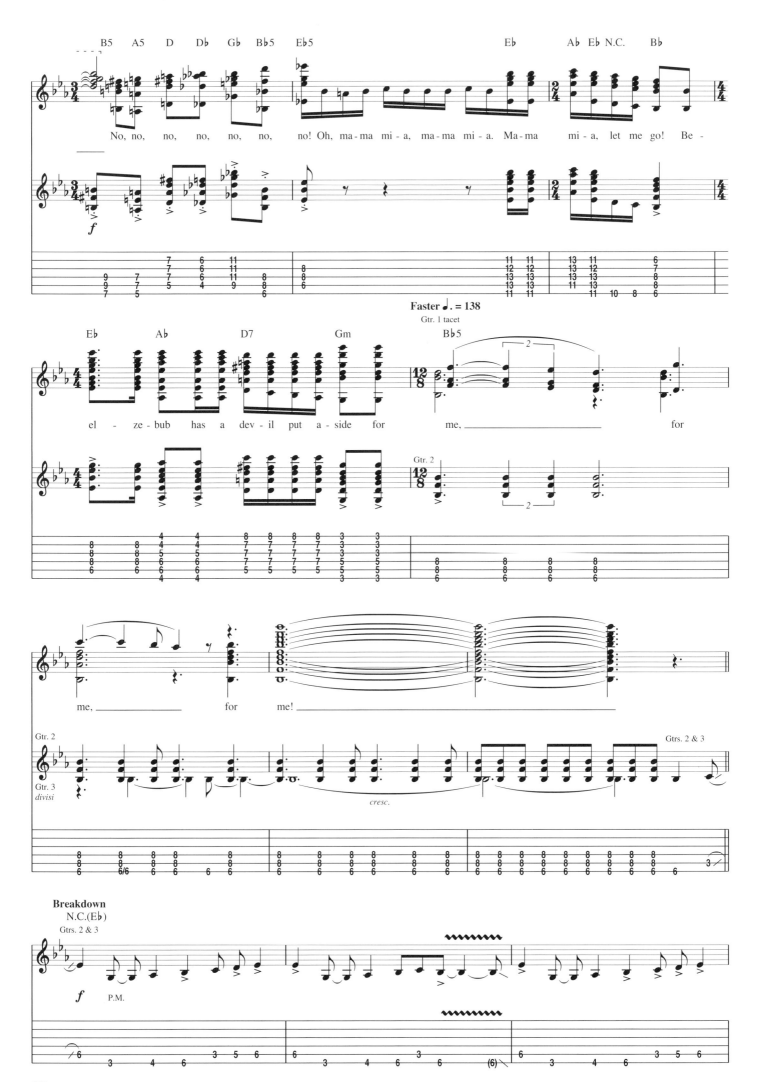

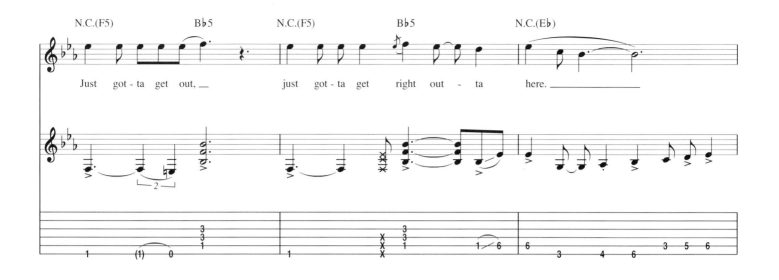

Just got-ta get out, ___ just got-ta get right out-ta here. _____

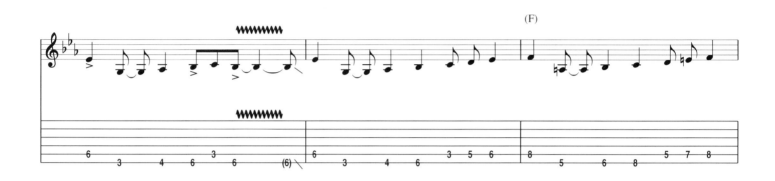

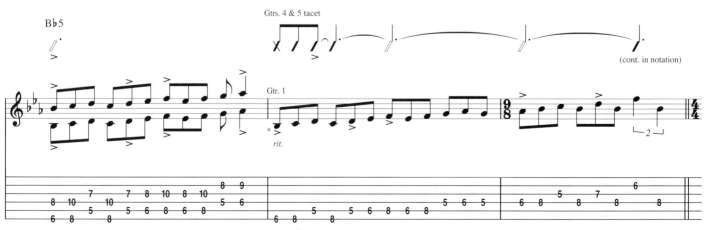

*Doubled by lower octave on recording.

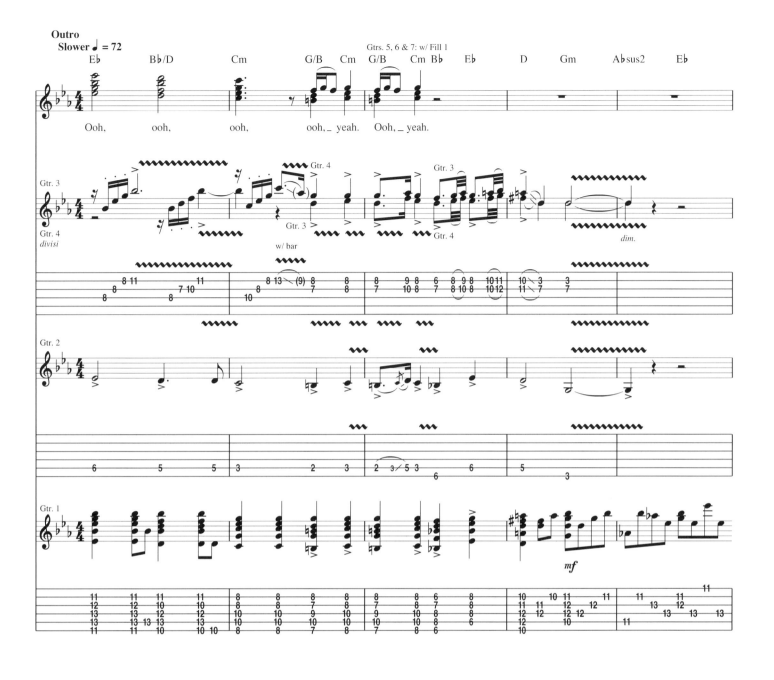

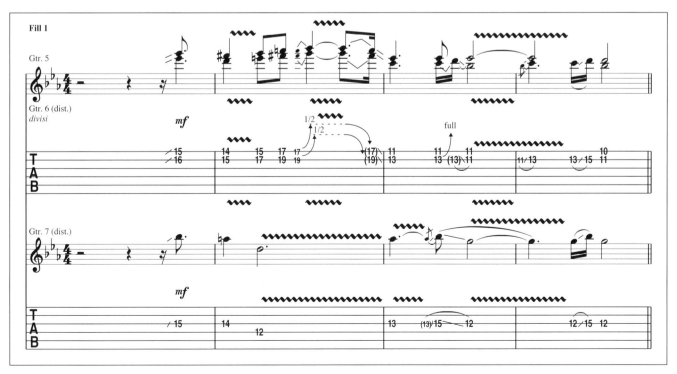

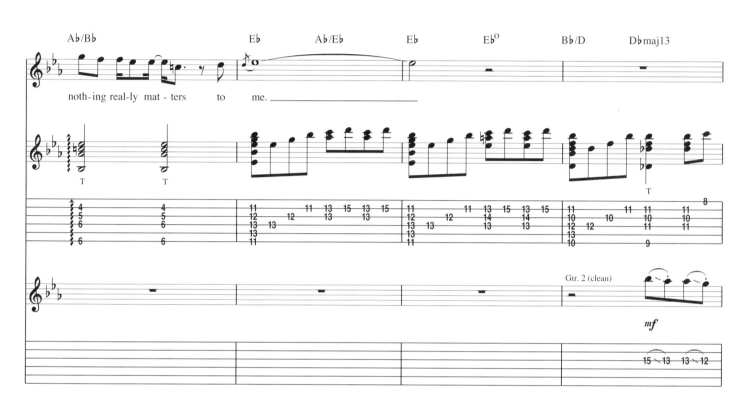

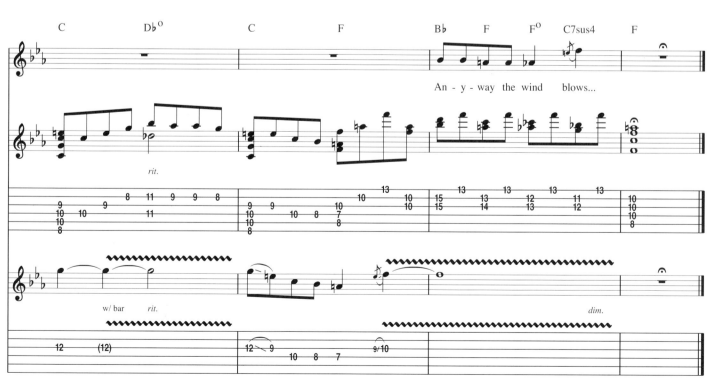

Born to Be Wild

Words and Music by Mars Bonfire

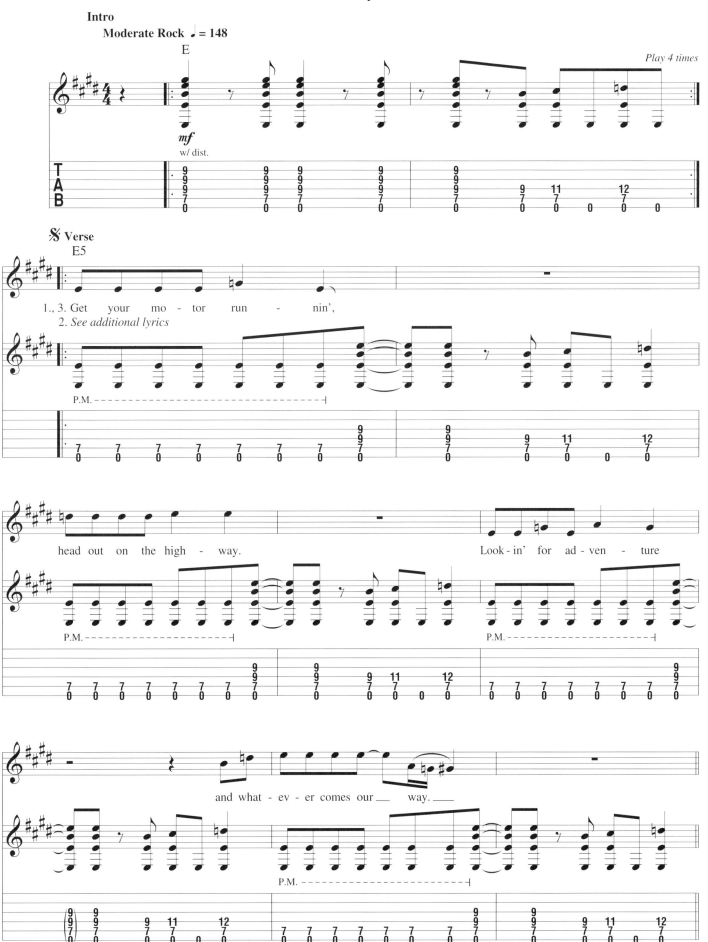

Pre-Chorus

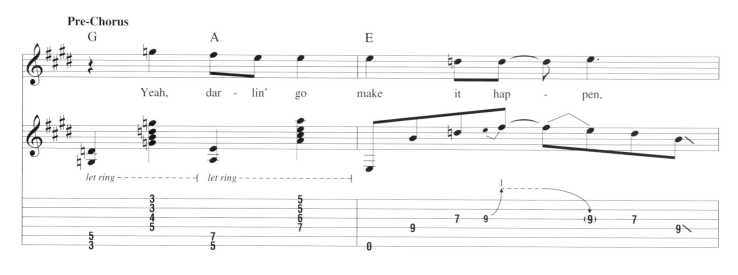

Yeah, dar - lin' go make it hap - pen,

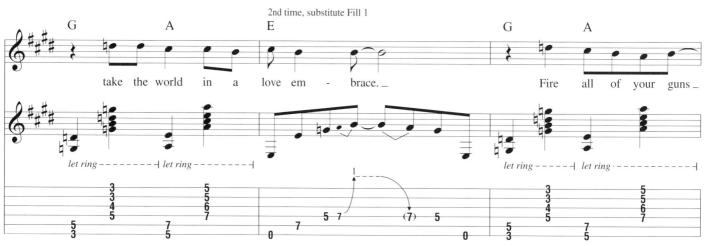

take the world in a love em - brace. _____ Fire all of your guns _____

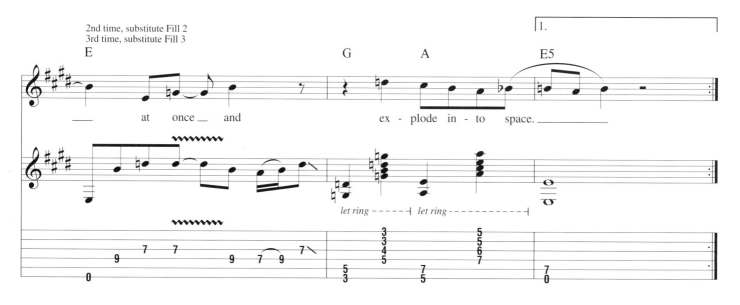

_____ at once _____ and ex - plode in - to space. _____

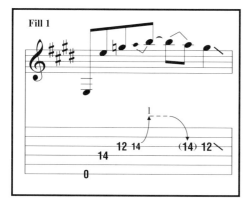

Fill 1

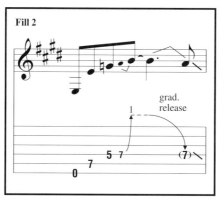

Fill 2

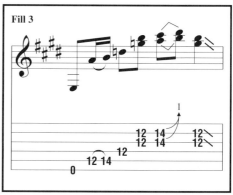

Fill 3

Additional Lyrics

2. I like smoke and lightning,
   Heavy metal thunder,
   Racin' with the wind,
   And the feelin' that I'm under.

Cause We've Ended as Lovers

Words and Music by Stevie Wonder

* Vol. swell

** Push down on string behind nut.

† Played w/ ring finger.

* Behind nut

grad. release

** As before

† As before

* Hammer onto note while manipulating vol. knob.

* Both strings caught and bent w/ ring finger.

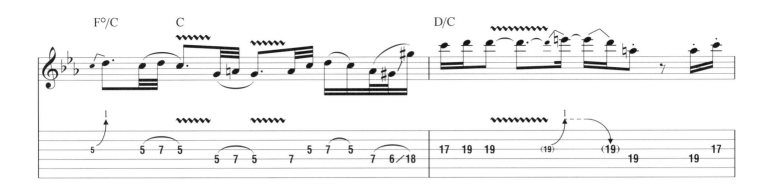

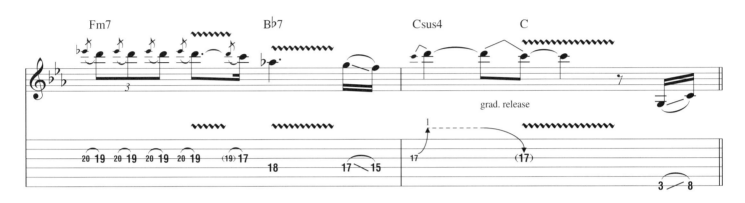

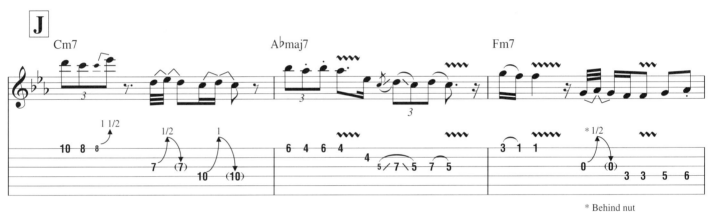

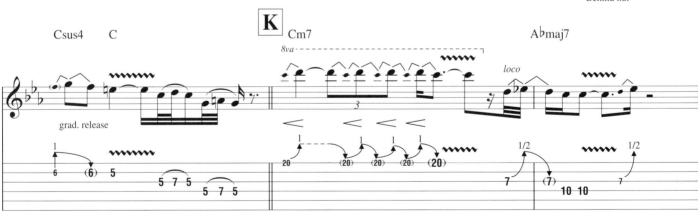

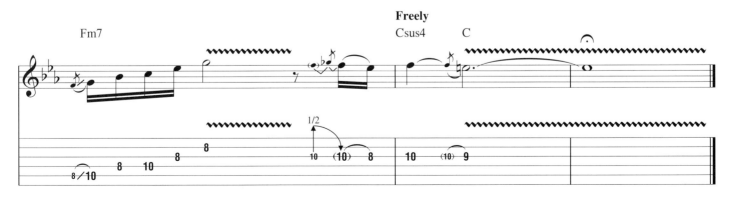

Cherry Pie

Words and Music by Jani Lane

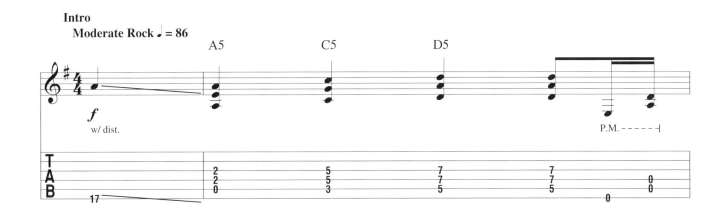

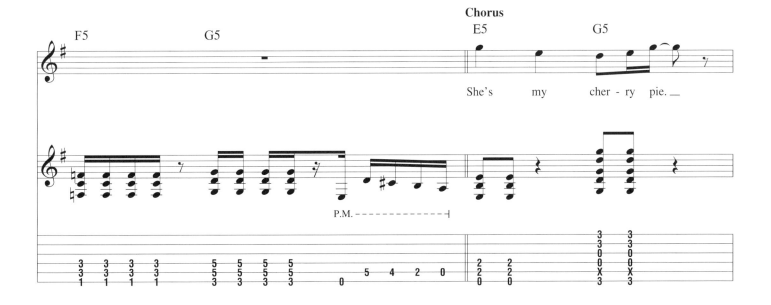

She's my cher - ry pie. _

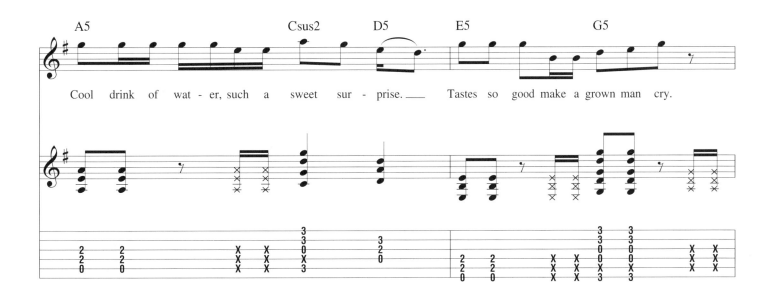

Cool drink of wat - er, such a sweet sur - prise. _ Tastes so good make a grown man cry.

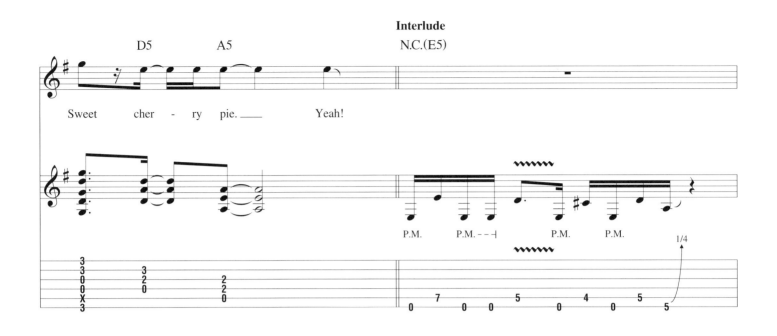

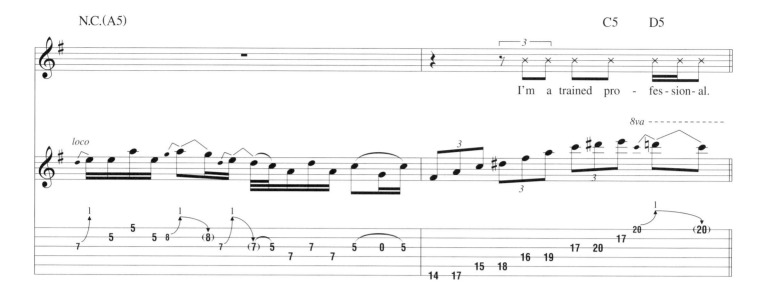

I'm a trained pro - fes - sion - al.

Verse

4. Swing-in' in the bath-room, swing-in' on the floor. Swing-in' so hard, _ for-got to lock the door. _

In walk her dad-dy stand-in' six foot four, said, "You ain't gon-na swing with my daugh-ter no more."

Outro-Chorus

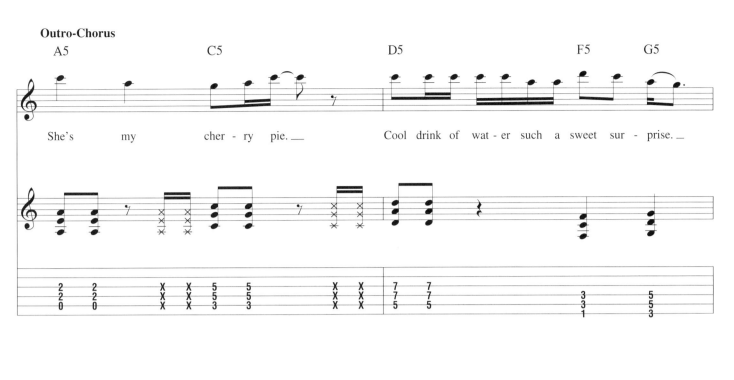

She's my cher - ry pie. __ Cool drink of wat - er such a sweet sur - prise. __

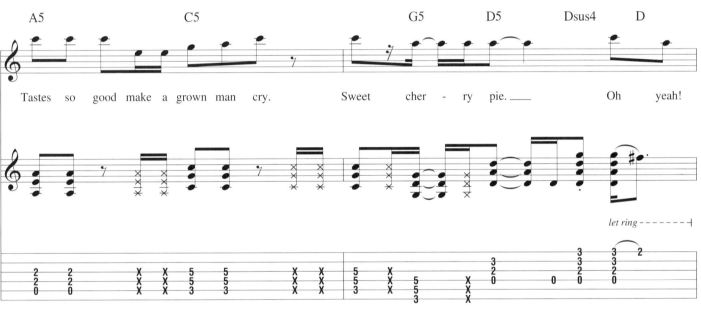

Tastes so good make a grown man cry. Sweet cher - ry pie. __ Oh yeah!

let ring - - - - - - -

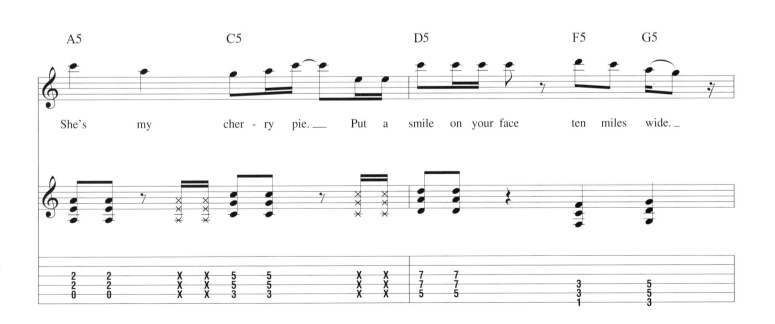

She's my cher - ry pie. __ Put a smile on your face ten miles wide. __

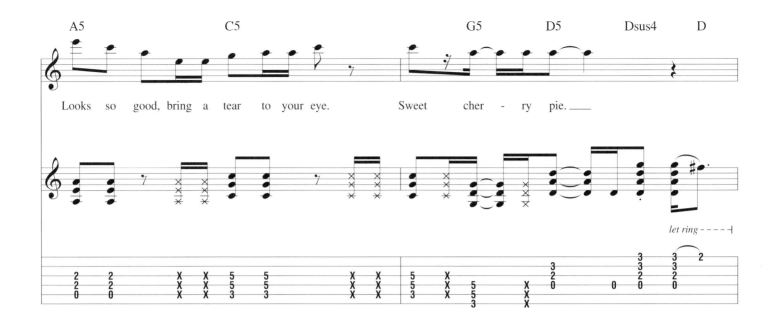

Looks so good, bring a tear to your eye. Sweet cher - ry pie. ___

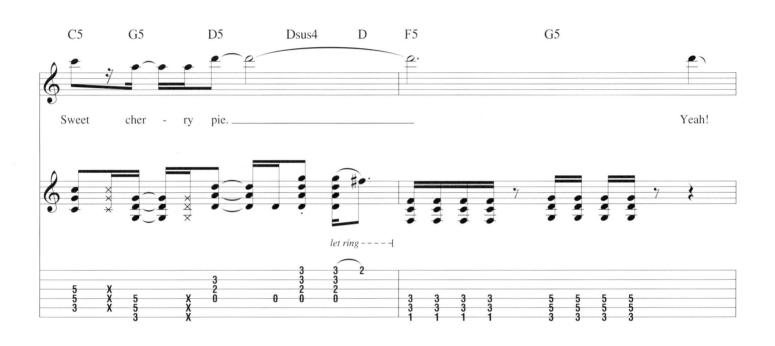

Sweet cher - ry pie. ___ Yeah!

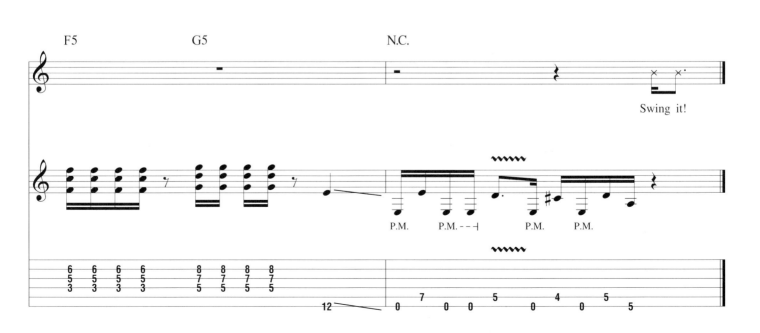

Swing it!

Creep

Words and Music by Albert Hammond, Mike Hazlewood, Thomas Yorke, Richard Greenwood, Philip Selway, Colin Greenwood and Edward O'Brian

Intro

Moderately slow ♩ = 80

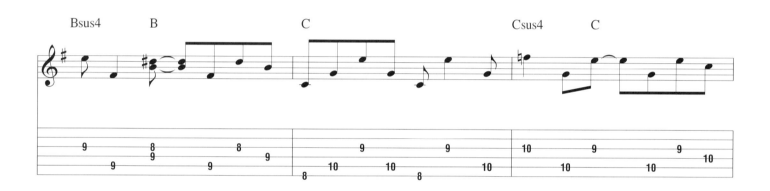

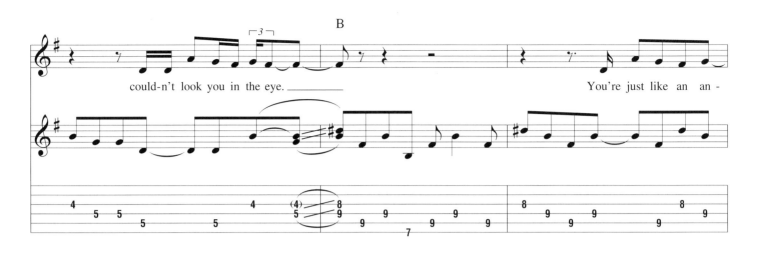

could-n't look you in the eye. _____ You're just like an an -

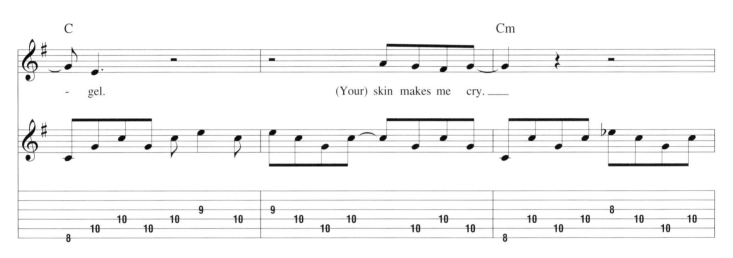

- gel. (Your) skin makes me cry. ____

You float like a feath - er _____ in a beau-ti-ful world. __

I wish I was spe - cial.

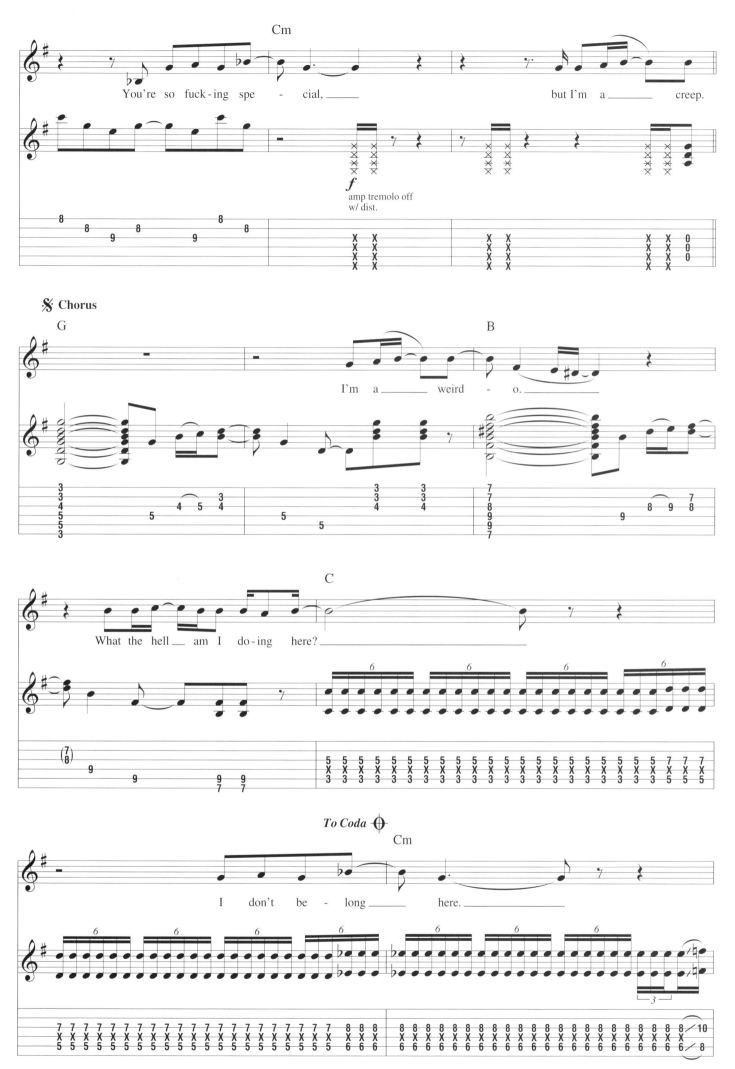

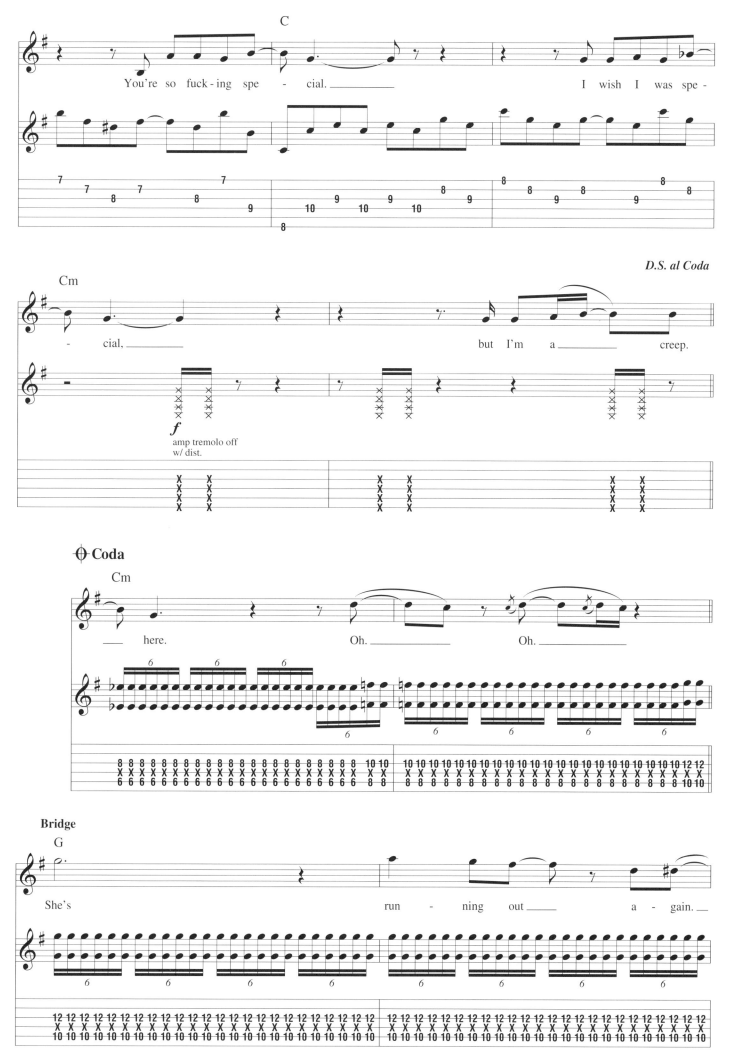

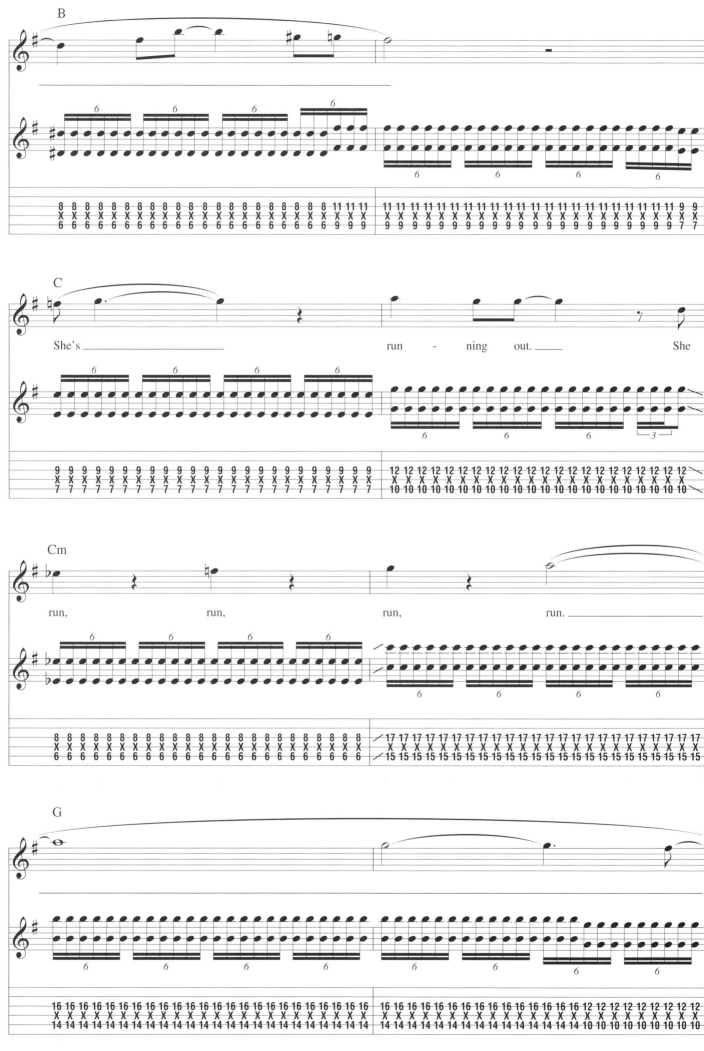

- cial. I wish I was spe - cial,

Outro-Chorus

but I'm a _____ creep. I'm a _____ weird-

- o. _____ What the hell am I do-ing here? _____

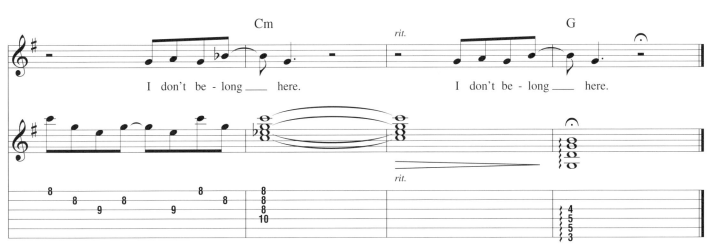

I don't be - long _____ here. I don't be - long _____ here.

Dream On

Words and Music by Steven Tyler

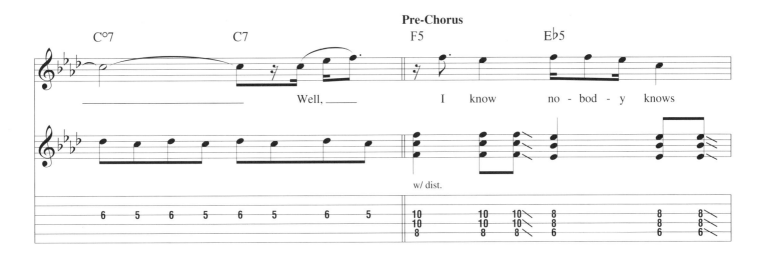

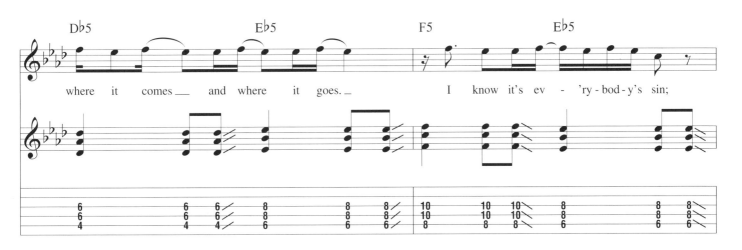

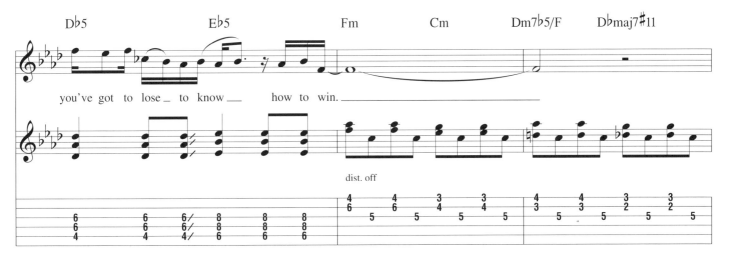

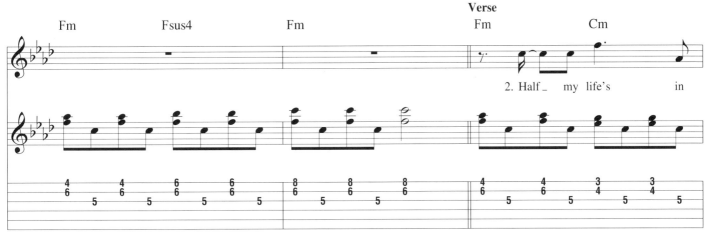

may-be to-mor-row the good Lord will take you a-way.

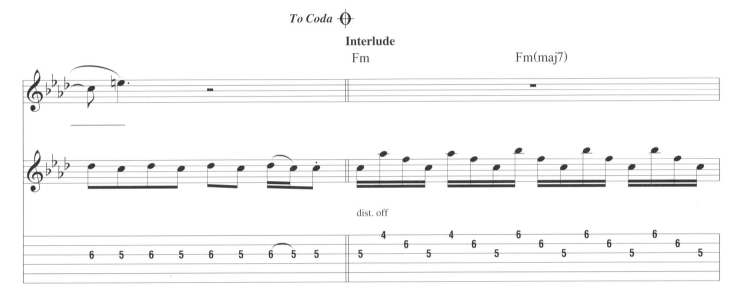

To Coda

Interlude

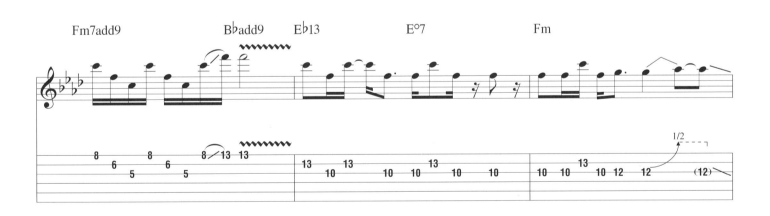

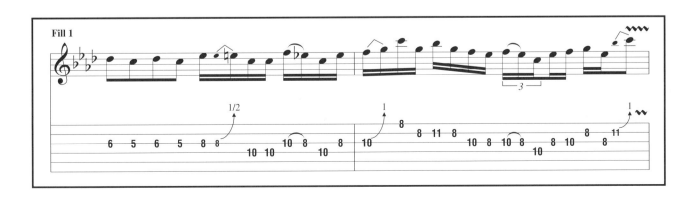

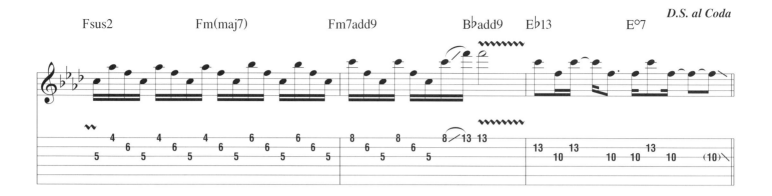

Fsus2   Fm(maj7)   Fm7add9   B♭add9   E♭13   E°7

Coda

Chorus

B♭5   C5   D♭5   E♭5

Dream on, __ 'n' dream on, __ 'n' dream on, __ dream your-self a dream come

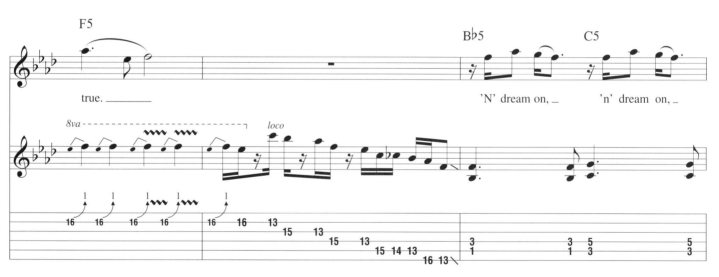

F5   B♭5   C5

true. _____   'N' dream on, __ 'n' dream on, __

D♭5   E♭5   F5

'n' dream on, __ 'n' dream un-til your dream come _____ true.

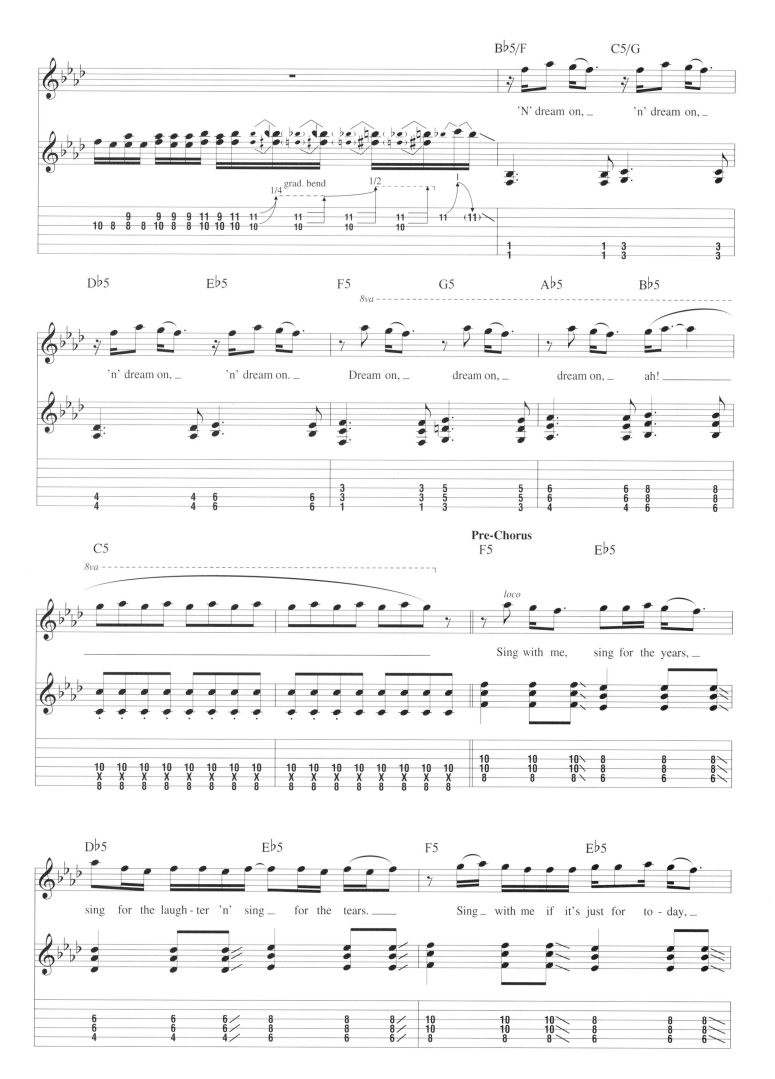

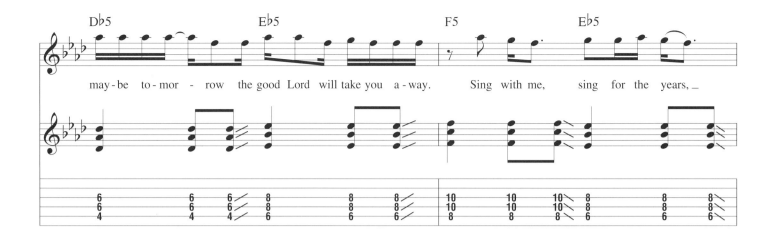

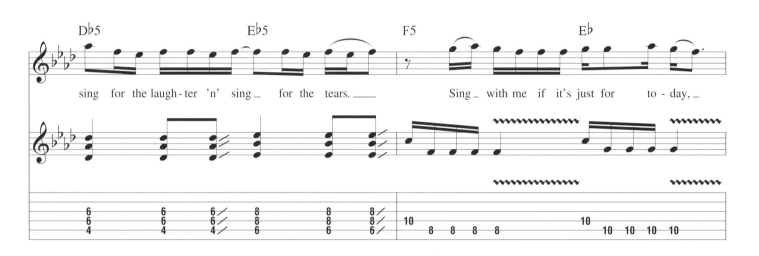

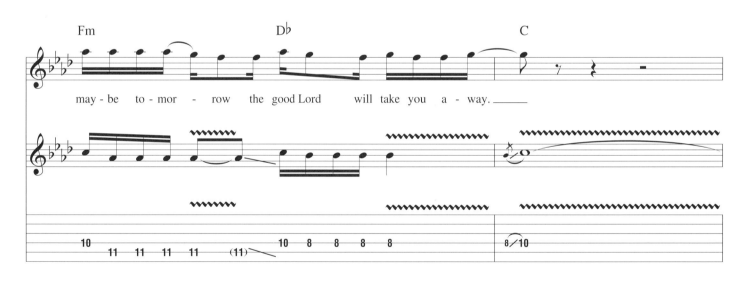

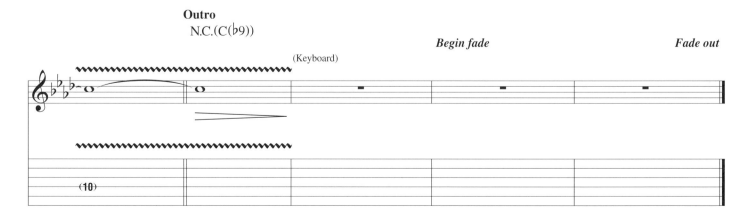

Drive

Words and Music by Brandon Boyd, Michael Einziger, Alex Katunich, Jose Pasillas II and Chris Kilmore

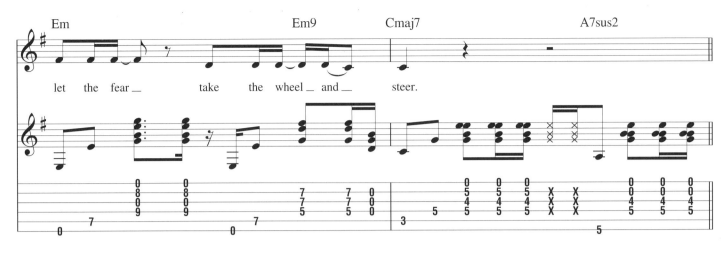

let the fear ___ take the wheel ___ and ___ steer.

Pre-Chorus

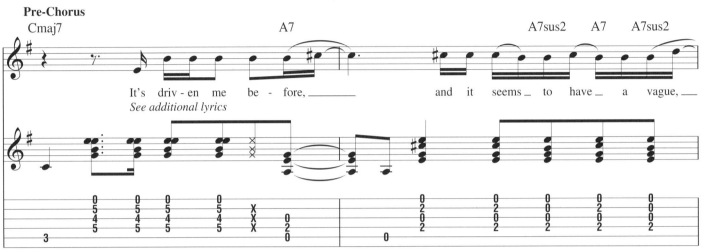

It's driv-en me be-fore, _____ and it seems ___ to have ___ a vague, ___

See additional lyrics

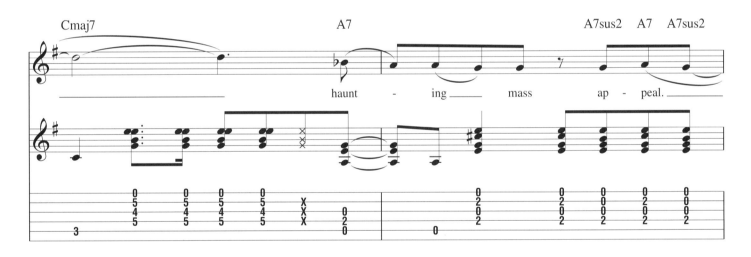

_____ haunt - ing ___ mass ap - peal. ___

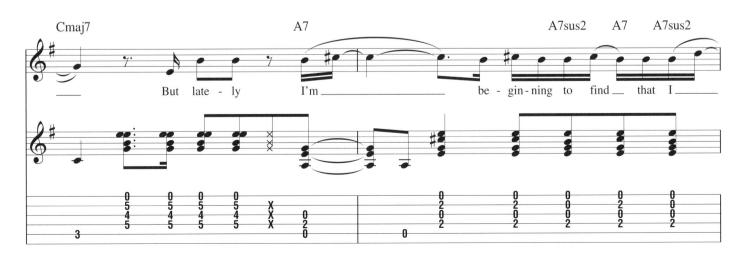

___ But late - ly I'm _____ be - gin-ning to find ___ that I _____

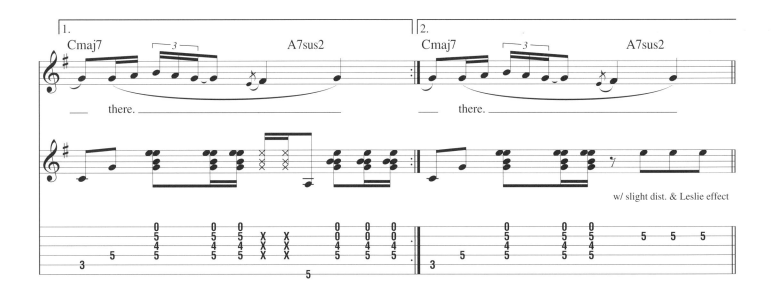

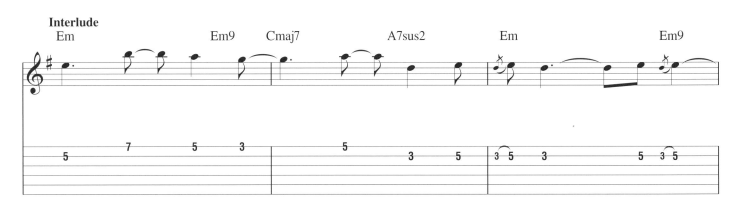

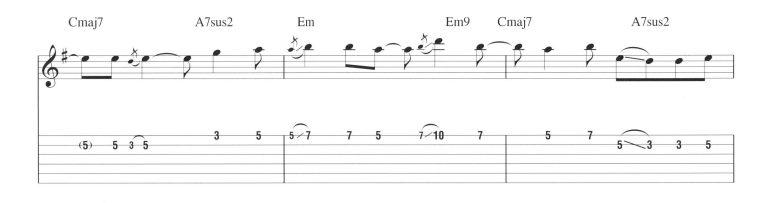

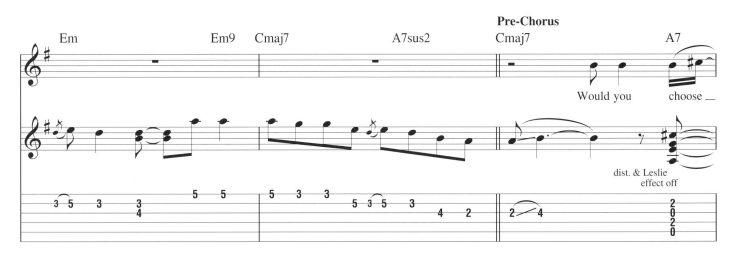

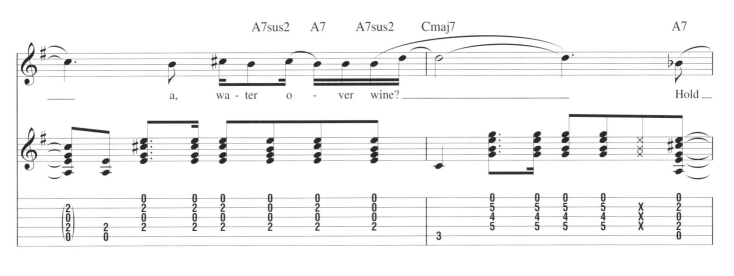

D.S. al Coda

*P.S.

*Rub edge of pick down the strings,
producing a scratchy sound.

Coda

Outro

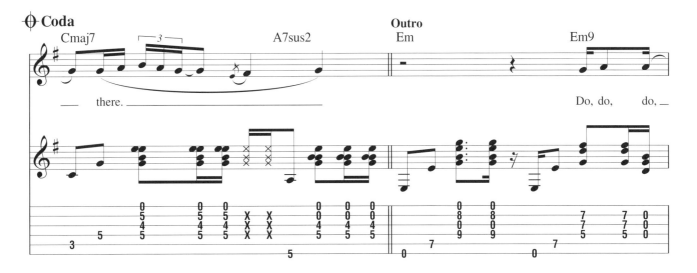

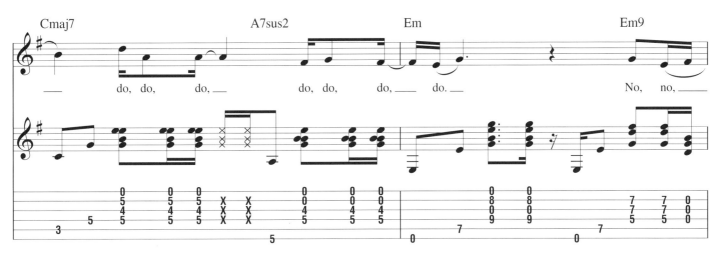

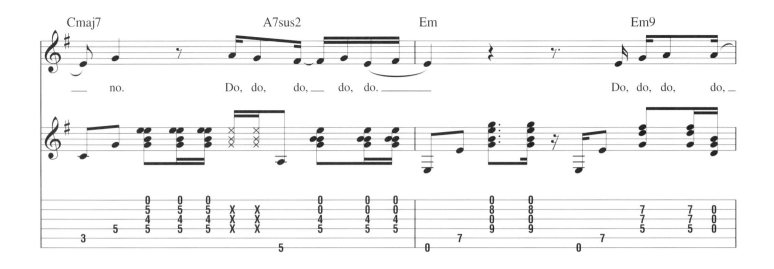

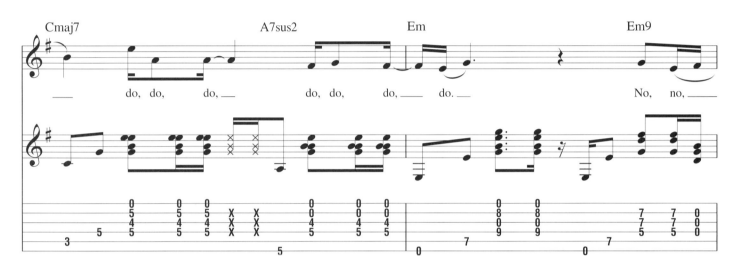

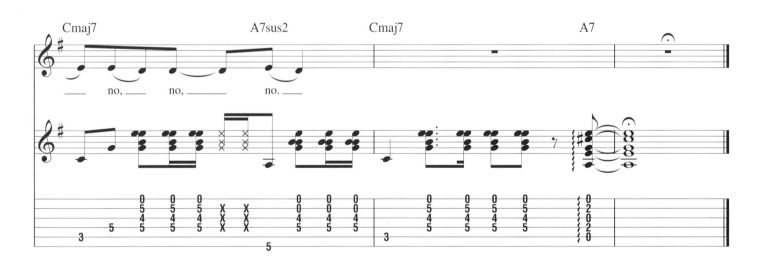

Additional Lyrics

2. So if I decide to waiver the
   Chance to be one of the hive,
   Will I choose water over wine
   And hold my own and drive?
   Oh, oh, oh.

Pre-Chorus It's driven me before,
   And it seems to be the way,
   That ev'ryone else gets around.
   But lately I'm beginning to find
   That when I drive myself my light is found.

Dust in the Wind

Words and Music by Kerry Livgren

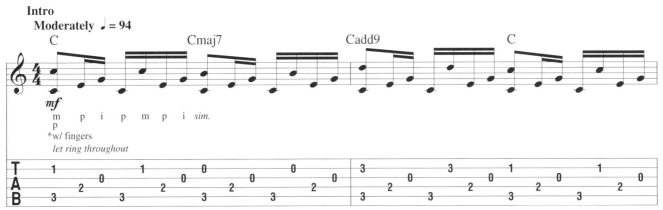

*p=thumb, i=index, m=middle

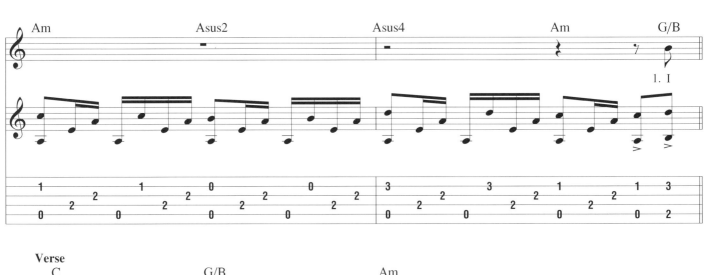

Verse

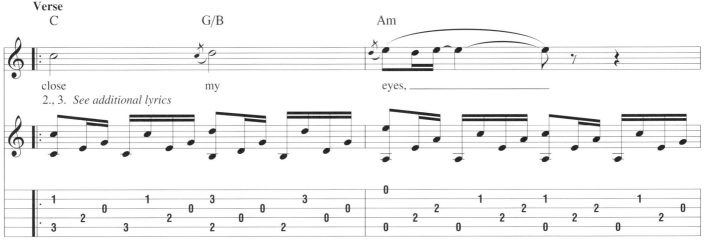

close ___ my ___ eyes, _____

2., 3. *See additional lyrics*

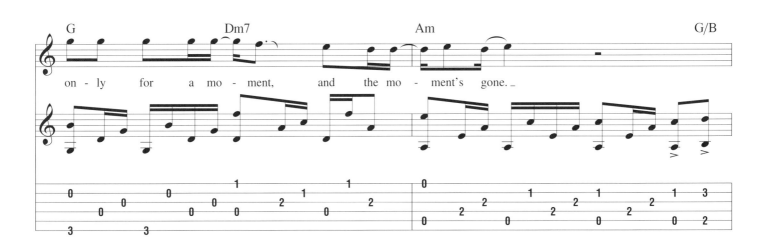

on - ly for a mo - ment, and the mo - ment's gone. __

All ___ my ___ dreams _____

Interlude

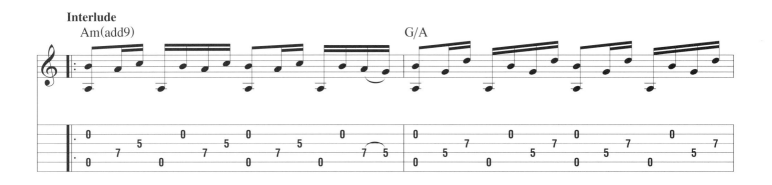

2nd time, D.C. al Coda

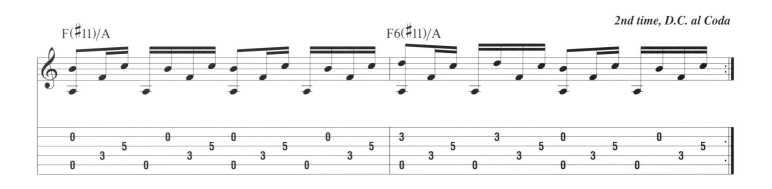

Coda

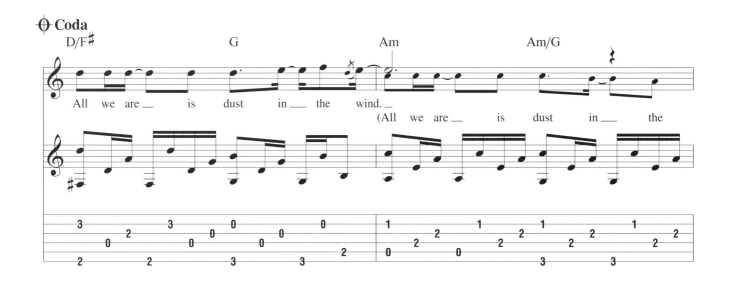

All we are __ is dust in __ the wind. __

(All we are __ is dust in __ the

Outro

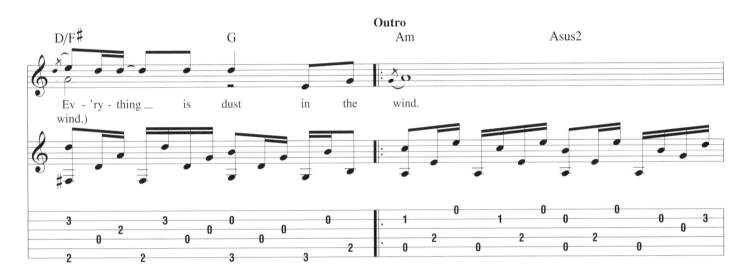

Repeat and fade

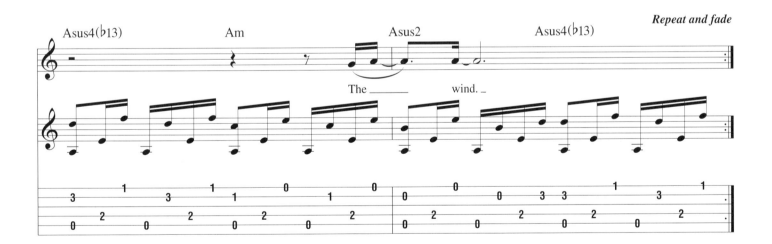

Additional Lyrics

2. Same old song.
   Just a drop of water in an endless sea.
   All we do
   Crumbles to the ground though we refuse to see.

3. Now don't hang on,
   Nothing lasts forever but the earth and sky.
   It slips away
   And all your money won't another minute buy.

Eye of the Tiger

Theme from ROCKY III

Words and Music by Frank Sullivan and Jim Peterik

* Chord symbols reflect overall tonality.

Verse

Gtr. 2 tacet · Gtr. 1: w/ Riff A, 2 times

Cm · Ab/C · Bb/C · Cm

1. Ris - in' up, back on the street__ did my time,__ took my chanc - es.

Ab/C · Bb/C · Cm

Went the dis - tance, now I'm back on __ my feet, just a man and his will to sur-vive. __

Verse

Gtr. 1: w/ Riff A, 2 times, 1st time
Gtr. 1 tacet, 2nd time

Cm · Ab · Bb · Cm

2. So man - y times __ it hap-pens too fast, __ you change your pas-sion for glo - ry.
4. Ris - in' up, __ straight to the top, __ had guts, _____ got the glo - ry.

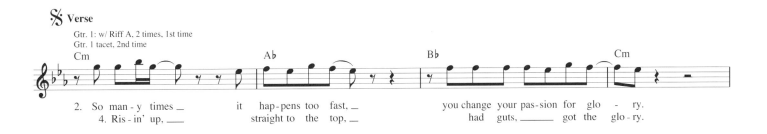

Gtr. 1: w/ Riff A, 2nd time

Ab · Bb · Cm · Bb · Cm7

Don't lose your grip __ on the dreams of __ the past, you must fight just to keep them a-live. __
Went the dis - tance, now I'm not gon - na stop, just a man and his will to sur-vive. __

It's the

Chorus

Fm · Bbsus4 · Bb · Fm

eye of the ti - ger, it's the thrill of the fight, ris - ing up to the chal-lenge of our

Gtr. 2 · **Rhy. Fig. 2**

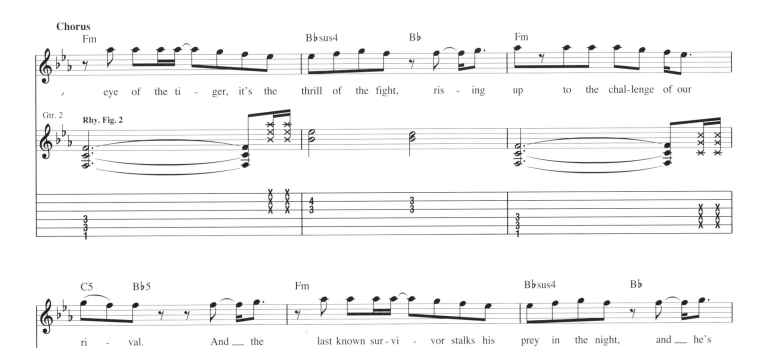

C5 · Bb5 · Fm · Bbsus4 · Bb

ri - val. And __ the last known sur - vi - vor stalks his prey in the night, and __ he's

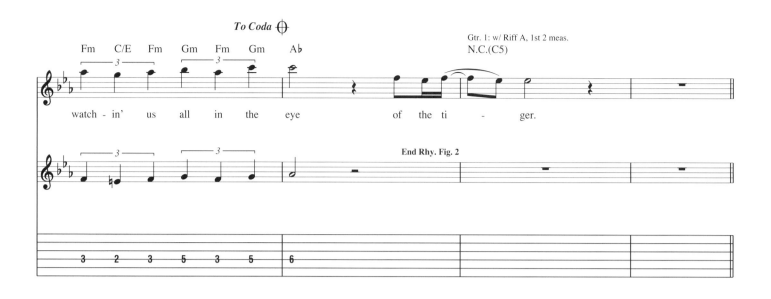

To Coda ⊕

Fm C/E Fm Gm Fm Gm Ab

Gtr. 1: w/ Riff A, 1st 2 meas.
N.C.(C5)

watch - in' us all in the eye of the ti - ger.

End Rhy. Fig. 2

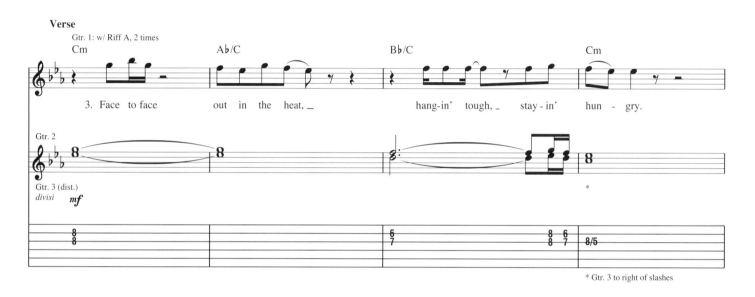

Verse
Gtr. 1: w/ Riff A, 2 times

Cm   Ab/C   Bb/C   Cm

3. Face to face out in the heat, __ hang-in' tough, __ stay - in' hun - gry.

Gtr. 2

Gtr. 3 (dist.)
divisi *mf*

* Gtr. 3 to right of slashes

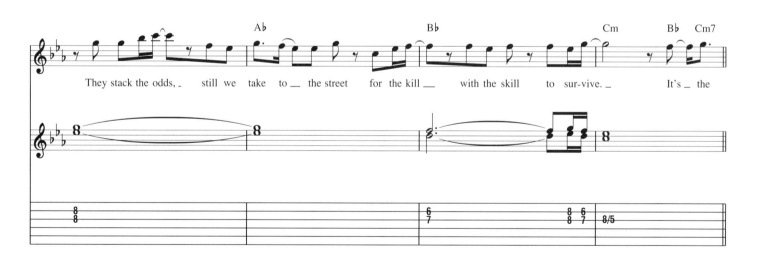

Ab   Bb   Cm   Bb   Cm7

They stack the odds, __ still we take to __ the street for the kill __ with the skill to sur-vive. __ It's __ the

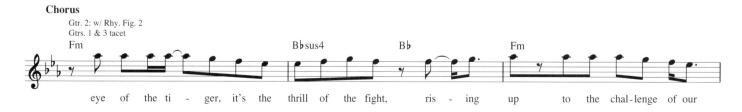

Chorus
Gtr. 2: w/ Rhy. Fig. 2
Gtrs. 1 & 3 tacet

Fm   Bbsus4   Bb   Fm

eye of the ti - ger, it's the thrill of the fight, ris - ing up to the chal - lenge of our

ri - val. And the last known sur - vi - vor stalks his prey in the night, and he's

D.S. al Coda

watch- in' us all in the eye of the ti - ger.

⊕ *Coda*

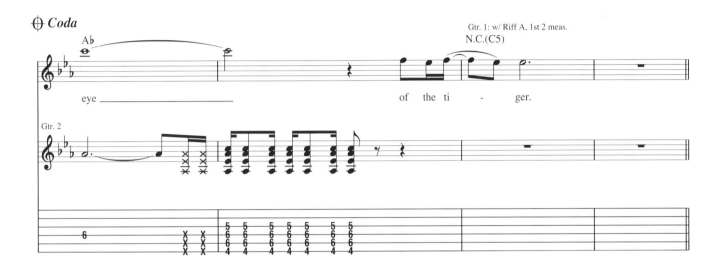

eye of the ti - ger.

Outro

The eye of the ti - ger.

The eye of the ti - ger.

The eye of the ti - ger.

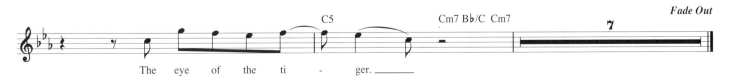

The eye of the ti - ger.

77

Fear of the Dark

Words and Music by Steven Harris

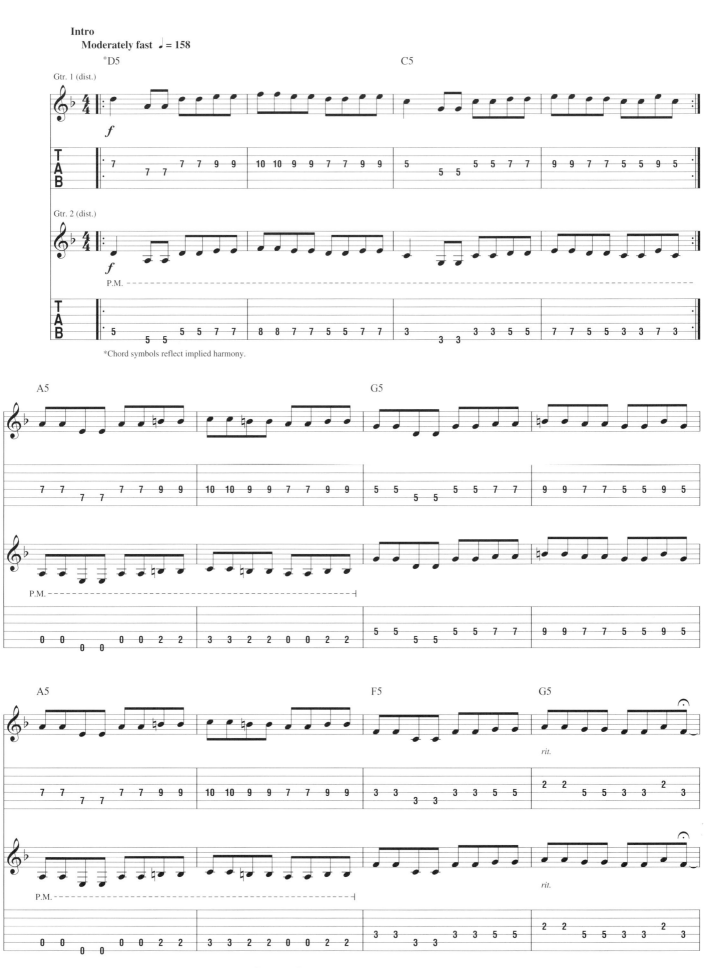

*Chord symbols reflect implied harmony.

79

*Bass plays notes to right of slashes.

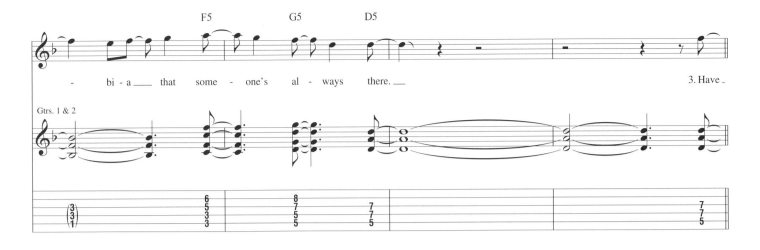

-bi - a ___ that some - one's al - ways there. ___ 3. Have -

𝄋 Verse

2nd time, Gtrs. 1 & 2: w/ Rhy. Fill 1

___ you ev - er been a - lone ___ at night, ___ thought you heard foot - steps be - hind, ___
-ing hor - ror films ___ the night be - fore, ___ de - bat - ing witch - es and ___ folk - lore. ___

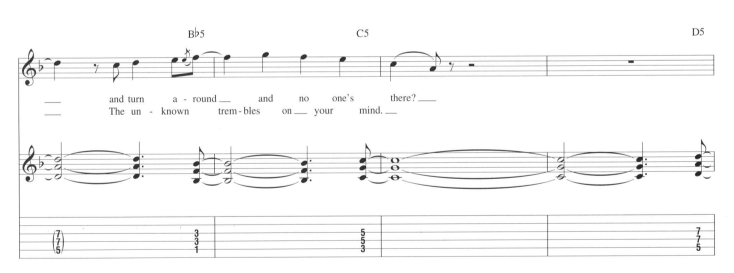

___ and turn a - round ___ and no one's there? ___
The un - known trem - bles on ___ your mind. ___

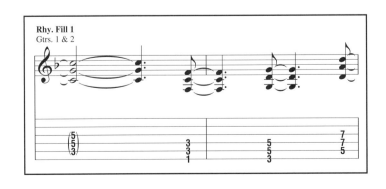

Rhy. Fill 1
Gtrs. 1 & 2

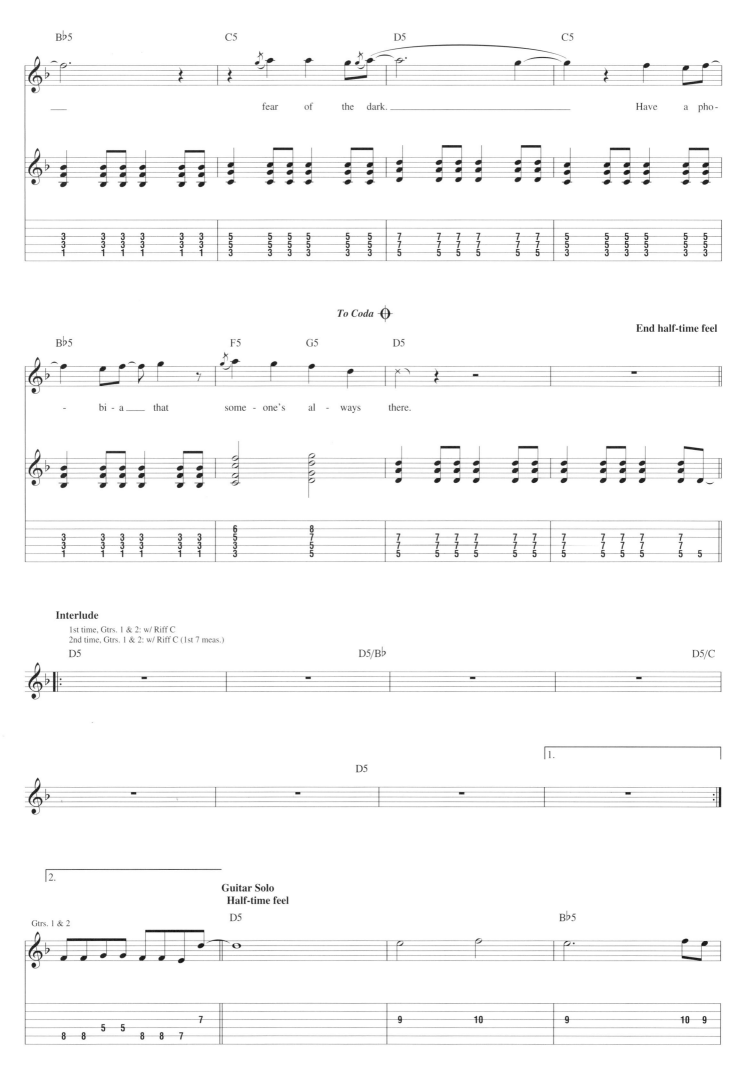

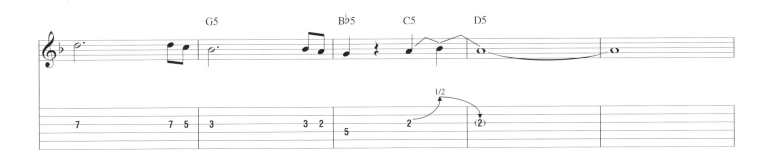

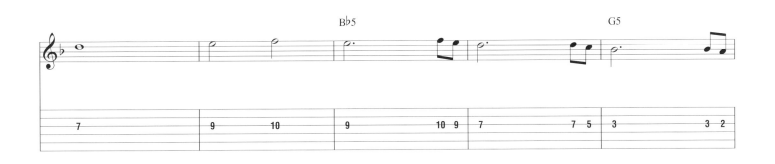

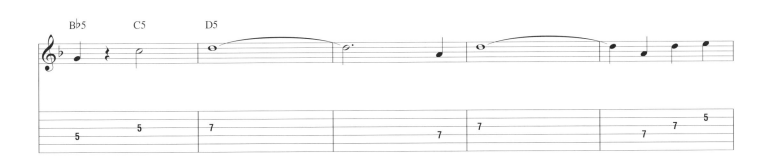

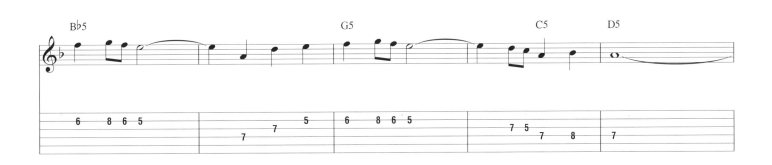

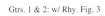

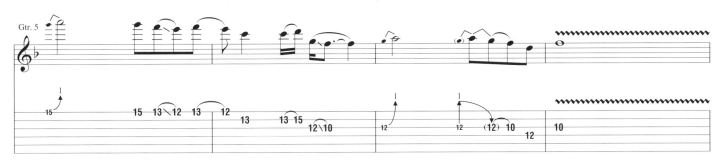

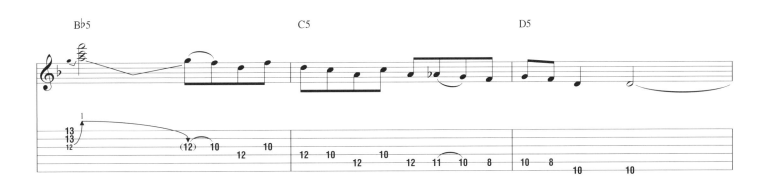

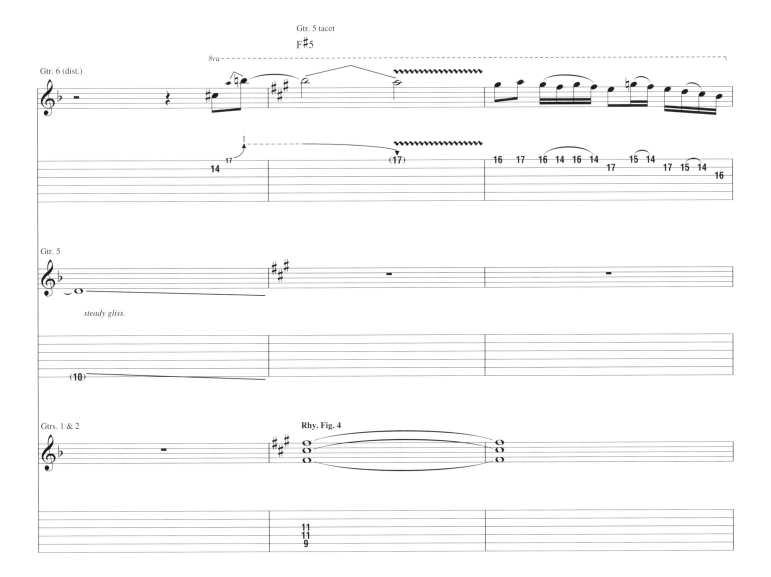

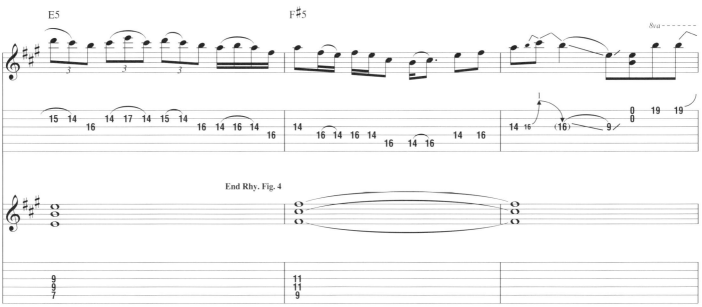

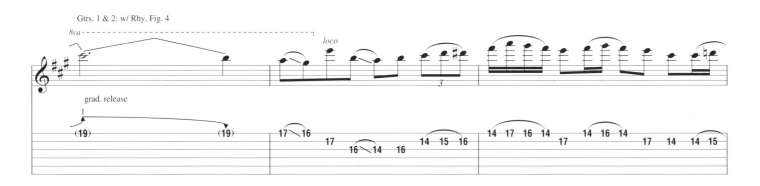

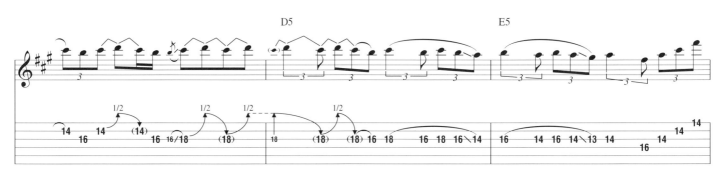

End Riff D

End Rhy. Fig. 5

Bridge

1st time, Gtrs. 1 & 2: w/ Riff D
2nd time, Gtrs. 1 & 2: w/ Riff D (1st 15 meas.)
Gtr. 7 tacet

D5

Fear   of   the   dark. _____

B♭5

Fear   of   the   dark. _____

G5   A5   Gtr. 7: w/ Rhy. Fig. 5   Dsus2

Fear   of   the   dark. _____   Fear   of   the   dark. __

1.

2.

End half-time feel

Gtrs. 1 & 2: w/ Fill 1

Fill 1
Gtrs. 1 & 2

Interlude

1st time, Gtrs. 1 & 2: w/ Riff C
2nd time, Gtrs. 1 & 2: w/ Riff C (1st 7 meas.)

D5   Bb5   C5

1.   2.   *D.S. al Coda*

Gtrs. 1 & 2: w/ Fill 2

D5

4. Watch -

⊕ Coda

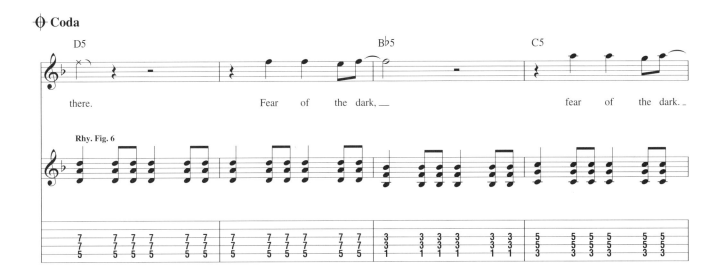

D5   Bb5   C5

there.   Fear   of   the   dark, ___   fear   of   the   dark. ___

Rhy. Fig. 6

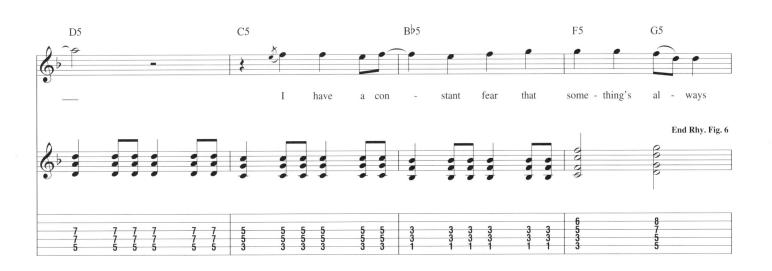

D5   C5   Bb5   F5   G5

___   I   have   a   con -   stant   fear   that   some - thing's   al -   ways

End Rhy. Fig. 6

Gtrs. 1 & 2: w/ Rhy. Fig. 6

D5   Bb5   C5

near.   Fear   of   the   dark, ___   fear   of   the   dark. ___

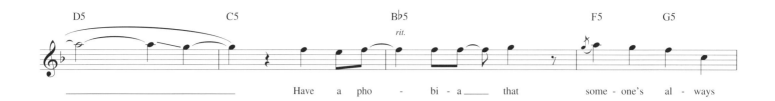

Have a pho - bi - a ___ that some-one's al - ways

Interlude
Faster ♩ = 144

Gtrs. 3 & 4: w/ Riffs A & A1

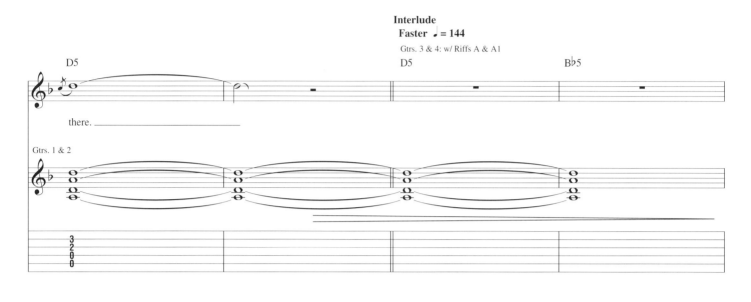

there. ____

Gtrs. 1 & 2

Gtrs. 1 & 2 tacet

Outro

When I'm walk - ing a dark ___ road, I am a man ___

Gtr. 3

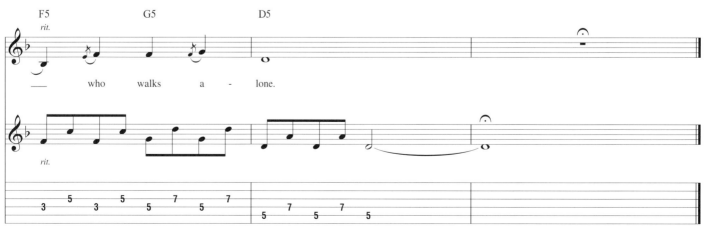

___ who walks a - lone.

Free Ride

Words and Music by Dan Hartman

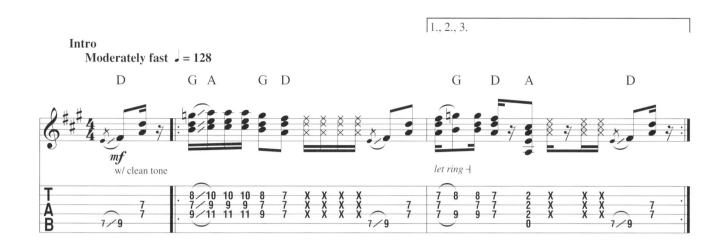

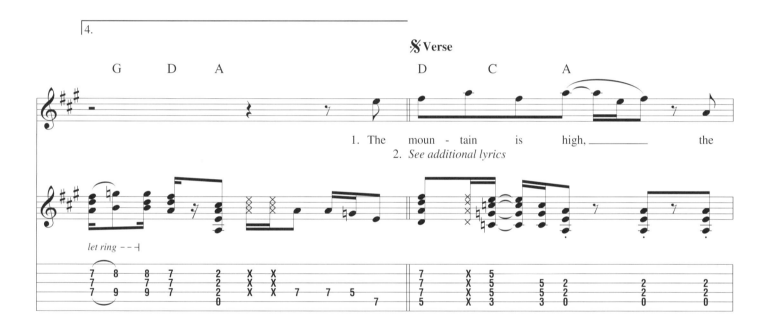

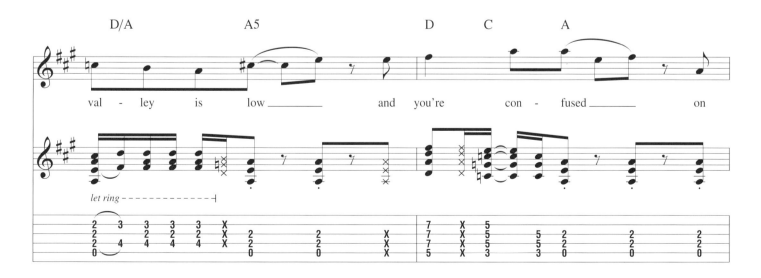

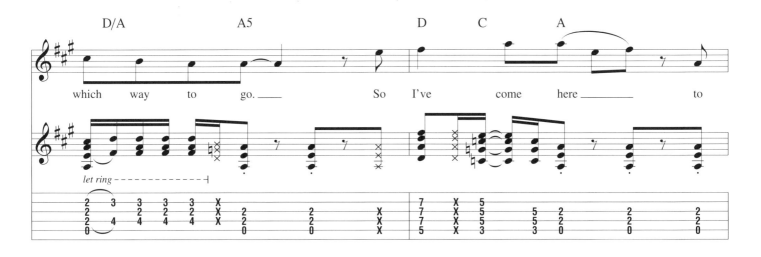

which way to go. ___ So I've come here ___ to

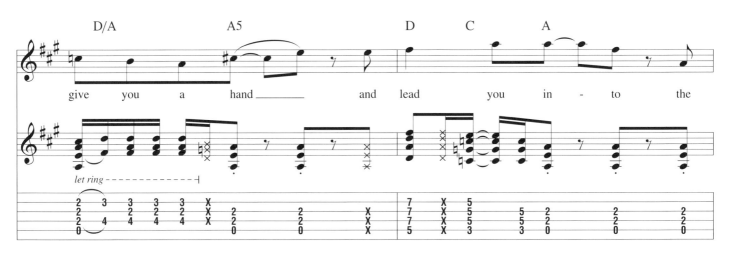

give you a hand ___ and lead you in - to the

Chorus

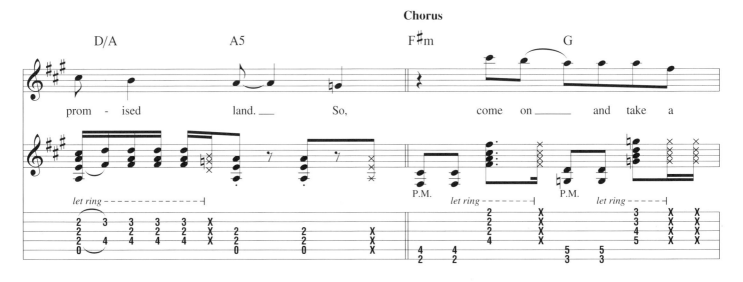

prom - ised land. ___ So, come on ___ and take a

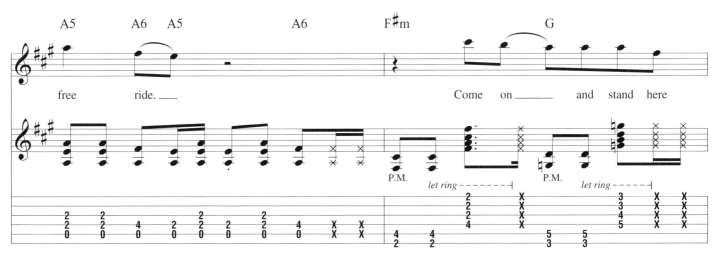

free ride. ___ Come on ___ and stand here

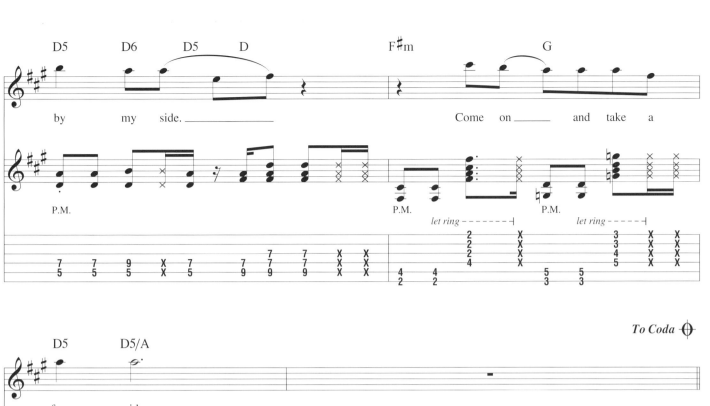

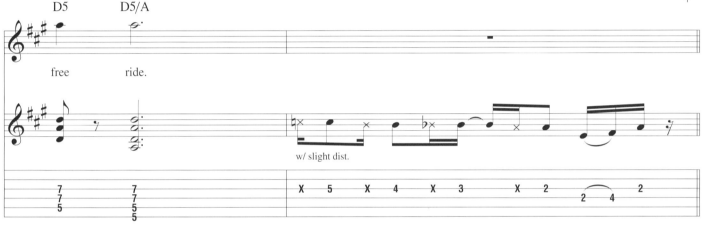

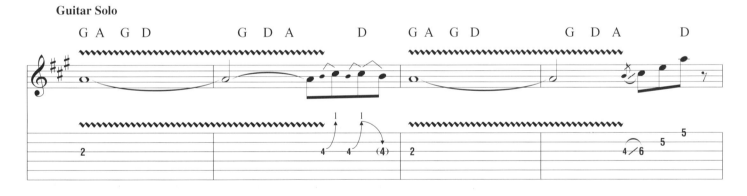

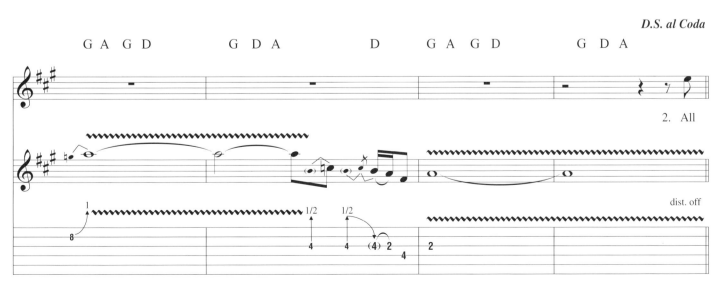

Coda

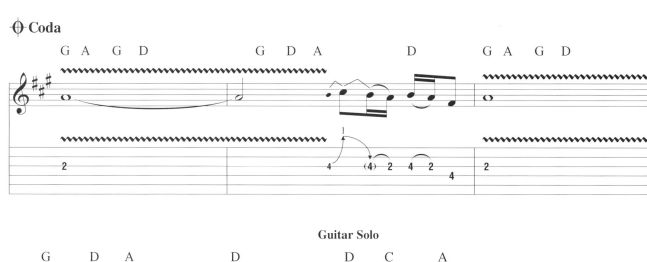

Guitar Solo

Yeah,   yeah,   yeah,   yeah.

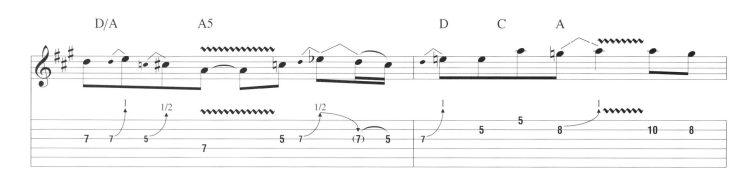

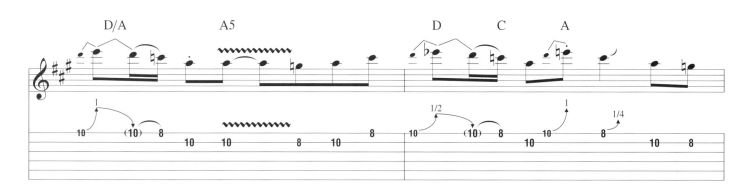

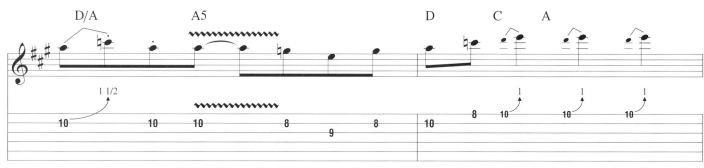

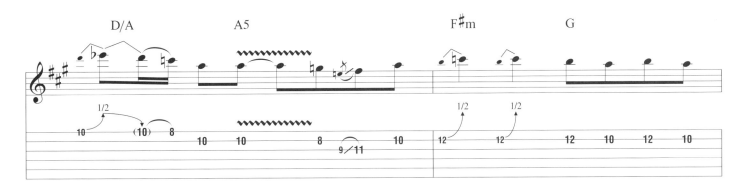

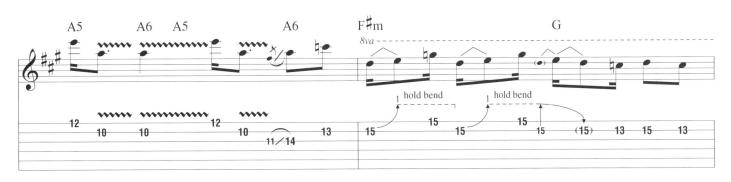

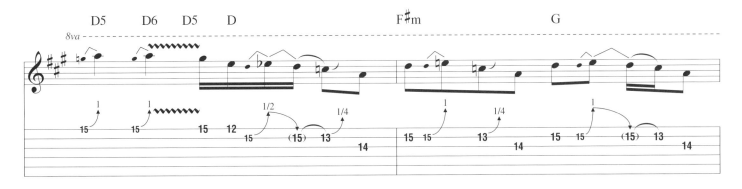

Interlude

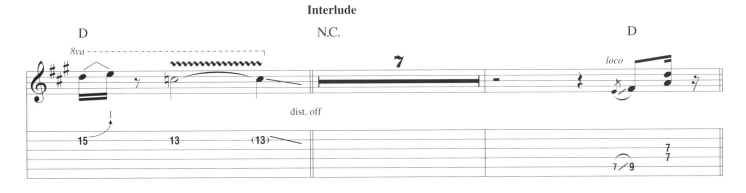

Outro

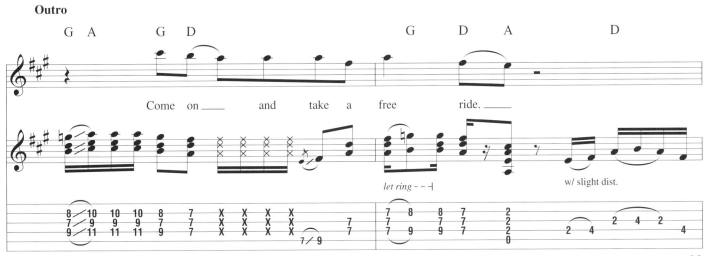

Come on ___ and take a free ride. ___

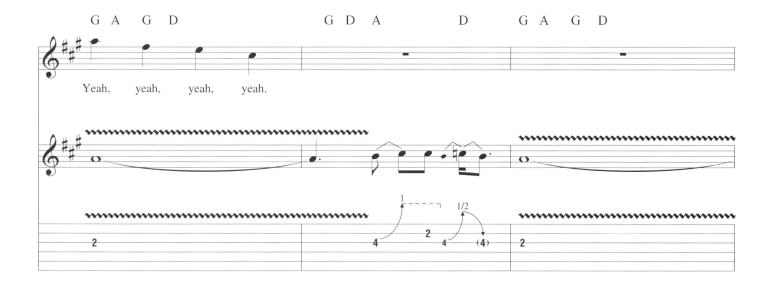

Yeah, yeah, yeah, yeah.

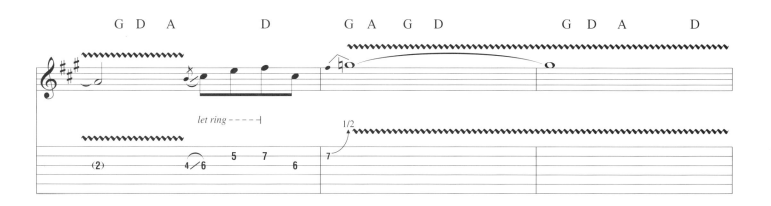

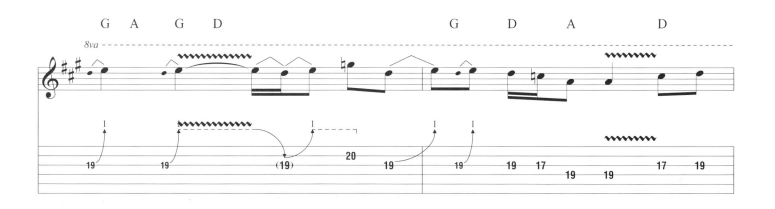

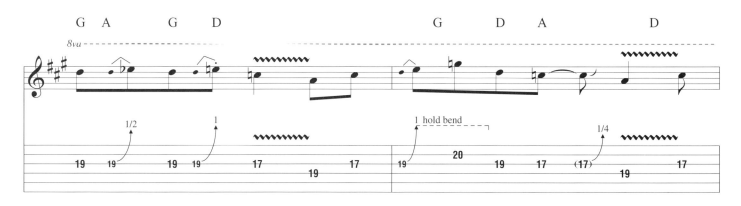

Hallelujah

Words and Music by Leonard Cohen

Capo V

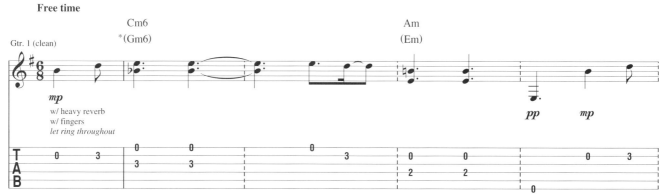

*Symbols in parentheses represent chord names respective to capoed guitar.
Symbols above reflect actual sounding chords. Capoed fret is "0" in tab.
Chord symbols reflect implied harmony.

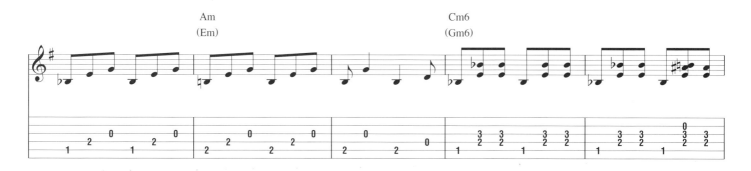

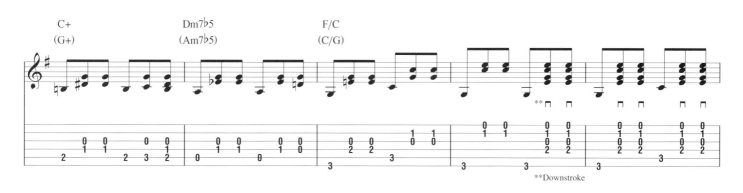

**Downstroke

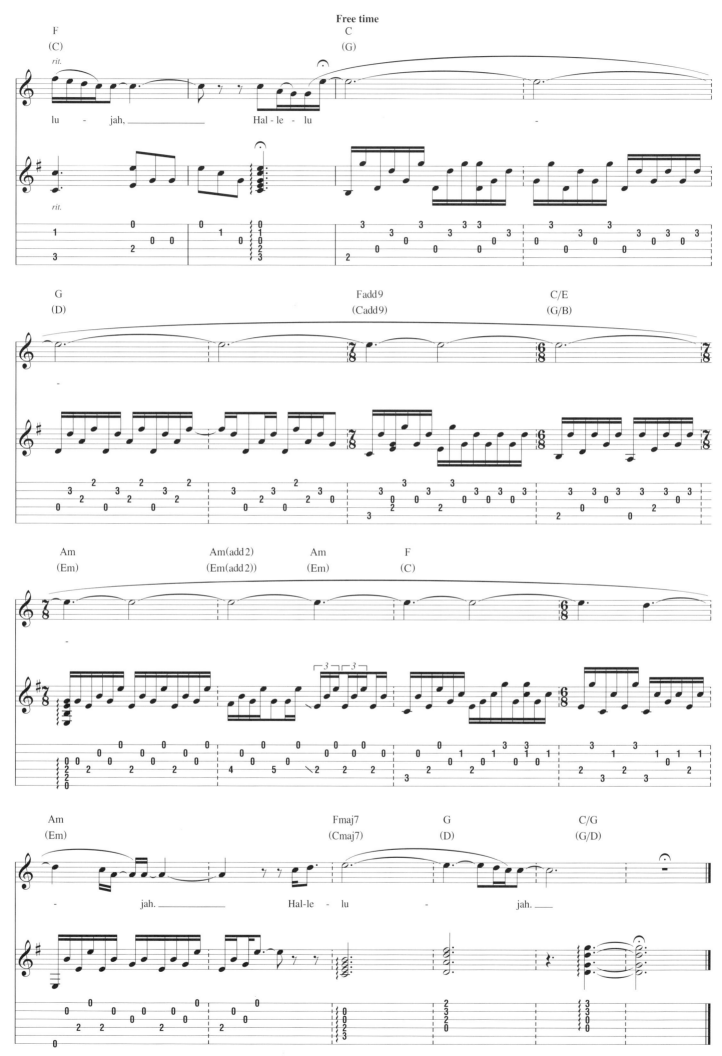

108

Here Without You

Words and Music by Matt Roberts, Brad Arnold, Christopher Henderson and Robert Harrell

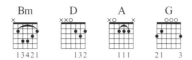

Tune down 1/2 step:
(low to high) Eb-Ab-Db-Gb-Bb-Eb

Intro

Moderately slow ♩ = 72

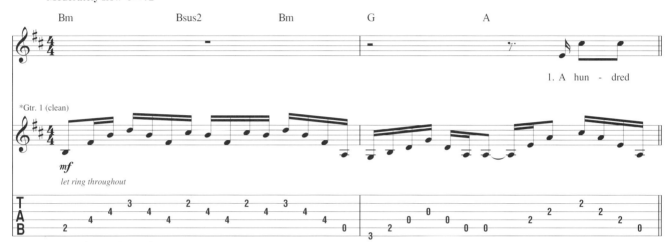

1. A hun-dred

*Gtr. 1 (clean)

mf
let ring throughout

*Two gtrs. (acous. & clean elec.) arr. for one.

Verse

days have made me old - er ___ since the last ___ time that ___ I saw ___ your ___ pret - ty face. ___

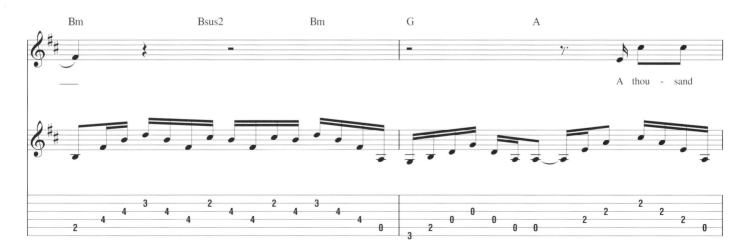

___ A thou - sand

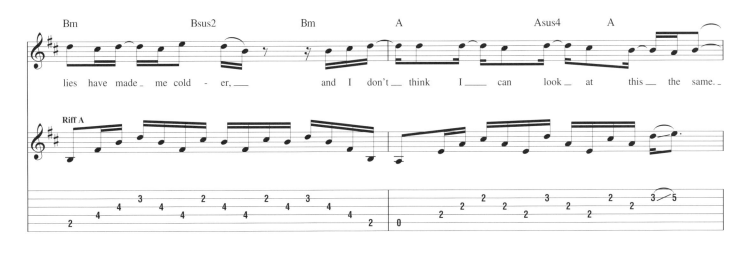

lies have made_ me cold - er, ___ and I don't ___ think I_ can look_ at this_ the same._

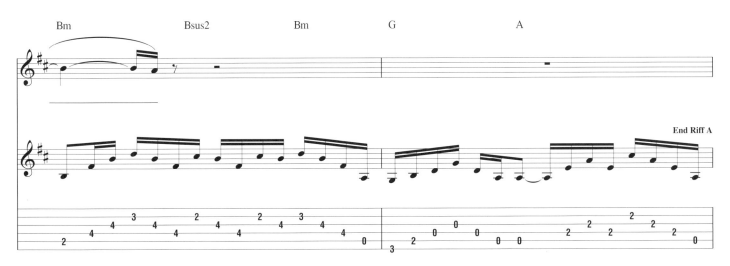

Gtr. 1: w/ Riff A

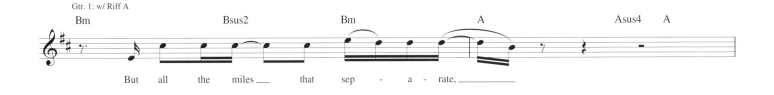

But all the miles ___ that sep - a - rate, _____

they dis - ap - pear ___ now when I'm dream - in' of ___ your face. ___

Chorus

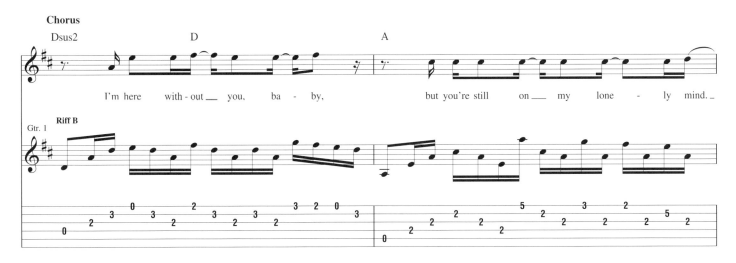

I'm here with - out ___ you, ba - by, but you're still on ___ my lone - ly mind. ___

Hey Joe

Words and Music by Billy Roberts

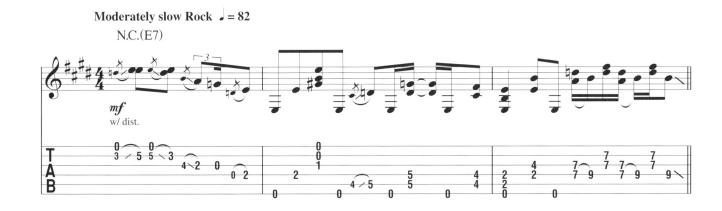

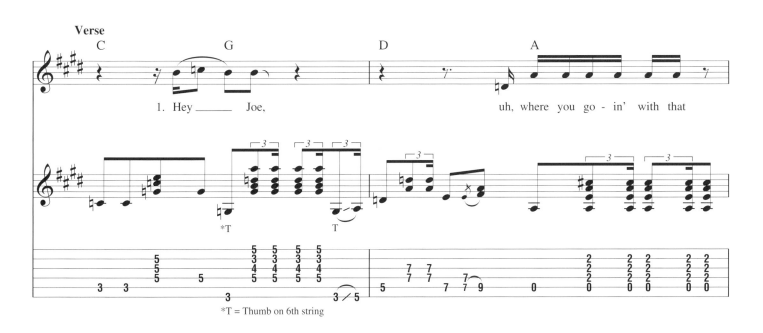

*T = Thumb on 6th string

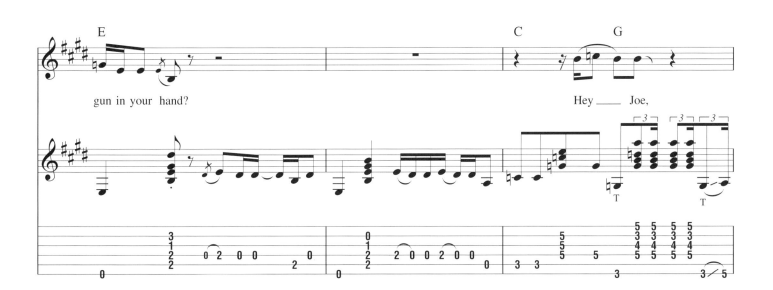

116

you know I caught her mess-in' 'round with an-oth-er man.___ Huh! And that ain't

Verse

too cool.

2. Uh, hey ___ Joe,

I heard you ___ shot your wom-an down, you shot her down now.___

Uh, hey ___ Joe,

I heard you ___ shot ___ your old la - dy down, you shot her down in the ground. ___

Yeah! ___   Yes, I ___ did, I shot her,

you know I caught her mess - in' 'round, mess - in' 'round town. ___

Uh, yes I did, I shot her,

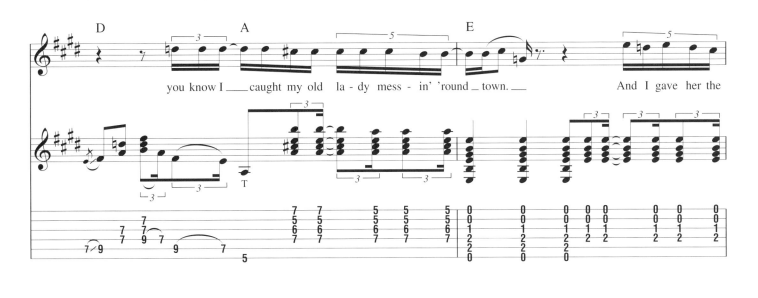

you know I ___ caught my old la - dy mess - in' 'round ___ town. ___ And I gave her the

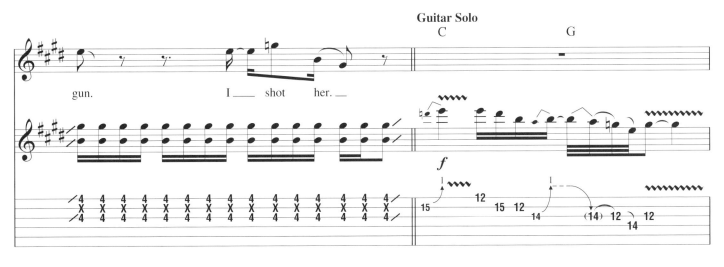

gun. I ___ shot her. ___

Guitar Solo

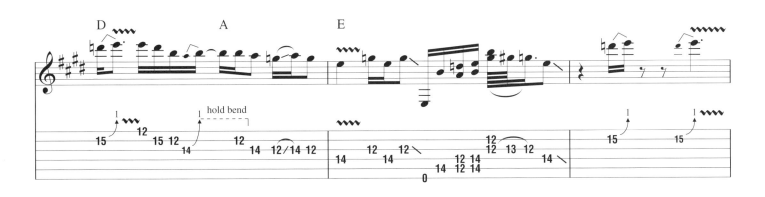

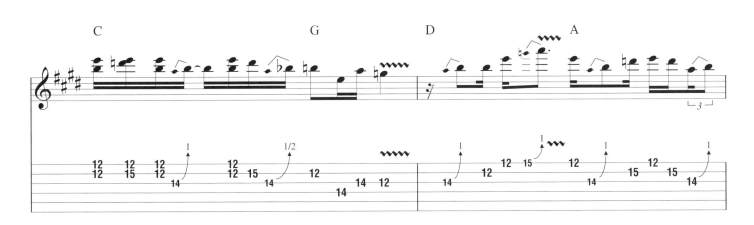

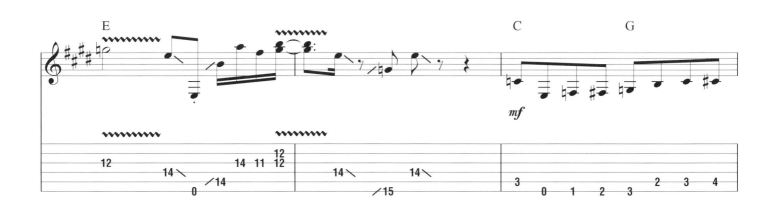

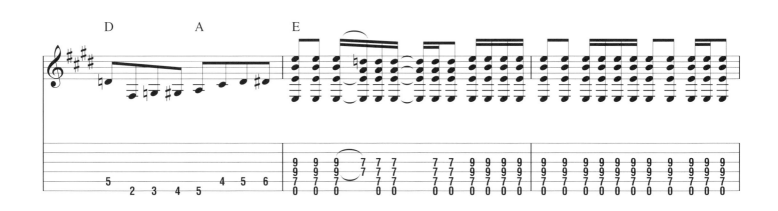

Verse

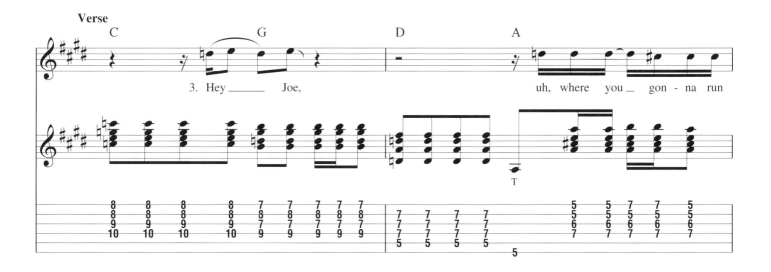

3. Hey _____ Joe,   uh, where you _ gon - na run

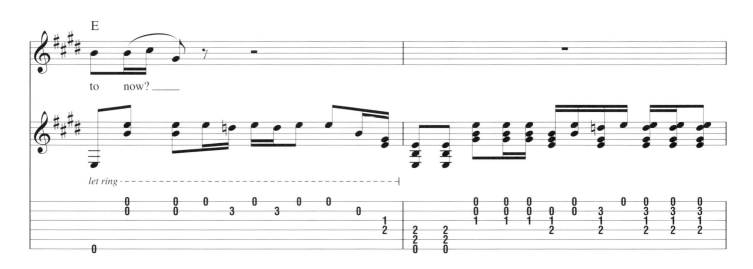

to   now? _____

The House of the Rising Sun

Words and Music by Alan Price

call _____ the Ris - ing Sun. ___ And it's

been _____ the ru - in _____ of man-y a _____ poor boy, ___ and

Interlude

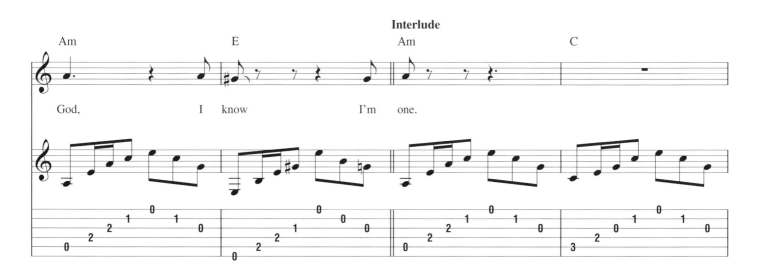

God, I know I'm one.

Interlude

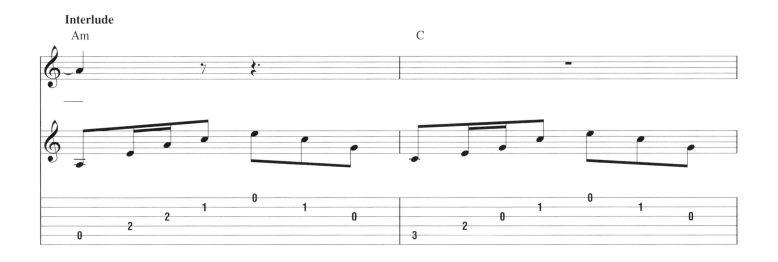

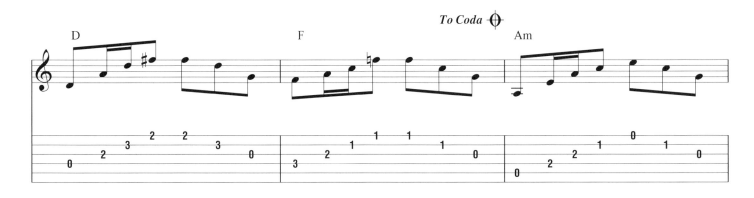

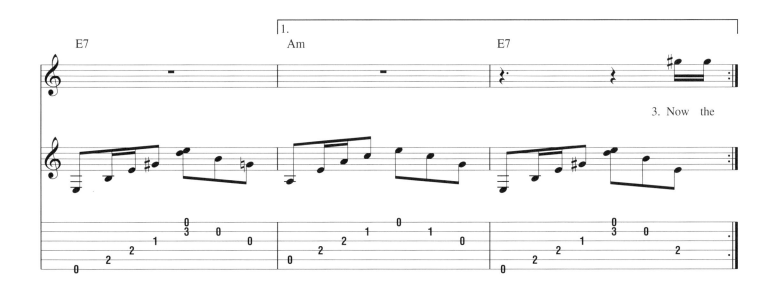

3. Now the

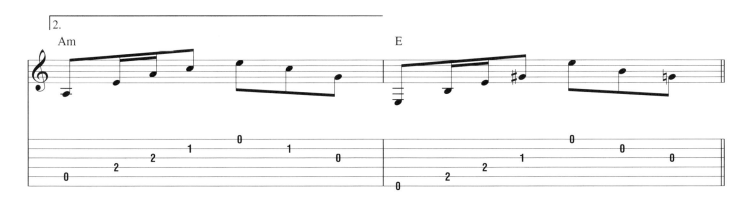

Organ Solo

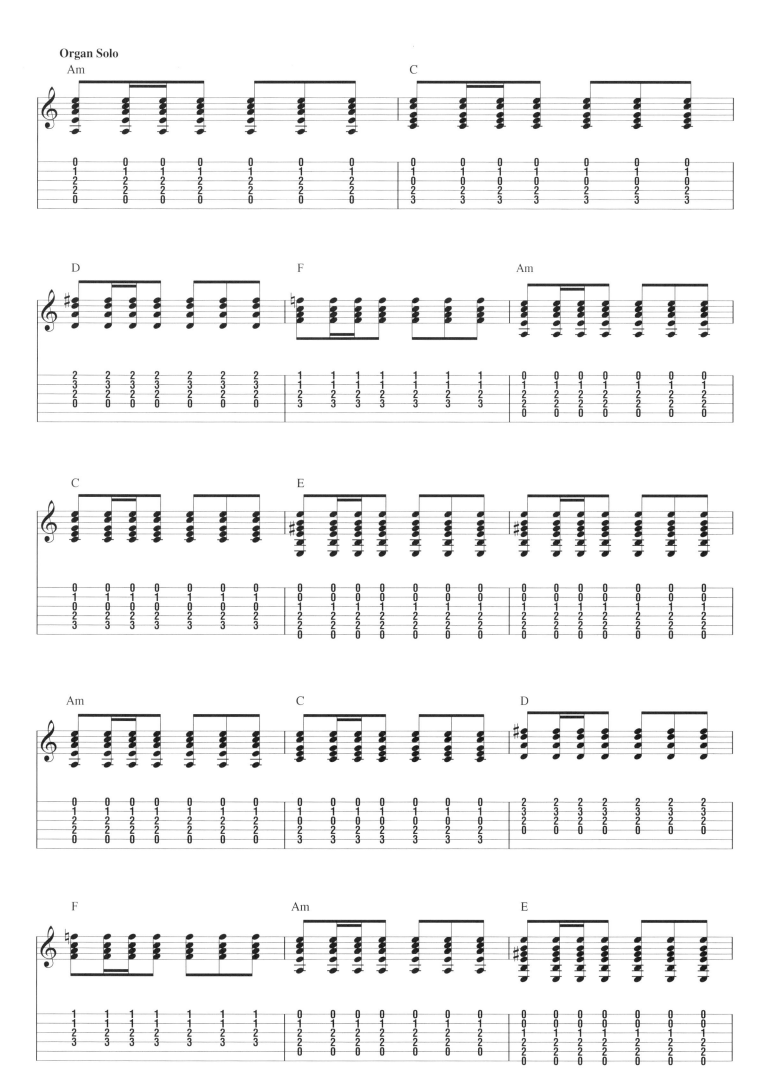

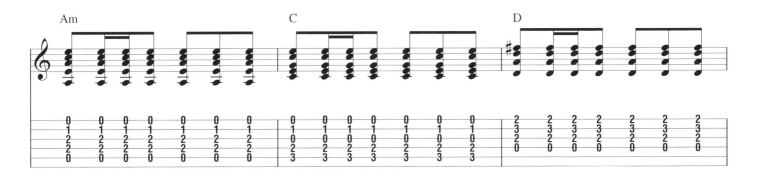

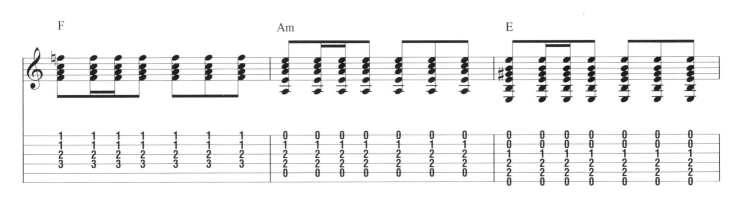

Coda

D.S. al Coda

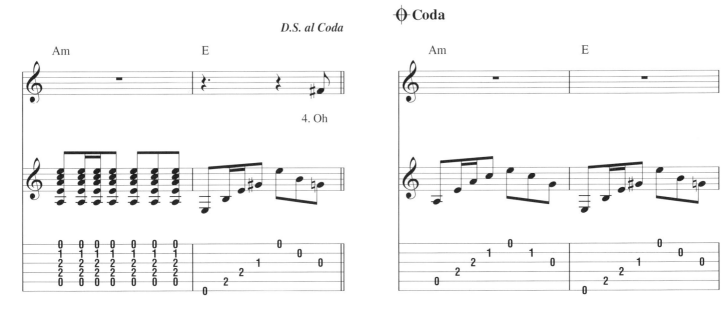

4. Oh

5. Well, _____ I got

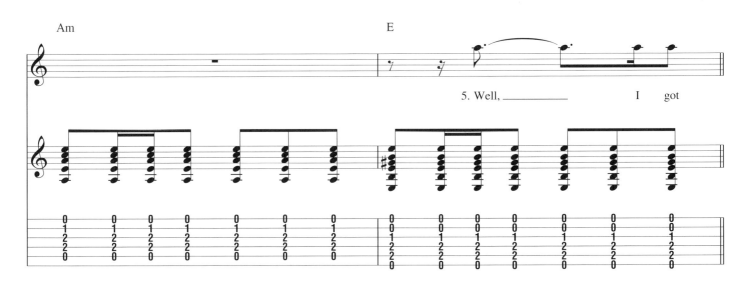

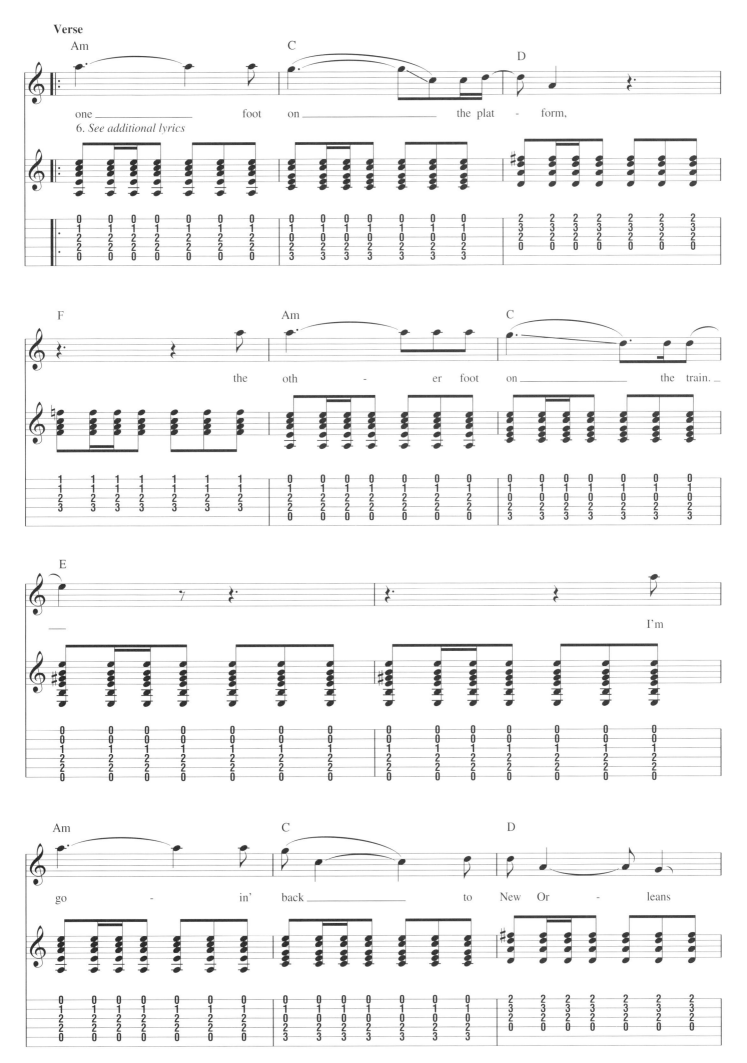

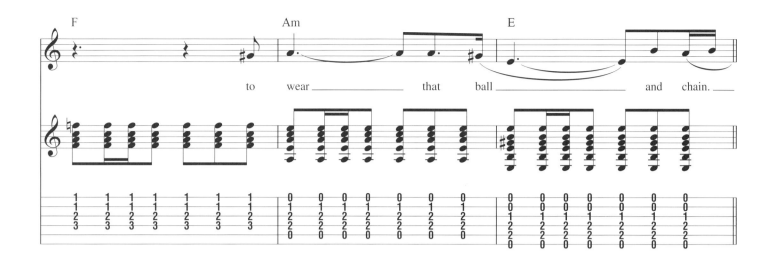

to   wear _____ that   ball _____ and   chain. ___

Interlude

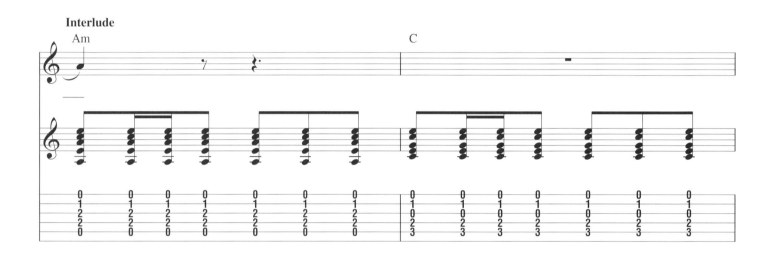

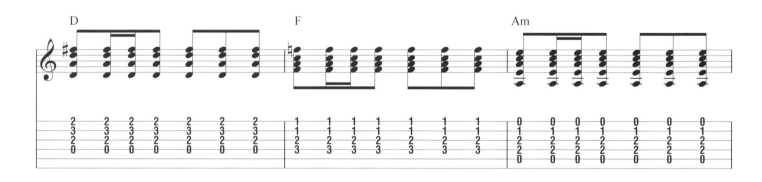

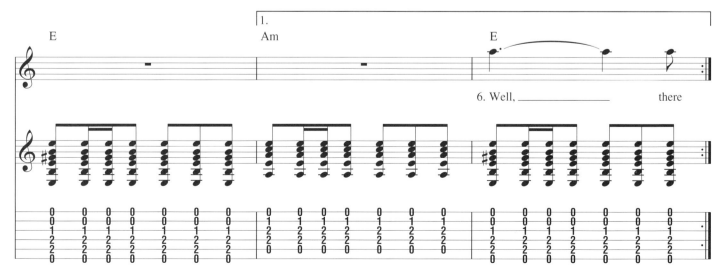

1.

6. Well, _____ there

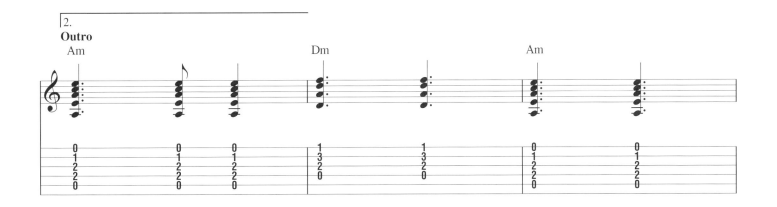

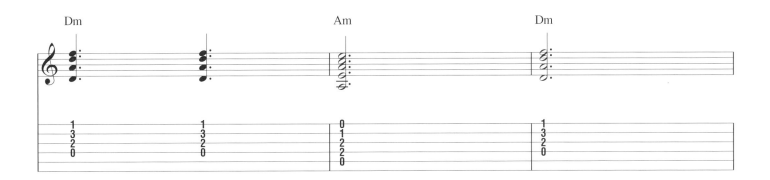

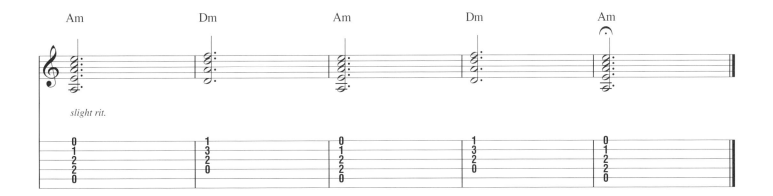

Additional Lyrics

3. Now the only thing a gambler needs
   Is a suitcase and a trunk.
   And the only time he's satisfied
   Is when he's on a drunk.

4. Oh mother, tell your children
   Not to do what I have done,
   Spend your lives in sin and misery
   In the House of the Rising Sun.

6. Well, there is a house in New Orleans
   They call the Rising Sun.
   And it's been the ruin of many a poor boy,
   And God, I know I'm one.

I Will Follow You Into the Dark

Words and Music by Benjamin Gibbard

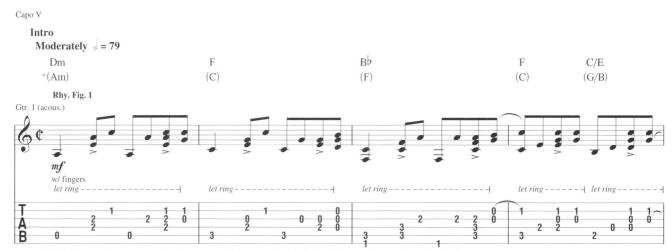

*Symbols in parentheses represent chord names respective to capoed guitar. Symbols above reflect actual sounding chords.
Capoed fret is "0" in tab. Chord symbols reflect implied harmony.

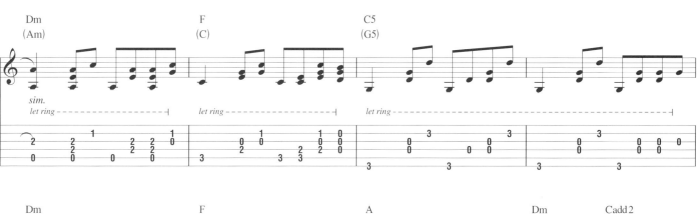

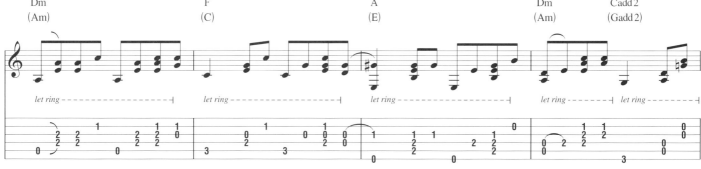

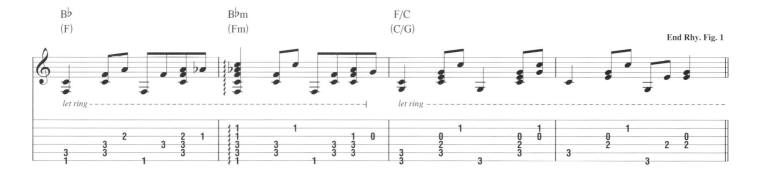

133

I Won't Back Down

Words and Music by Tom Petty and Jeff Lynne

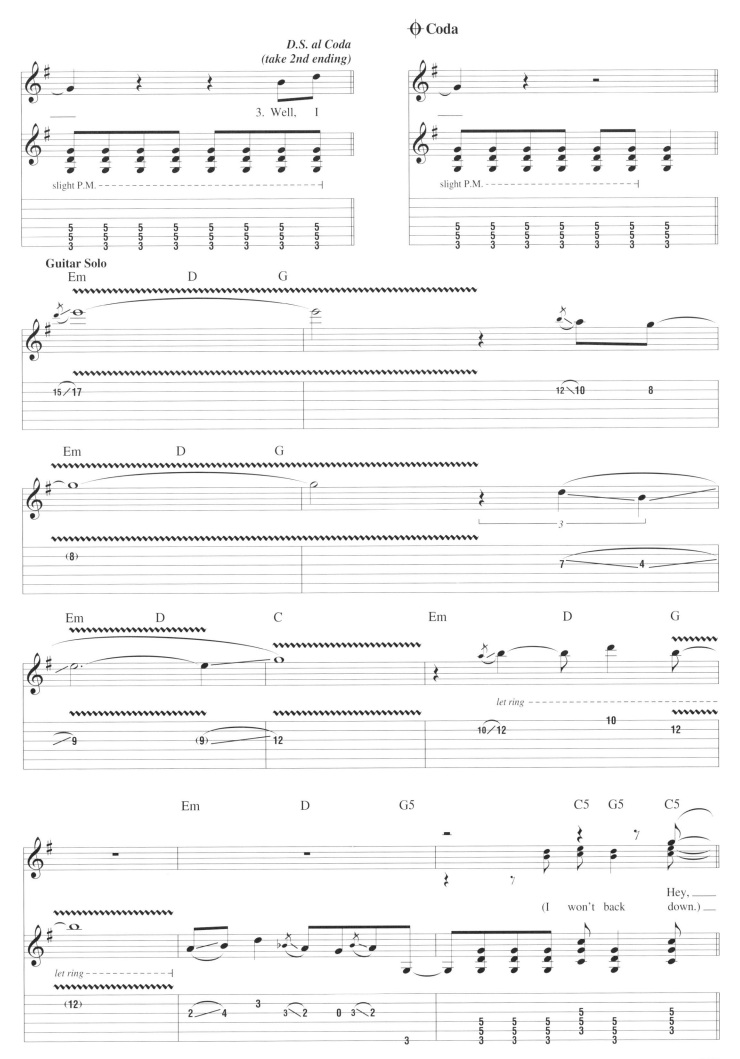

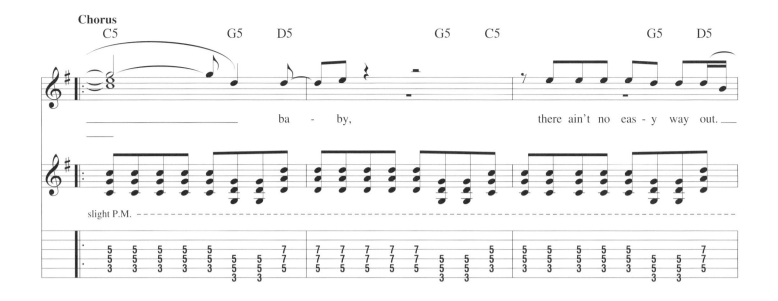

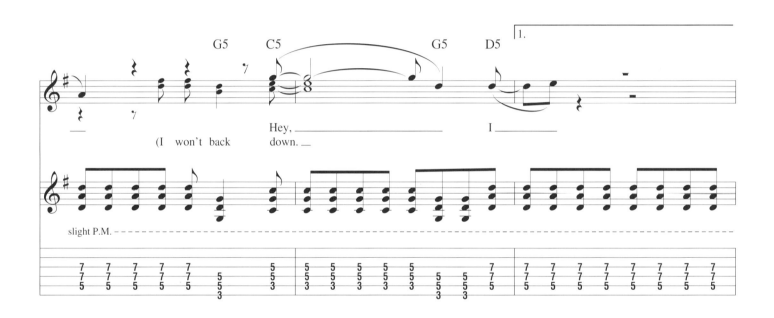

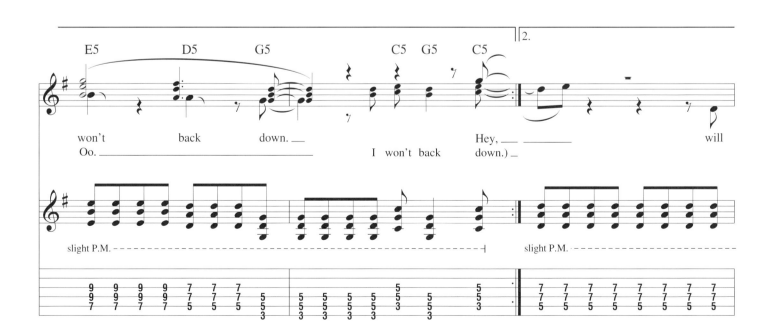

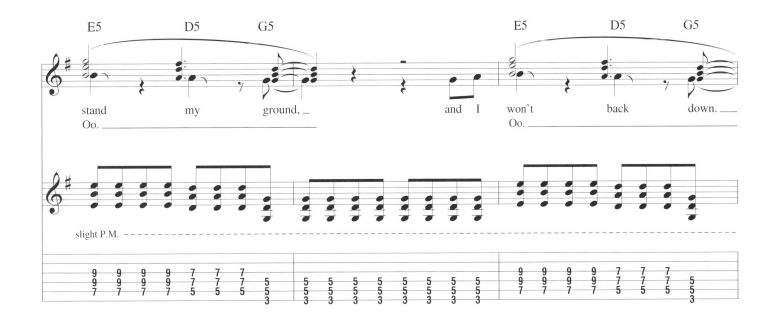

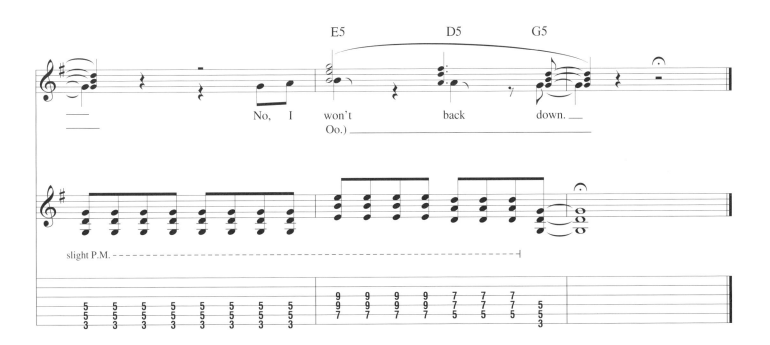

Additional Lyrics

2. No, I'll stand my ground.
   Won't be turned around.
   And I'll keep this world from draggin' me down,
   Gonna stand my ground.
   And I won't back down.

3. Well, I know what's right.
   I got just one life
   In a world that keeps on pushin' me around.
   But I'll stand my ground,
   And I won't back down.

Iris

from the Motion Picture CITY OF ANGELS

Words and Music by John Rzeznik

Tuning:
(low to high) B♭-D♭-D-D♭-D♯-D

Intro

Moderately slow ♩. = 51

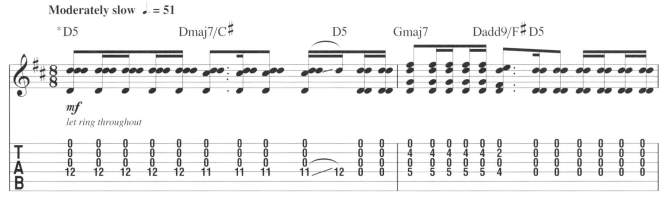

*Chord symbols reflect implied harmony.

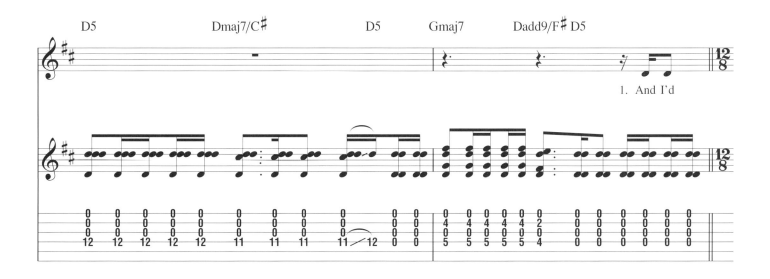

Verse

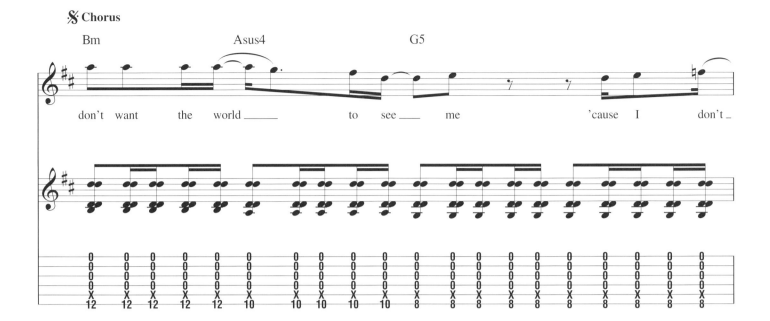

don't want the world ____ to see ____ me 'cause I don't _

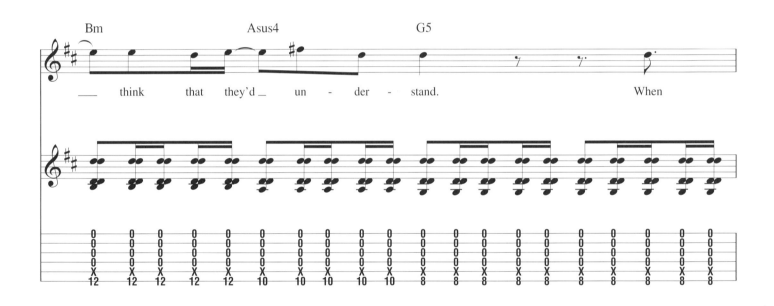

____ think that they'd _ un - der - stand. When

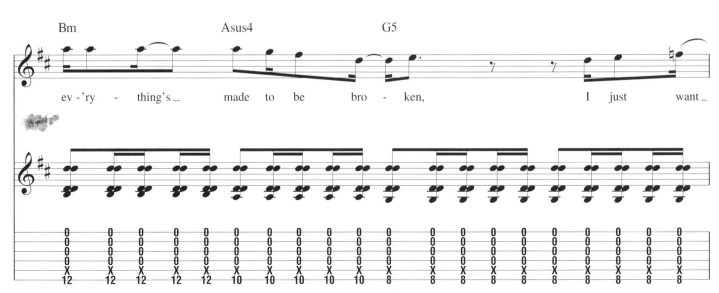

ev - 'ry - thing's _ made to be bro - ken, I just want _

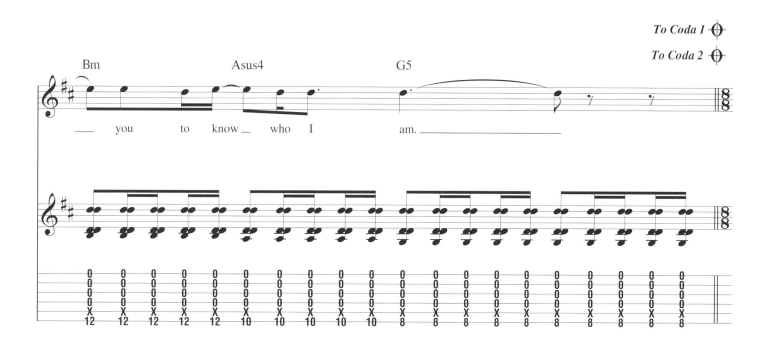

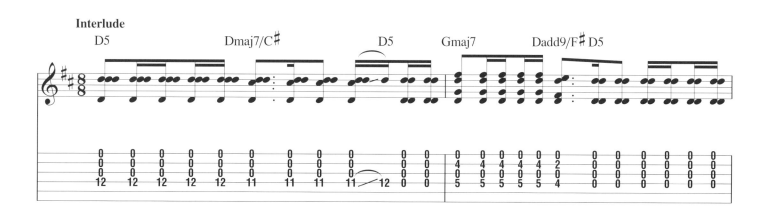

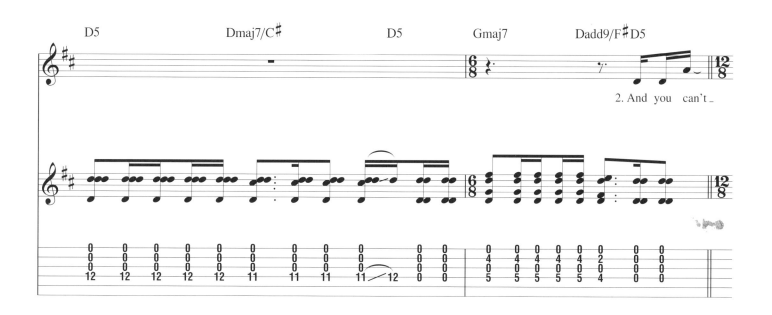

_____ fight the tears _ that ain't com-in'   or   the mo - ment of truth _ in your lies. _   When

D.S. al Coda 1

ev-'ry - thing _ feels like the mov - ies,   yeah, you bleed _ just to know _ you're a - live. _   And I

Coda 1

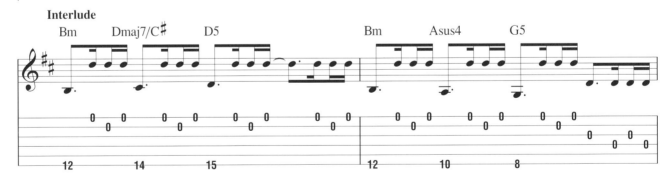

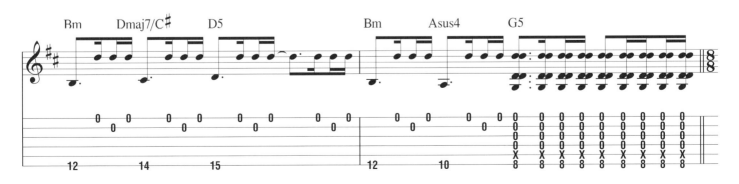

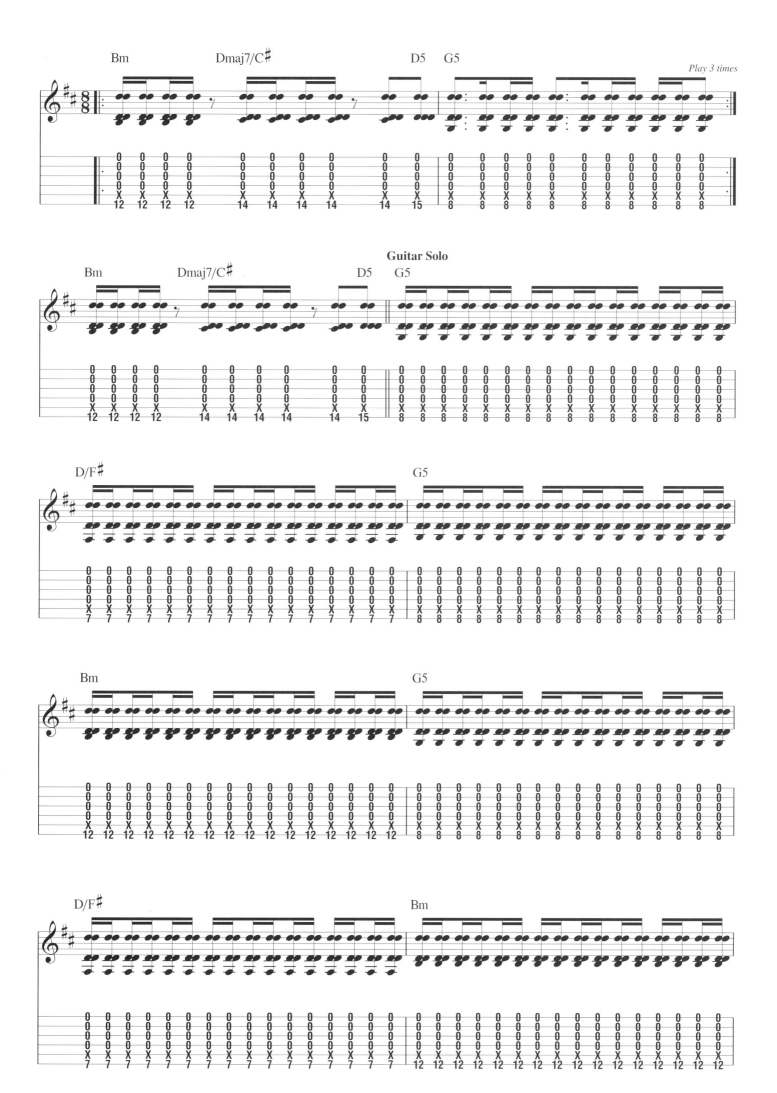

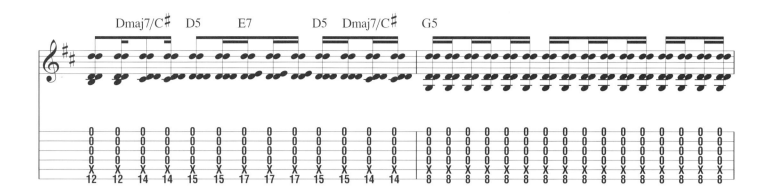

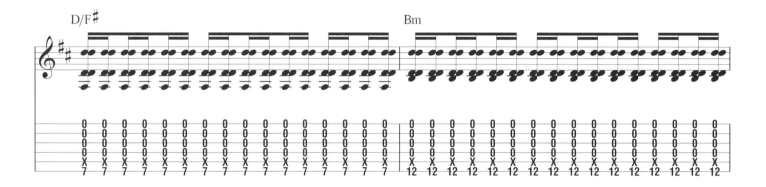

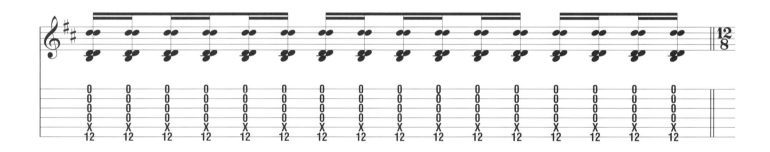

Interlude

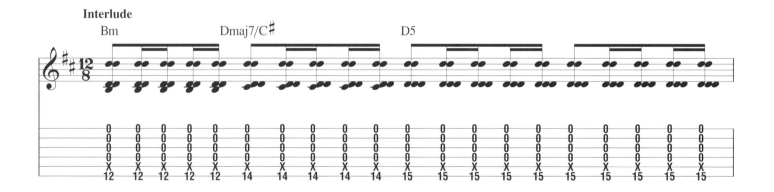

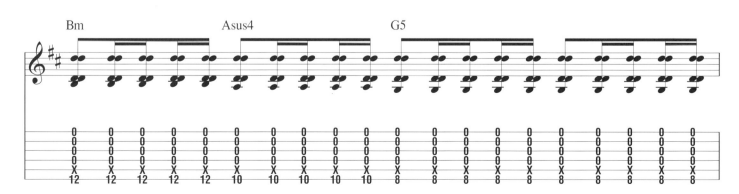

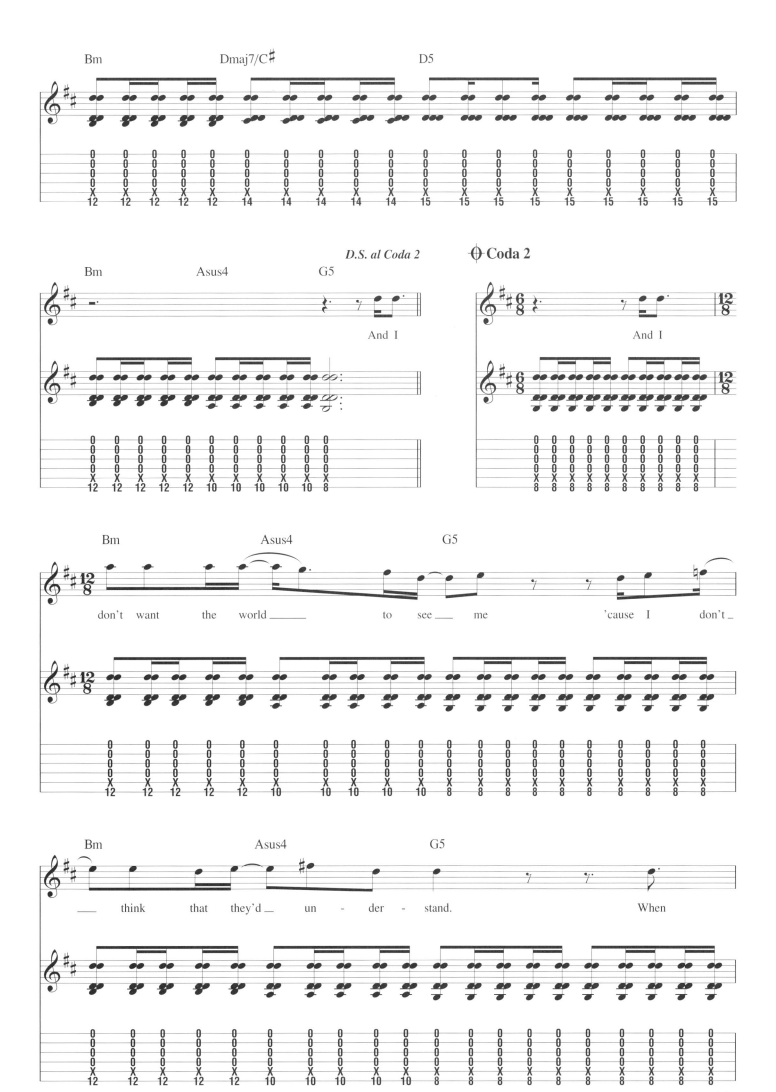

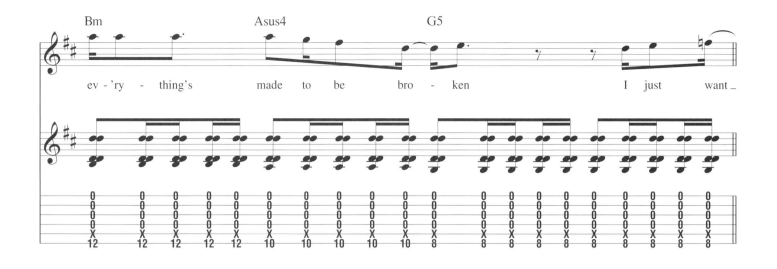

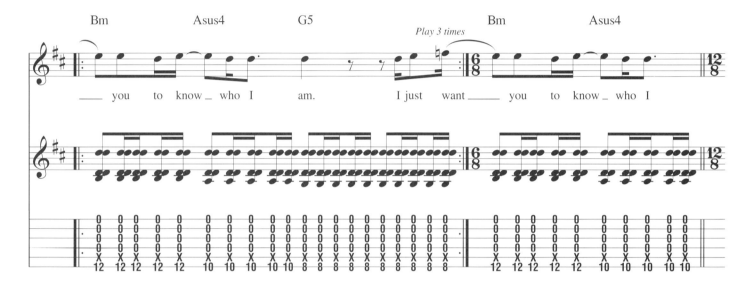

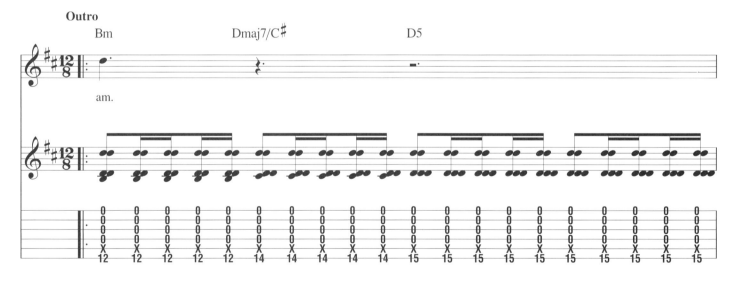

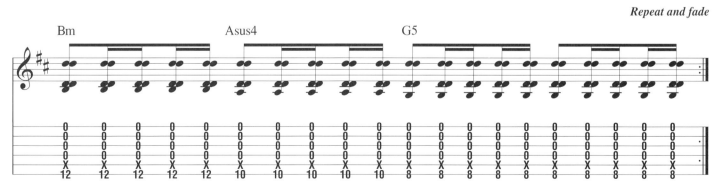

Iron Man

Words and Music by Frank Iommi, John Osbourne, William Ward and Terence Butler

Intro
Slow Rock ♩ = 69

N.C.(Em)

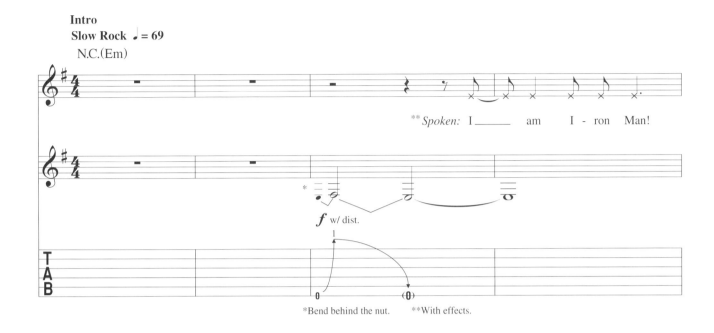

** *Spoken:* I ___ am I - ron Man!

*Bend behind the nut.   **With effects.

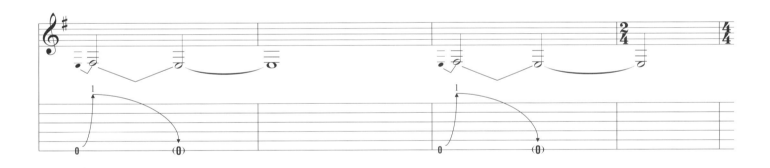

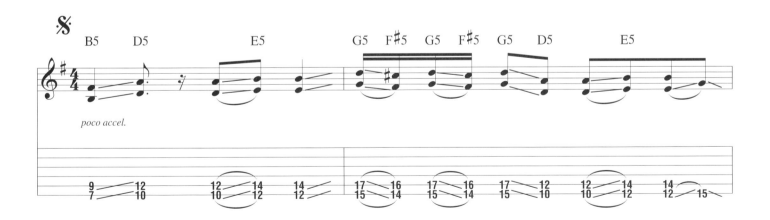

poco accel.

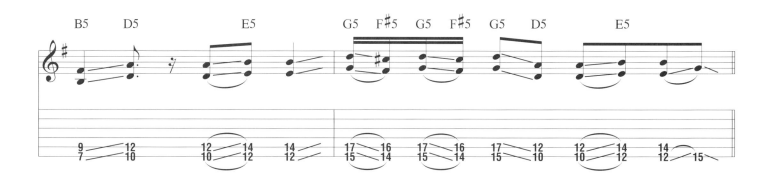

Verse
Slightly faster ♩ = 76

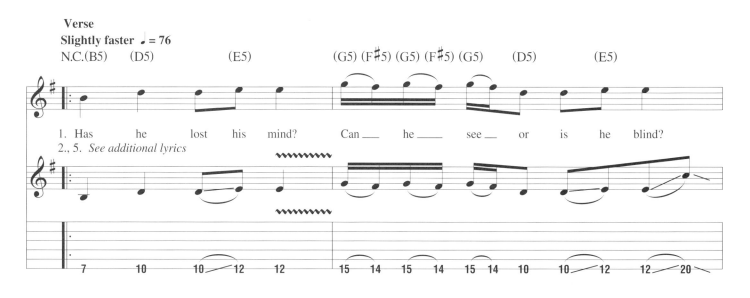

1. Has he lost his mind? Can __ he __ see __ or is he blind?
2., 5. See additional lyrics

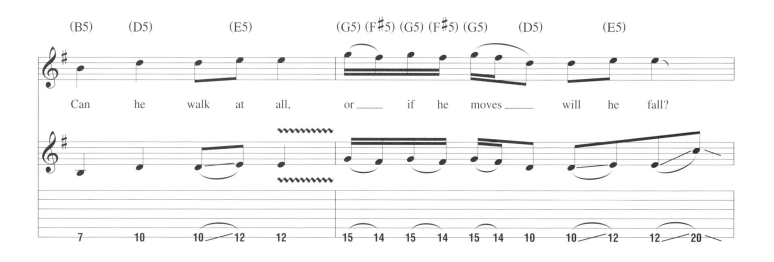

Can he walk at all, or __ if he moves __ will he fall?

1.

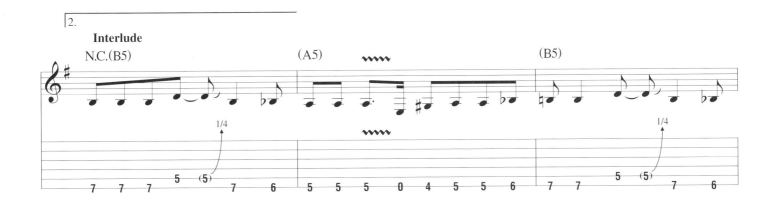

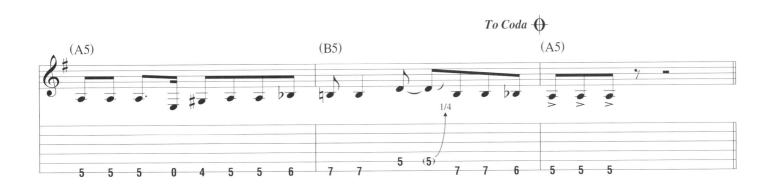

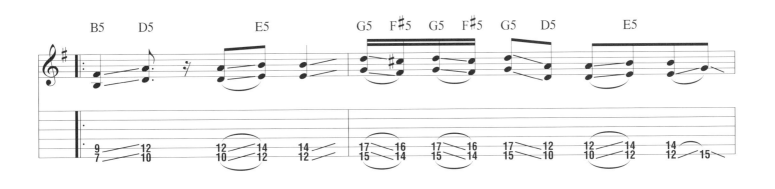

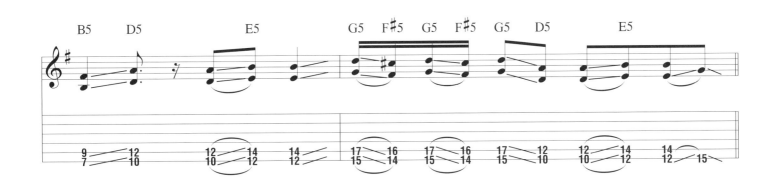

Verse

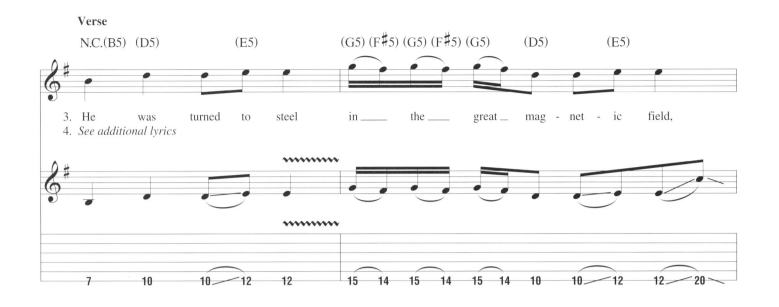

3. He was turned to steel in ___ the ___ great ___ mag - net - ic field,
4. *See additional lyrics*

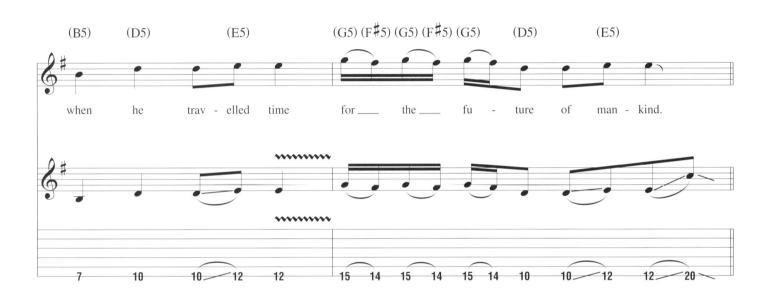

when he trav - elled time for ___ the ___ fu - ture of man - kind.

Bridge

No-bod- y wants ___ him, ___ he just stares ___ at the world. ___
See additional lyrics

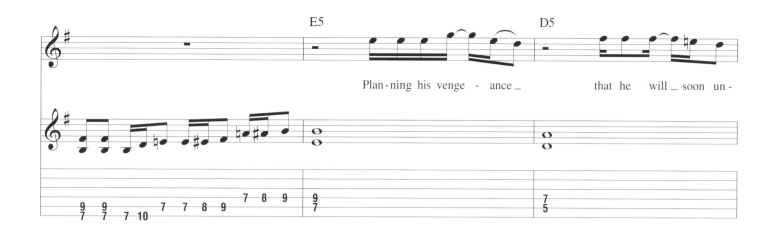

Plan-ning his venge - ance _ that he will _ soon un -

furl. _

Interlude
Double-time ♩ = 164

N.C.(C♯m)

Guitar Solo

N.C.(C♯m)

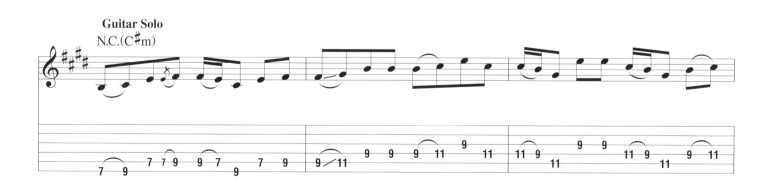

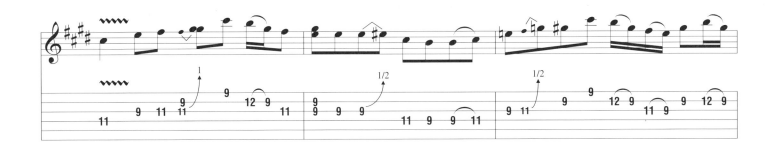

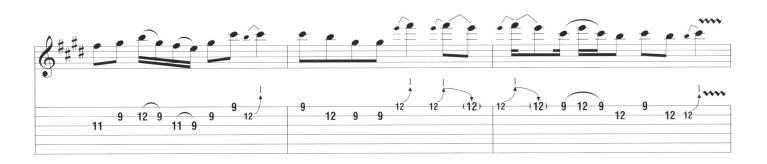

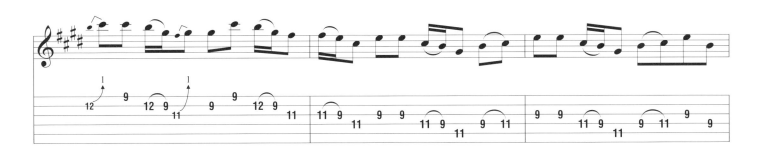

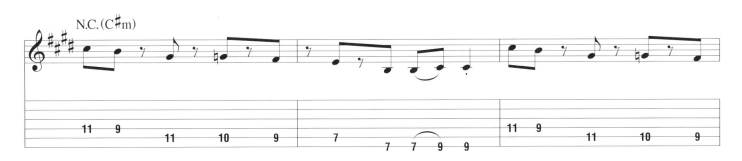

Half-time feel ♩ = 76

B5

Coda

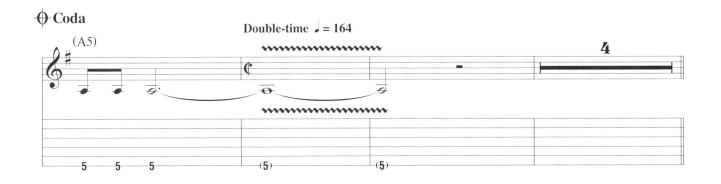

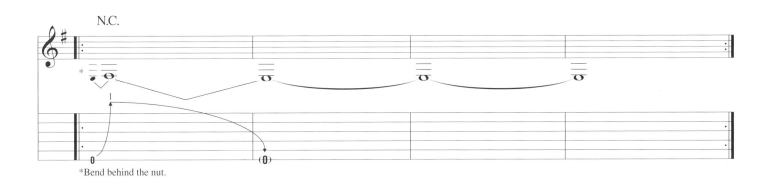

*Bend behind the nut.

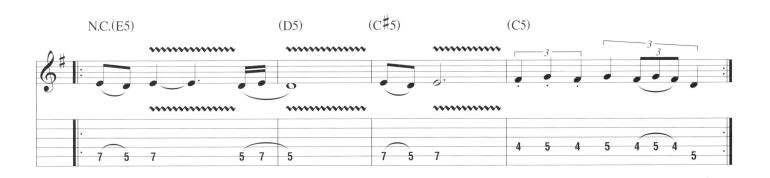

Guitar Solo

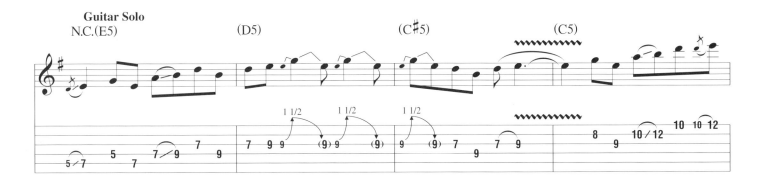

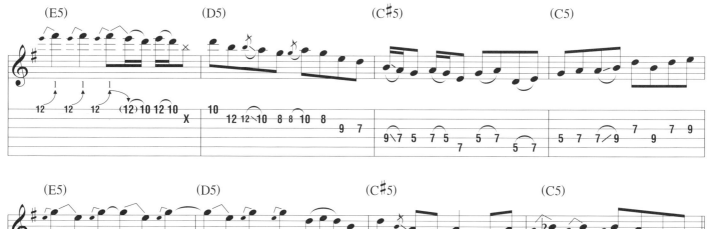

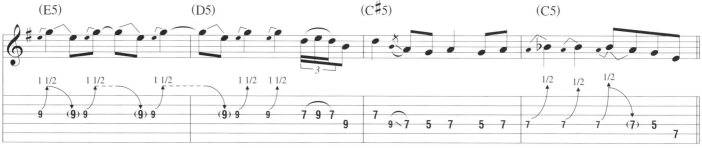

Outro

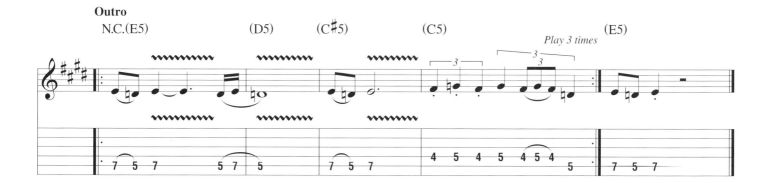

Additional Lyrics

2. Is he live or dead?
   I see thoughts within his head.
   We'll just pass him there.
   Why should we even care?

4. Now the time is here
   For Iron Man to spread fear.
   Vengeance from the grave,
   Kills the people he once saved.

Bridge Nobody wants him,
   They just turn their heads.
   Nobody helps him,
   Now he has his revenge.

5. Heavy boots of lead,
   Fills his victims full of dread,
   Running as fast as they can;
   Iron Man lives again.

The Kill

(Bury Me)

Words and Music by Jared Leto

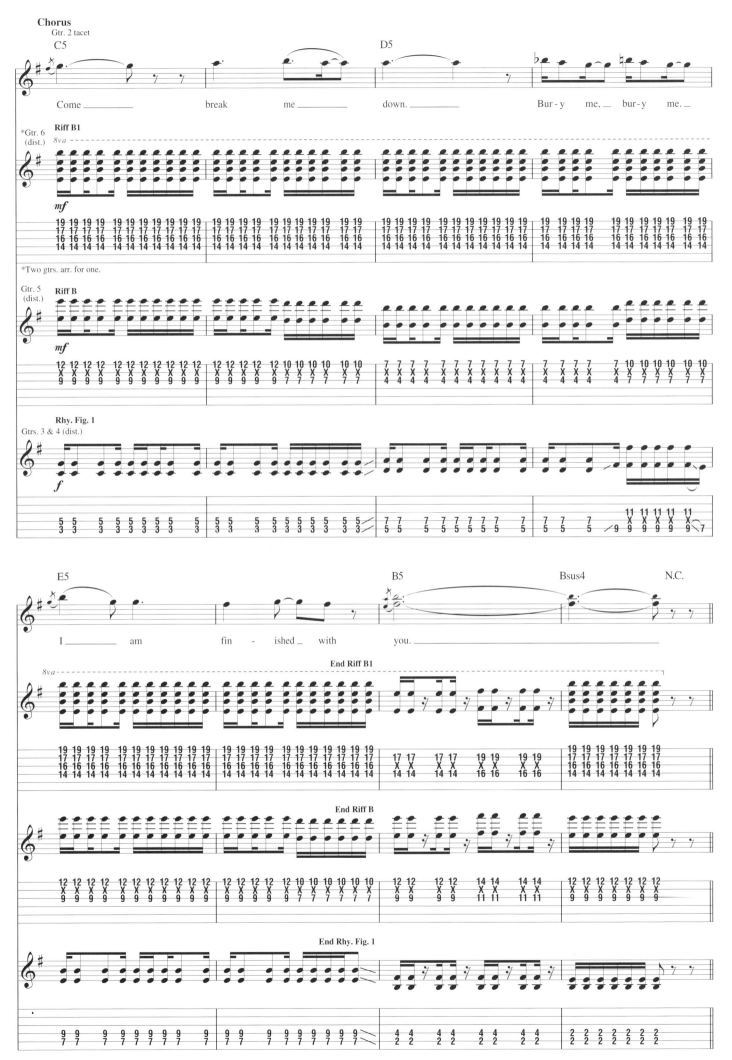

Verse

Gtrs. 3 - 6 tacet

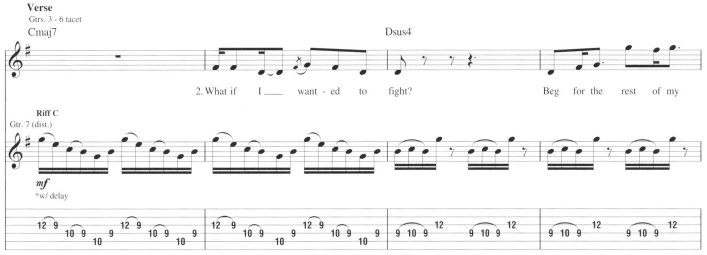

2. What if I ___ want - ed to fight? Beg for the rest of my

Riff C

Gtr. 7 (dist.)

mf

*w/ delay

*Delay set for eighth-note regeneration w/ 1 repeat.

life. What ___ would you ___ do? You

End Riff C

**w/ echo set for dotted quarter-note regeneration w/ 2 repeats.

Gtr. 1: w/ Riff A
Gtr. 7: w/ Riff C

say _____ you _____ want - ed _____ more. What _____ are you wait - ing _____ for?

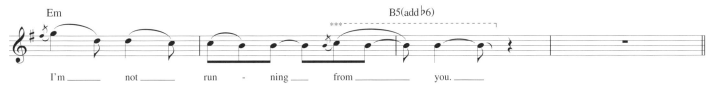

I'm _____ not _____ run - ning ___ from _____ you. ___

***w/ echo set for dotted half-note regeneration w/ 1 repeat.

Chorus

Gtrs. 3 & 4: w/ Rhy. Fig. 1
Gtrs. 5 & 6: w/ Riffs B & B1

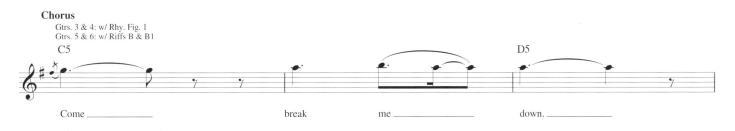

Come _____ break me down. _____

Bur - y me, Bur - y me. ___ I _____ am fin - ished ___ with

159

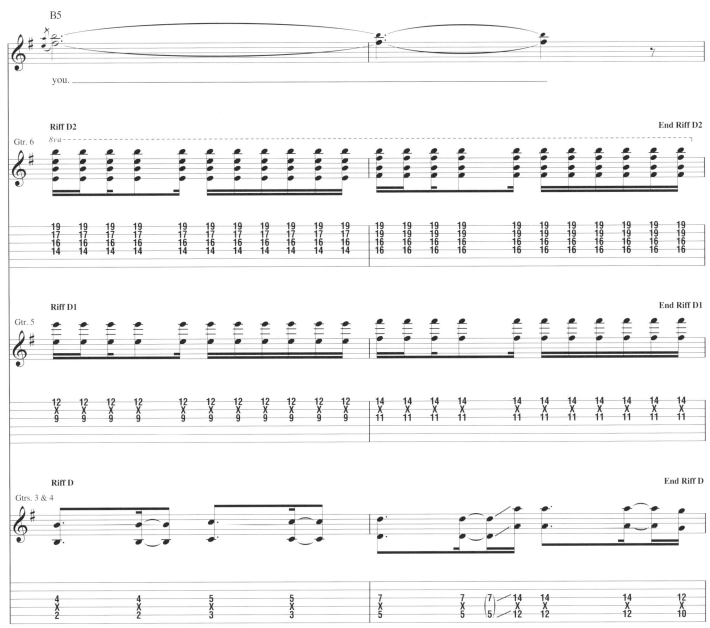

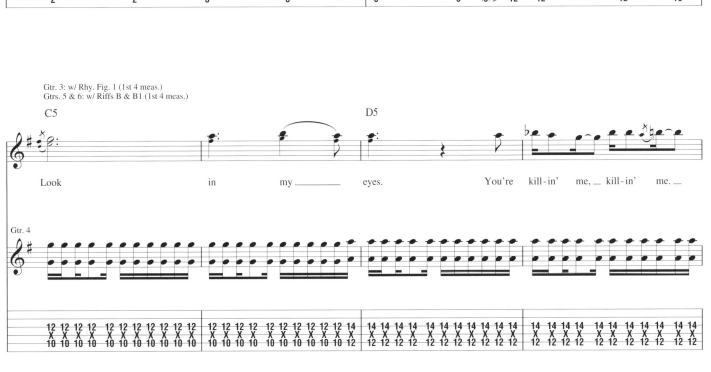

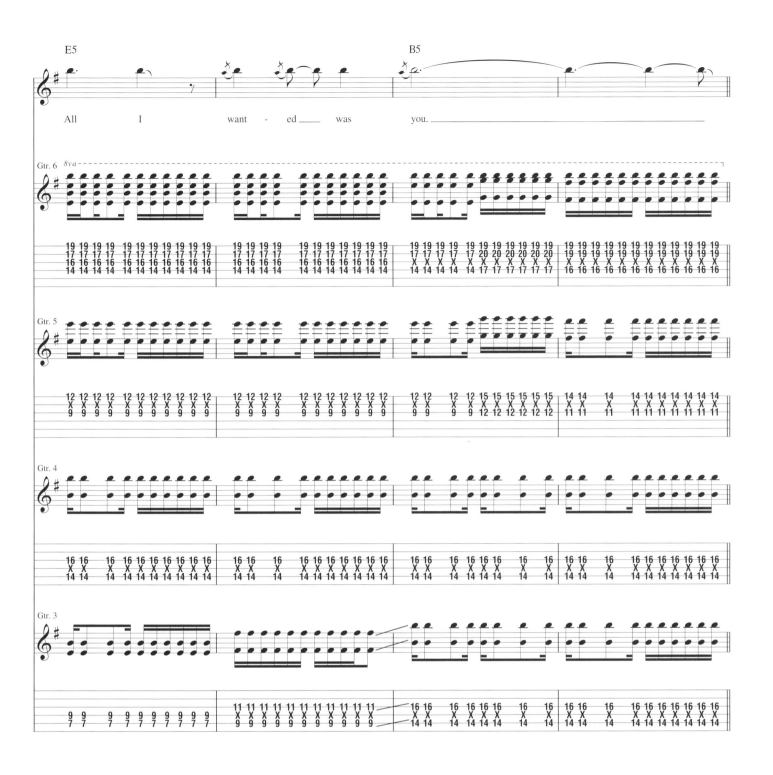

Bridge

*Chord symbols reflect overall harmony.

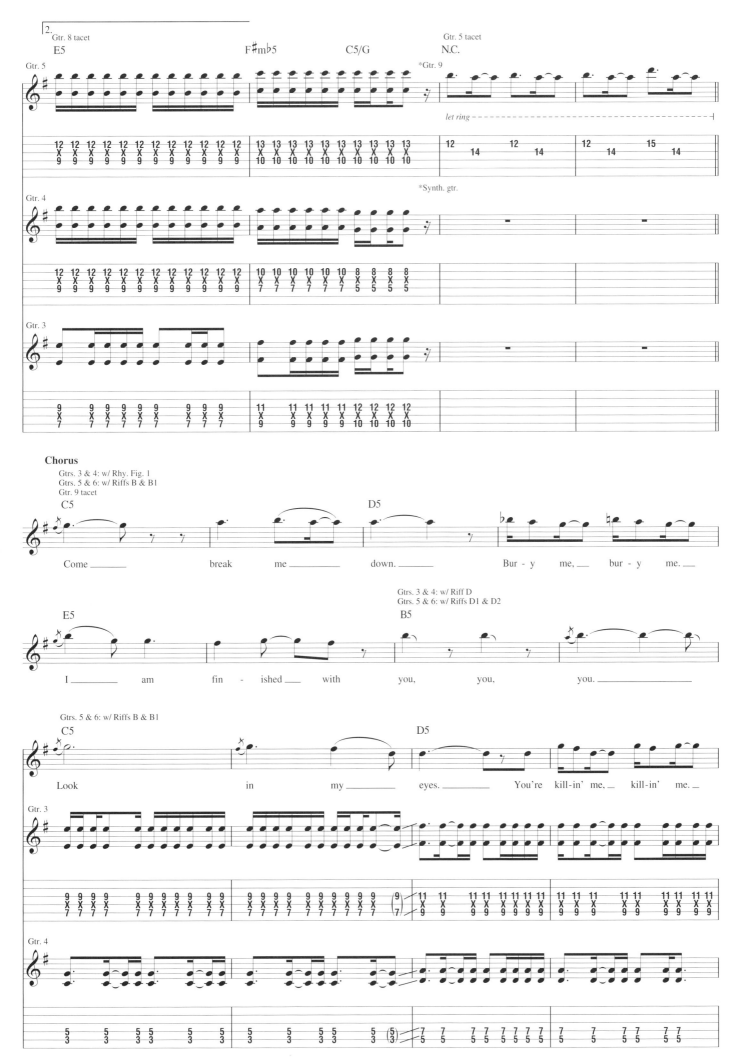

163

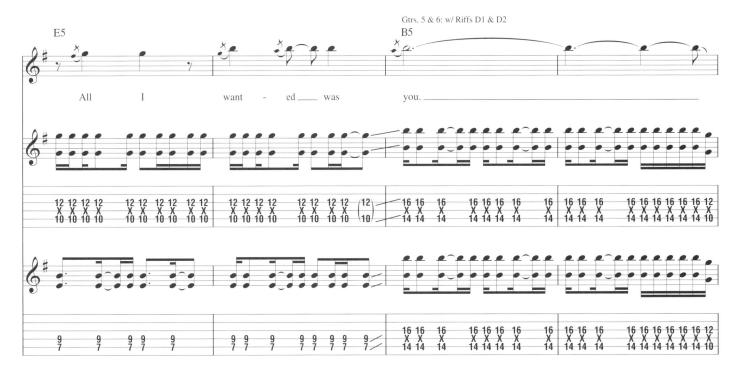

All I want - ed___ was you. _____

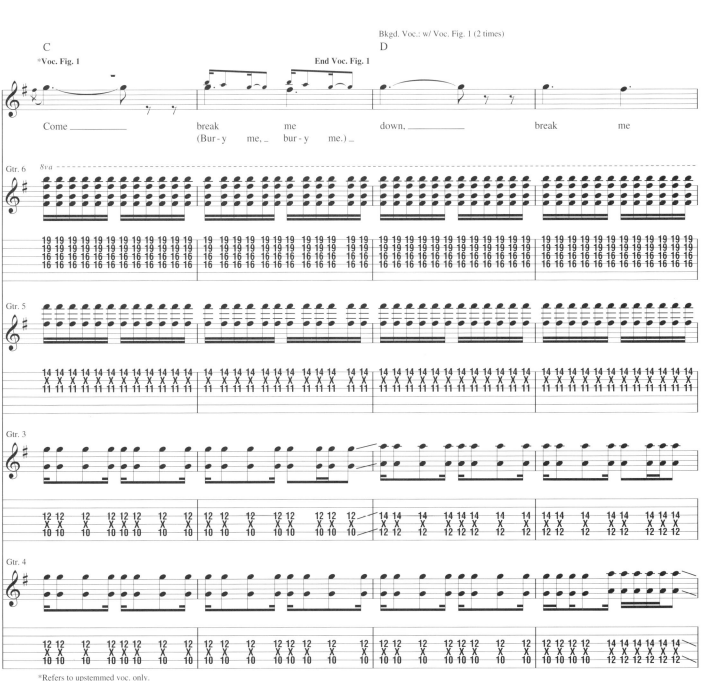

Come _____ break me down, _____ break me
(Bur - y me, _ bur - y me.) _

*Refers to upstemmed voc. only.

164

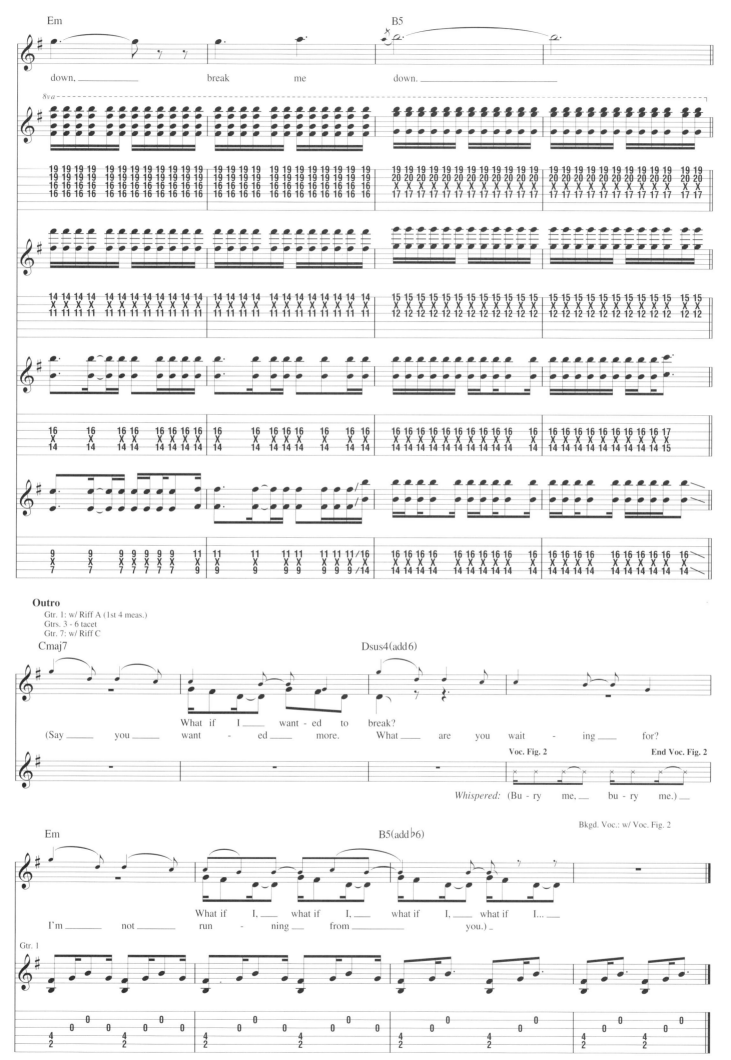

Let Me Hear You Scream

Words and Music by Ozzy Osbourne and Kevin Churko

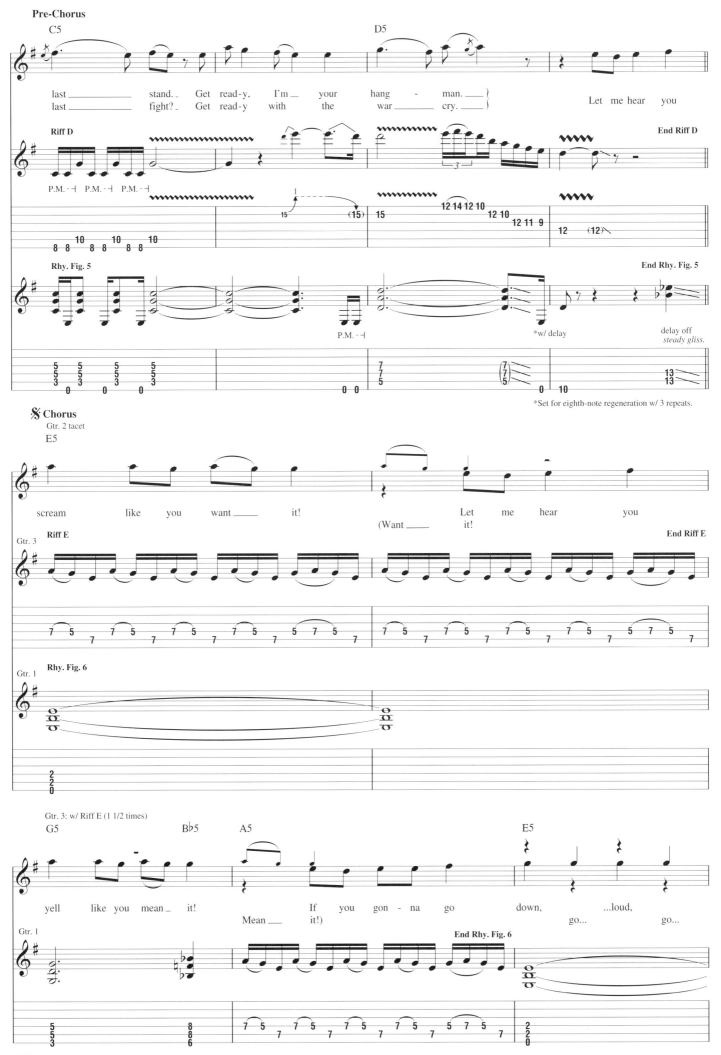

Lonely Day

Words and Music by Daron Malakian and Serj Tankian

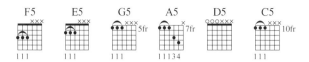

Gtrs. 1 & 3–7: Tune down 1/2 step:
(low to high) E♭-A♭-D♭-G♭-B♭-E♭

Gtr. 2: Drop D tuning, down 1/2 step:
(low to high) D♭-A♭-D♭-G♭-B♭-E♭

Intro
Moderately ♩ = 76

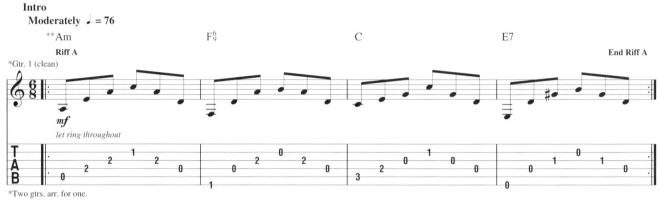

*Two gtrs. arr. for one.

**Chord symbols reflect implied harmony.

Verse

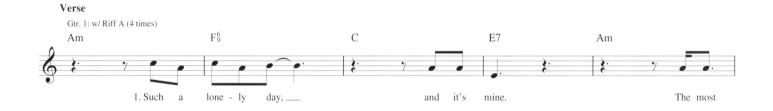

Chorus

The most lone-li-est day of my life. _____ The most

Rhy. Fig. 1
*Gtr. 2 (dist.)

End Rhy. Fig. 1

*Doubled throughout

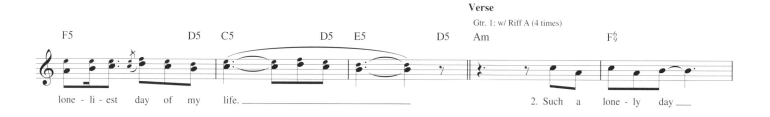

lone-li-est day of my life. _____

Verse

Gtr. 1: w/ Riff A (4 times)

2. Such a lone-ly day ___

should-n't ex - ist. _____ It's a day that I'll nev-er miss. _____

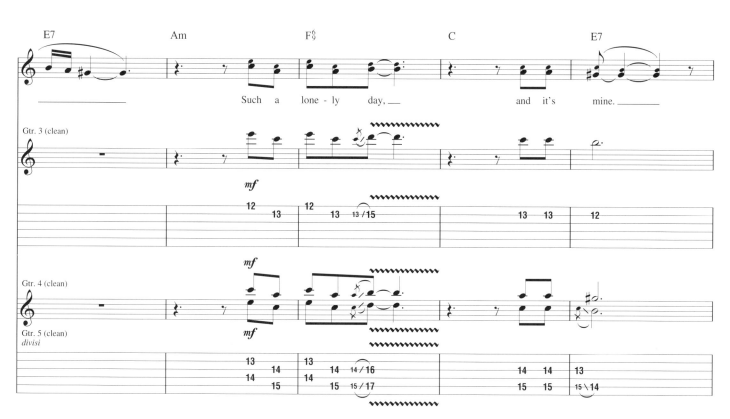

Such a lone-ly day, ___ and it's mine. _____

Gtr. 3 (clean)

Gtr. 4 (clean)

Gtr. 5 (clean)
divisi

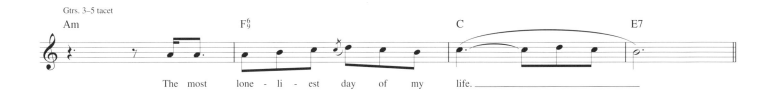

Guitar Solo

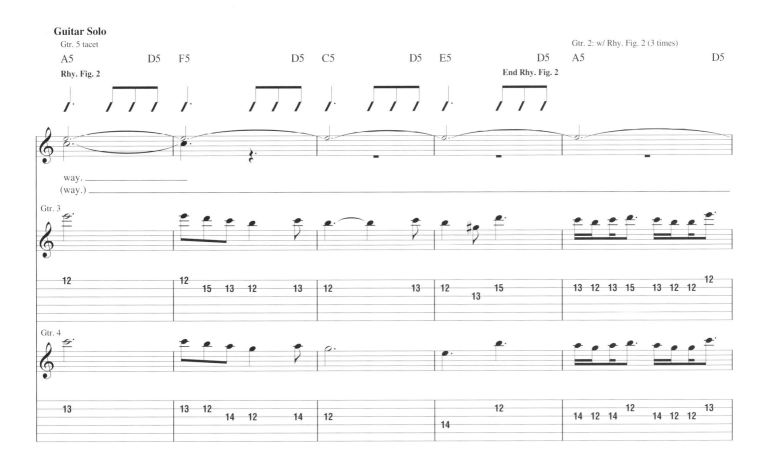

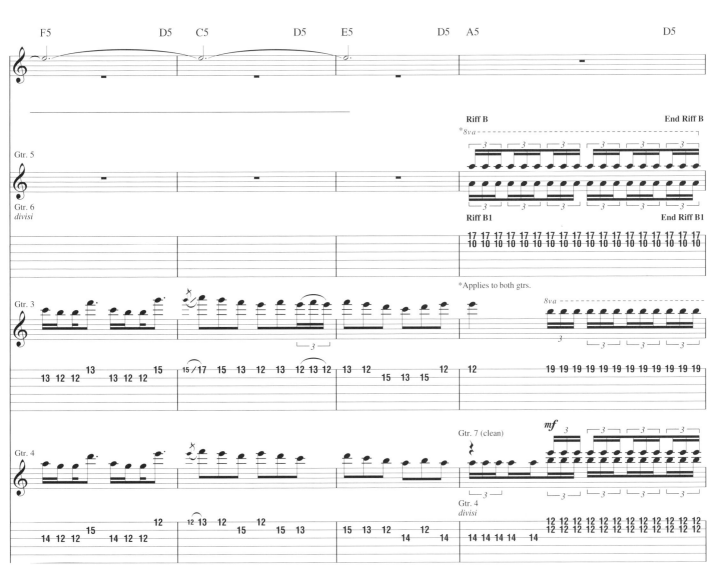

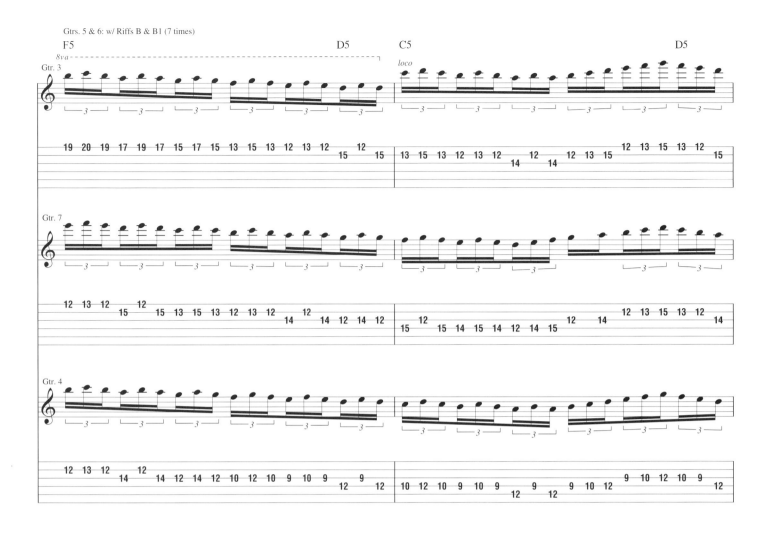

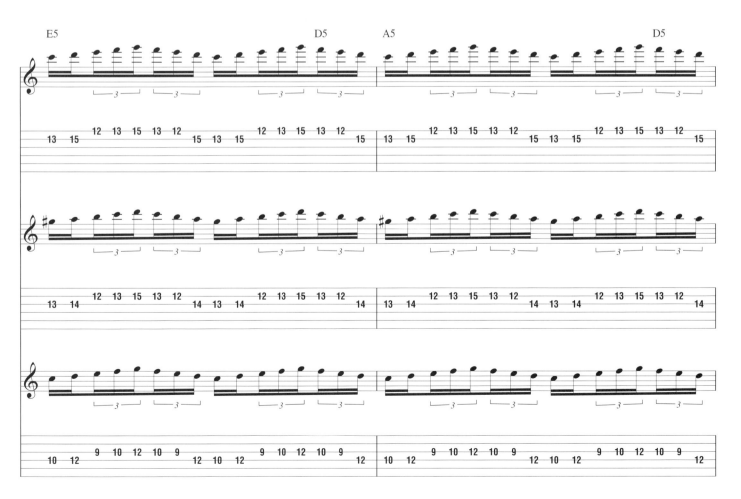

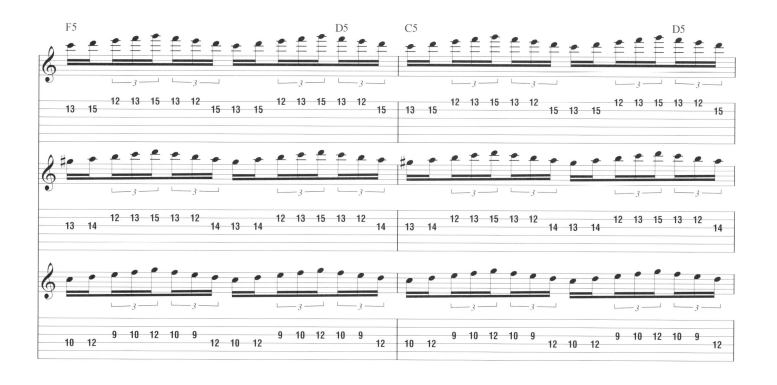

Chorus

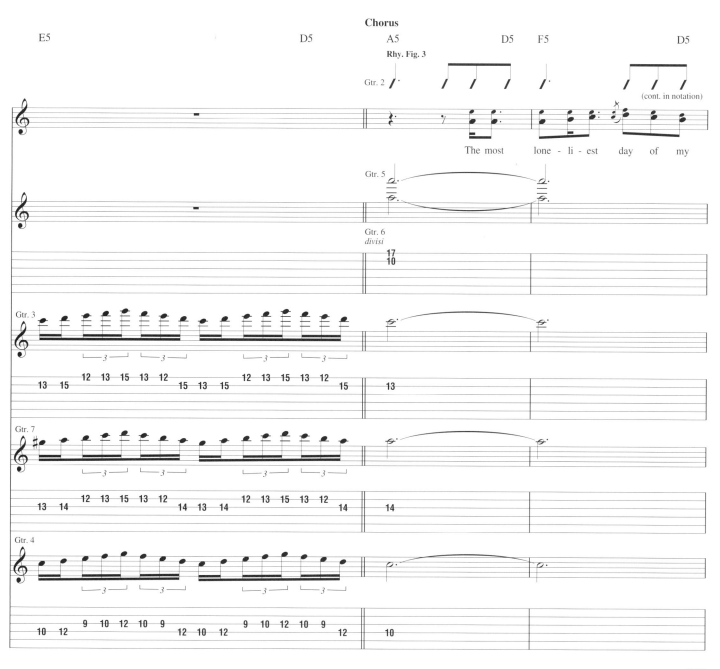

The most lone - li - est day of my

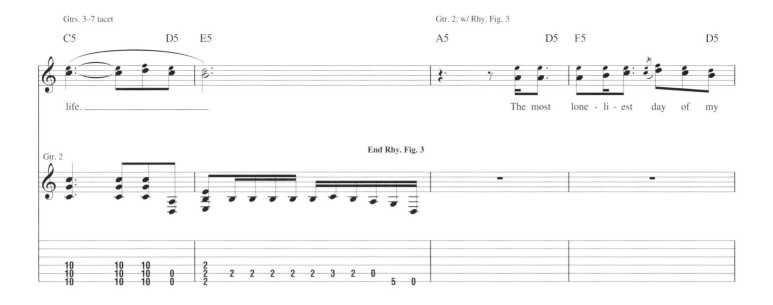

Outro-Verse

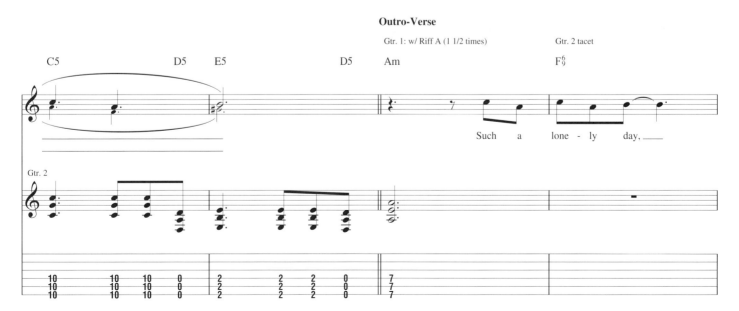

and it's mine. It's a day that I'm glad I ___ sur-

Slowly ♩ = 65

vived.

Gtr. 3

8va

Harm.

Pitch: E

Gtr. 4

mp *p*

w/ dist.
w/ slide

*Vol. swell

Gtr. 5

mp *p*

w/ dist.
w/ slide

**Vol. swell

Gtr. 1

Maggie May

Words and Music by Rod Stewart and Martin Quittenton

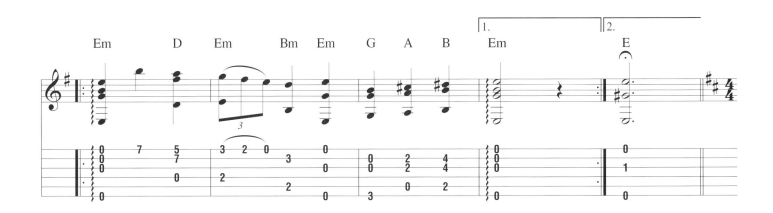

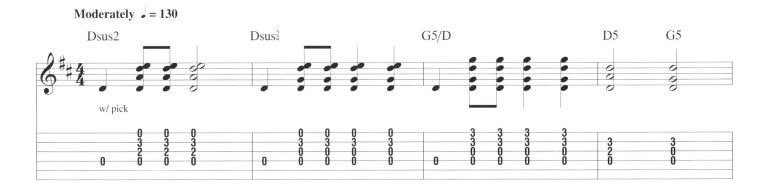

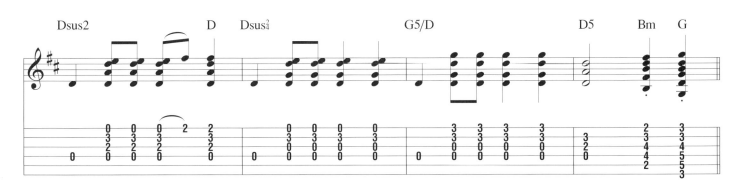

183

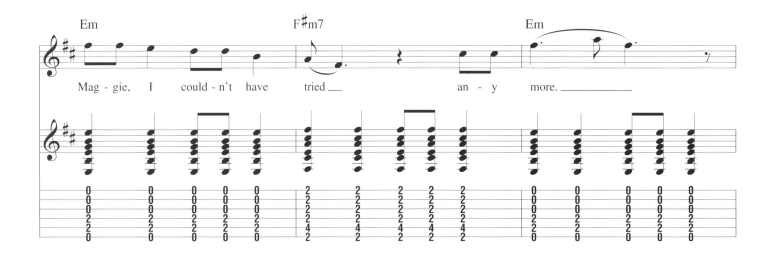

Verse
A
G5
D
1. Wake up, Mag - gie, I think I got some - thin' to say to you.
2., 3., 4. See additional lyrics
A
G5
It's late Sep - tem - ber and I real - ly should be back
D
G5
at school.
I know I keep you a - mused,
D
G5
A
but I feel I'm be - ing used.
Oh,

Mag - gie, I could-n't have tried ___ an - y more. _____

2nd & 3rd times, substitute Fill 1
4th time, substitute Fill 3

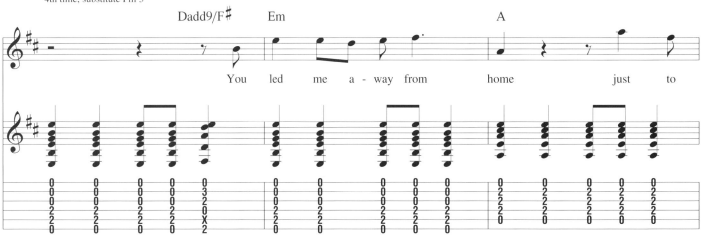

You led me a - way from home ___ just to

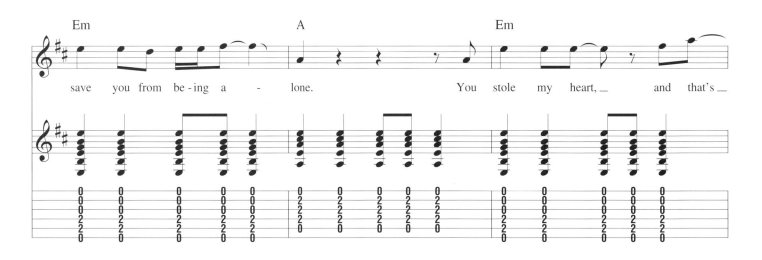

save you from be -ing a - lone. You stole my heart, ___ and that's ___

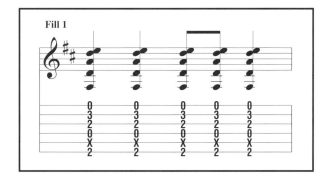

Fill 1

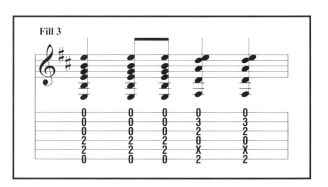

Fill 3

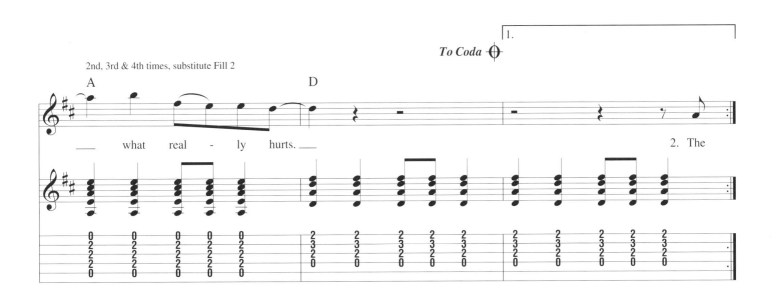

2nd, 3rd & 4th times, substitute Fill 2

To Coda ⊕

1.

___ what real - ly hurts. ___

2. The

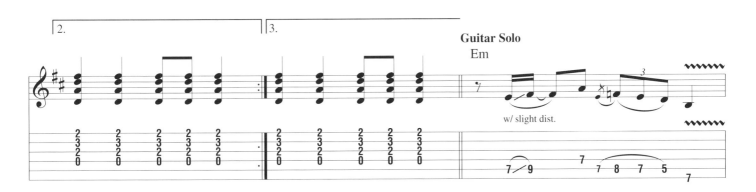

2.

3.

Guitar Solo

Em

w/ slight dist.

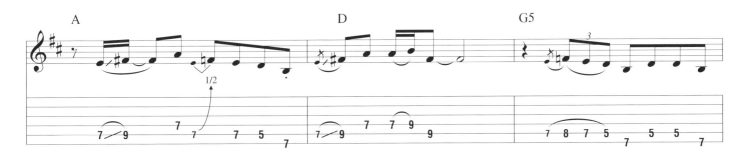

A

D

G5

D.S. al Coda

Em

D

G5

D

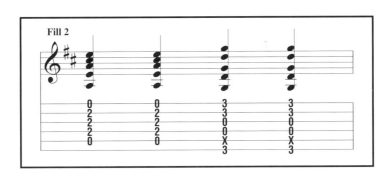

Fill 2

185

⊕ Coda

Guitar Solo

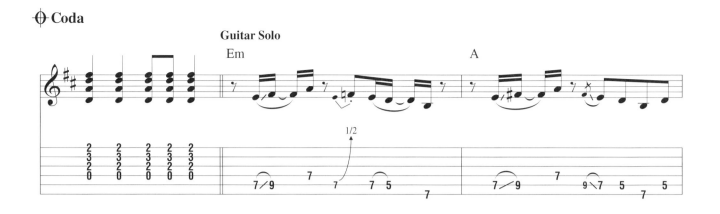

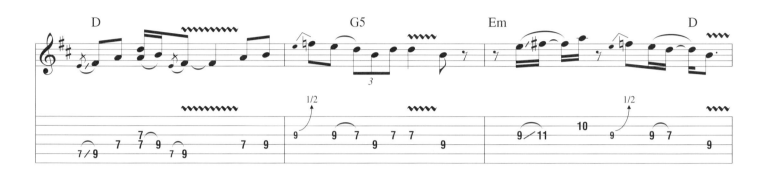

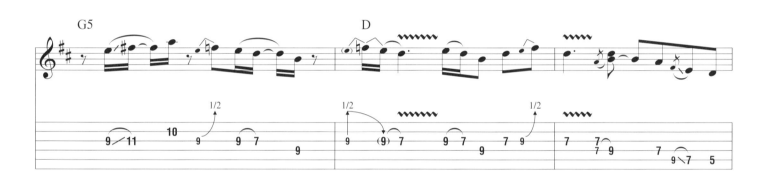

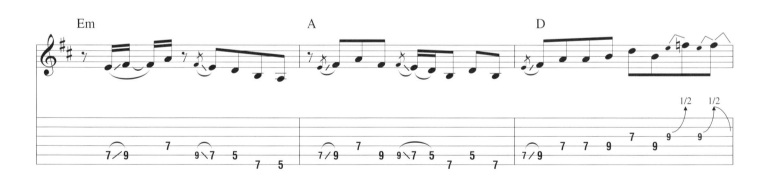

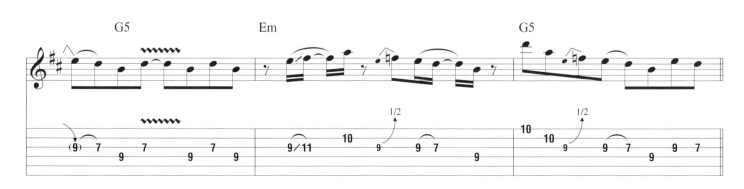

Mandolin Solo

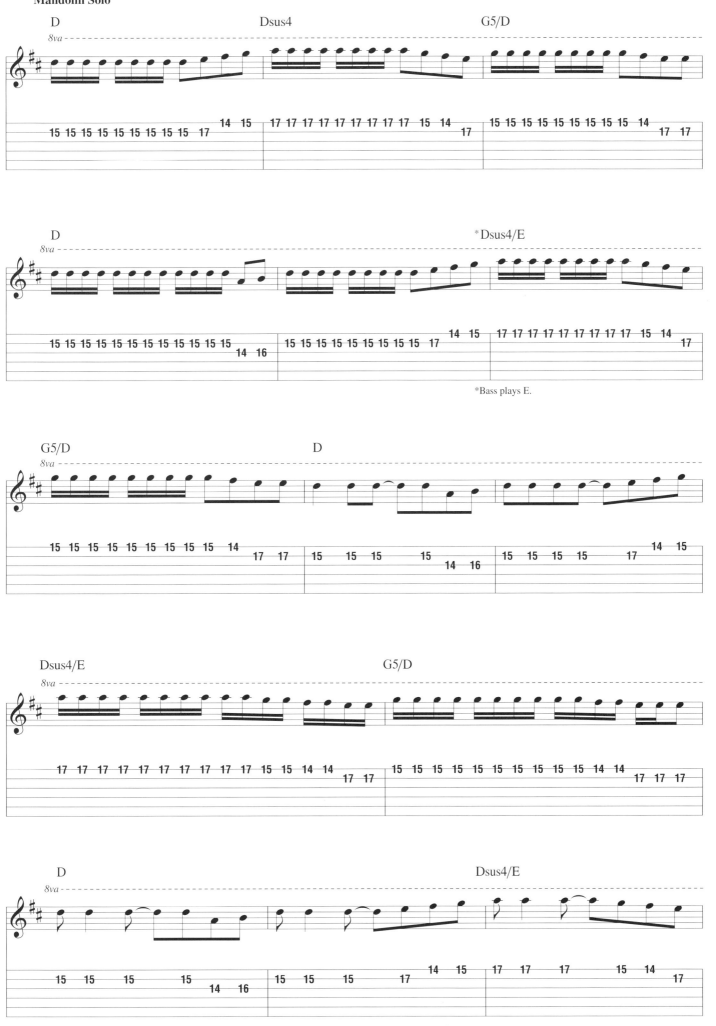

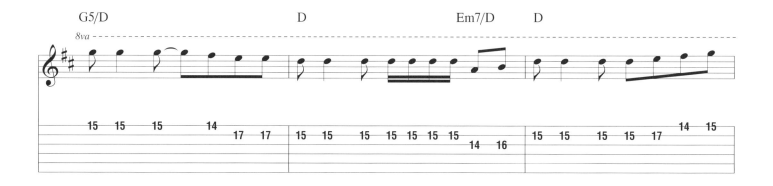

Outro

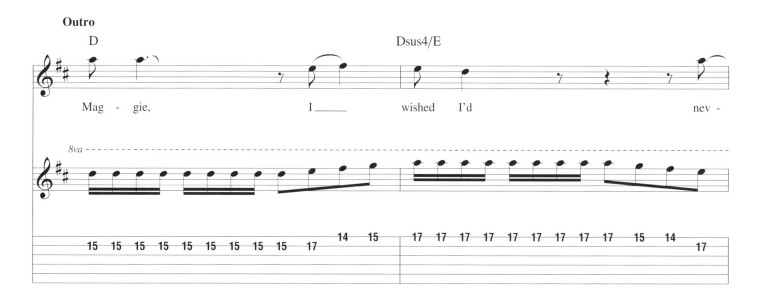

Mag - gie, I _____ wished I'd nev -

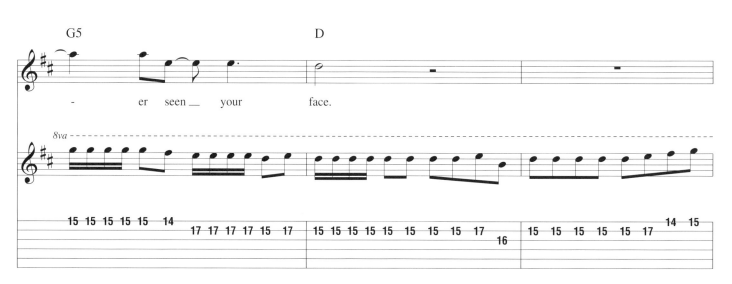

- er seen _ your face.

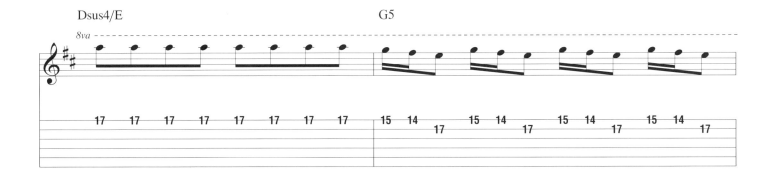

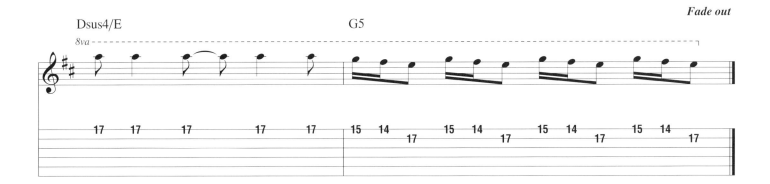

Additional Lyrics

2. The morning sun, when it's in your face, really shows your age.
   But that don't worry me none. In my eyes, you're everything.
   I laughed at all of your jokes.
   My love you didn't need to coax.
   Oh, Maggie, I couldn't have tried any more.
   You led me away from home
   Just to save you from being alone.
   You stole my soul, and that's a pain I can do without.

3. All I needed was a friend to lend a guiding hand.
   But you turned into a lover and, mother, what a lover! You wore me out.
   All you did was wreck my bed,
   And, in the morning, kick me in the head.
   Oh, Maggie, I couldn't have tried any more.
   You led me away from home
   'Cause you didn't want to be alone.
   You stole me heart; I couldn't leave you if I tried.

4. I suppose I could collect my books and get on back to school.
   Or steal my daddy's cue and make a living out of playing pool.
   Or find myself a rock 'n' roll band
   That needs a helping hand.
   Oh, Maggie, I wish I'd never seen your face.
   You made a first-class fool out of me.
   But I'm as blind as a fool can be.
   You stole me heart, but I love you anyway.

Message in a Bottle

Music and Lyrics by Sting

1. Just a cast - a - way, _ an is - land lost _ at sea, _
2.,3. *See additional lyrics*

_ oh. _ An - oth - er lone - ly day, _

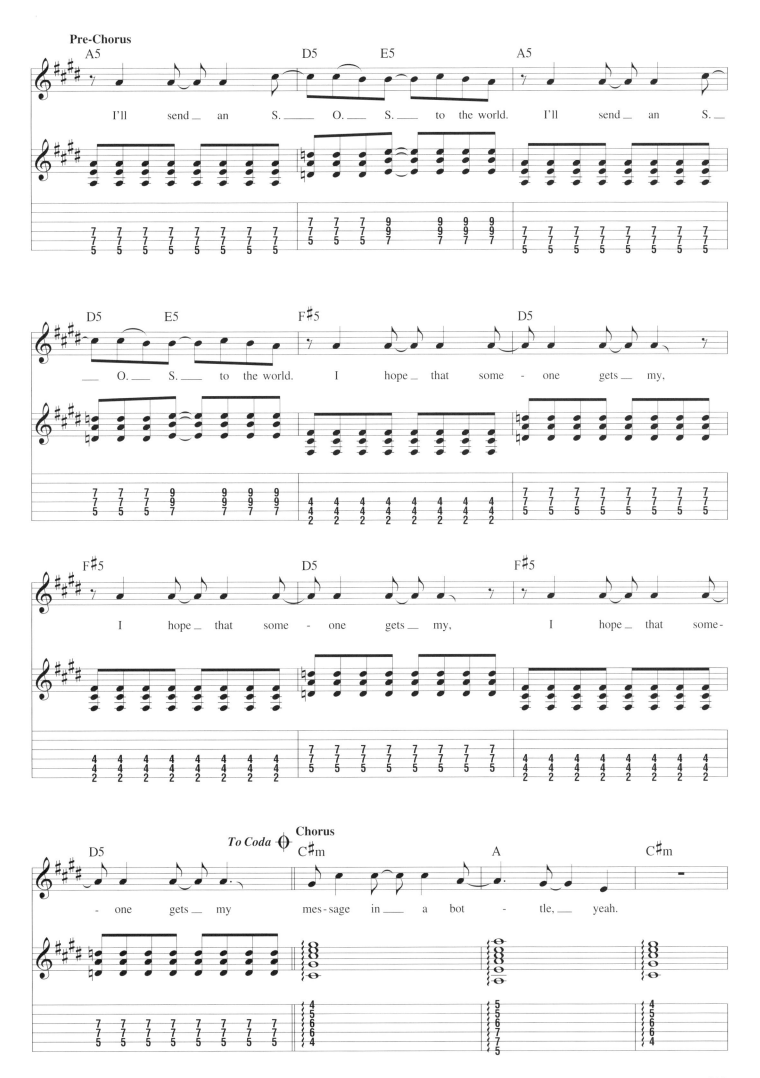

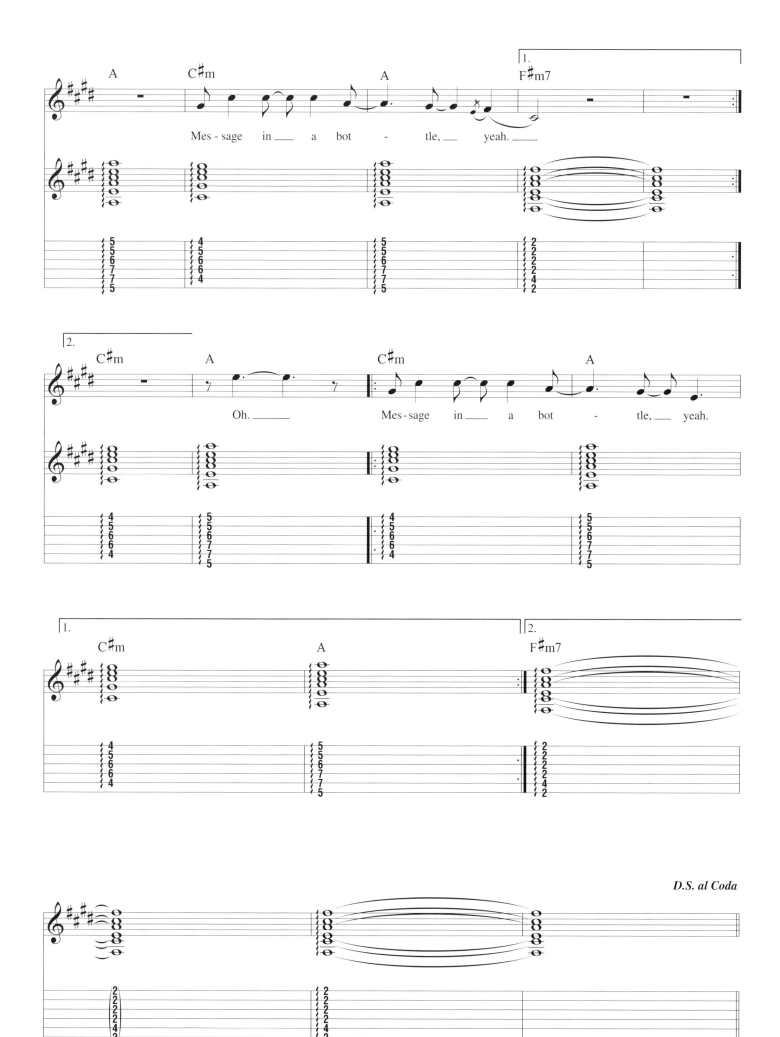

Additional Lyrics

2. A year has passed since I wrote my note.
   I should have known this right from the start.
   Only hope can keep me together.
   Love can mend your life, but love can break your heart.

3. Woke up this morning, I don't believe what I saw,
   Hundred billion bottles washed up on the shore.
   Seems I never noticed being alone.
   Hundred billion castaways, looking for a home.

More Than Words

Words and Music by Nuno Bettencourt and Gary Cherone

Tune down 1/2 step:
(low to high) Eb-Ab-Db-Gb-Bb-Eb

Intro

Moderately slow ♩ = 96

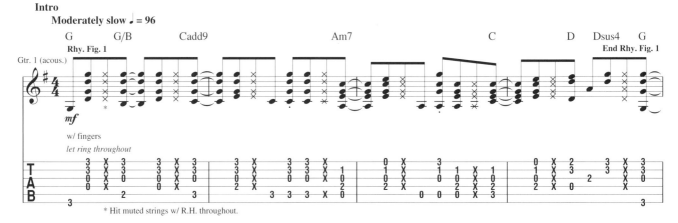

* Hit muted strings w/ R.H. throughout.

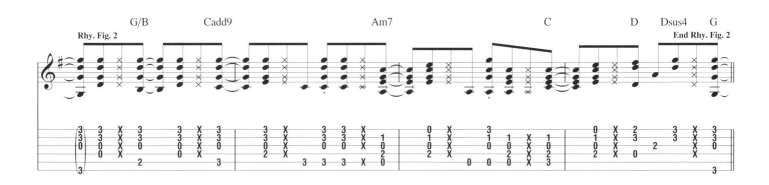

Verse

Gtr. 1: w/ Rhy. Fig. 2

1. Say - ing "I ___ love ___ you" is not the words ___ I want ___ to ___ hear ___ from you. ___

___ It's not that I ___ want ___ you not to say, ___ but if

Gtr. 1

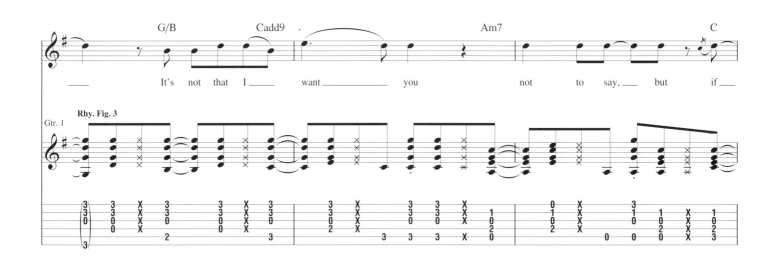

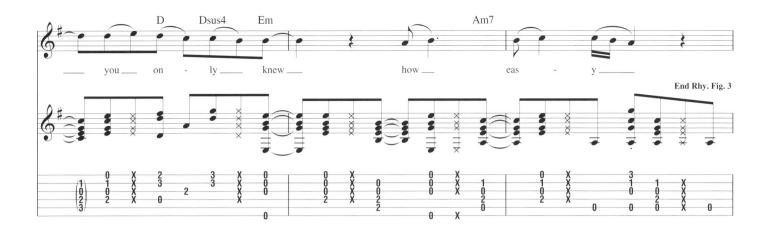

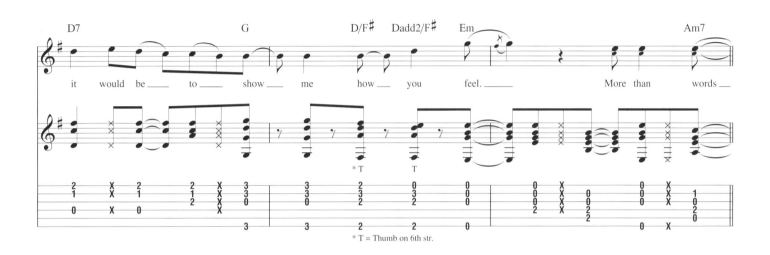

* T = Thumb on 6th str.

Chorus

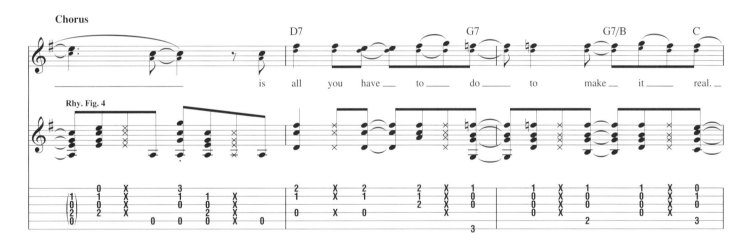

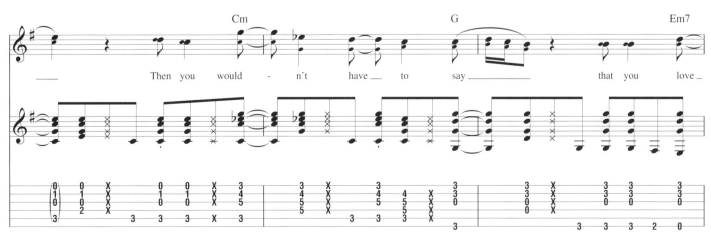

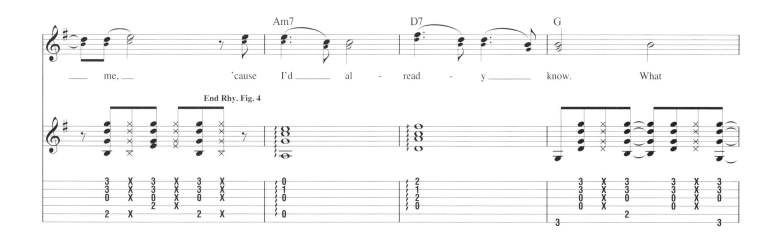

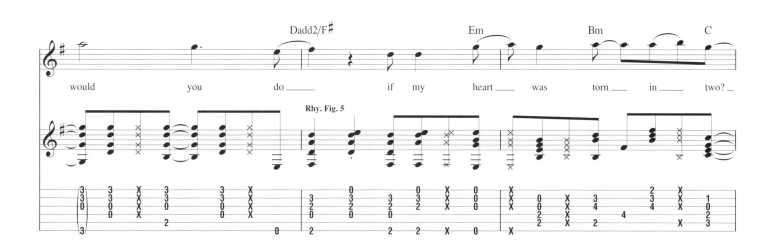

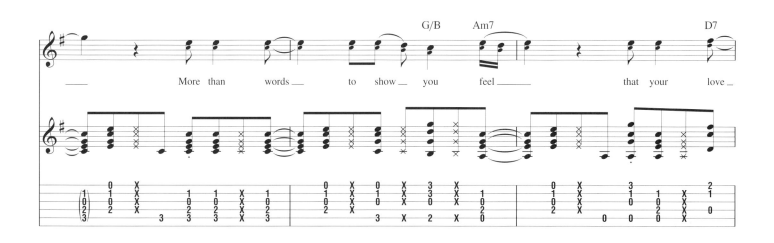

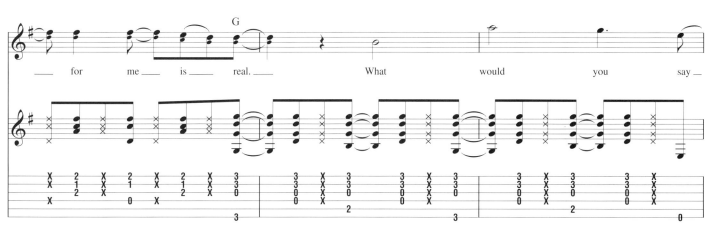

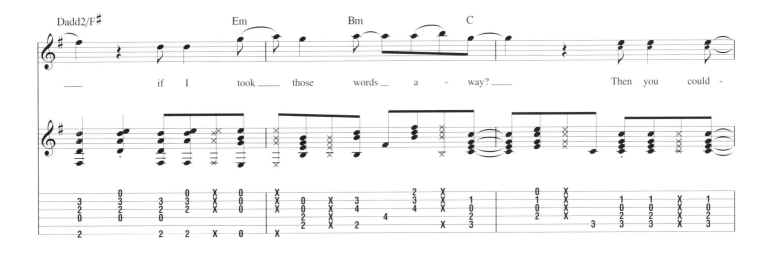

if I took those words a - way? Then you could -

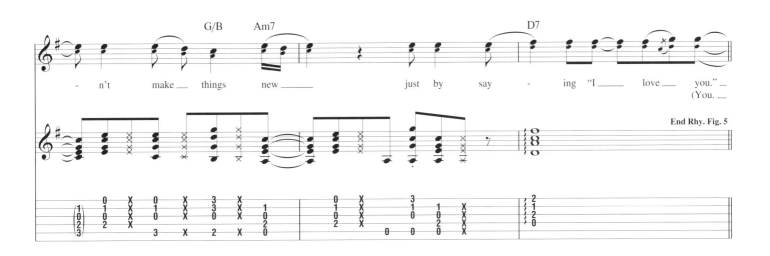

-n't make things new just by say - ing "I love you." (You.

End Rhy. Fig. 5

Interlude
Gtr. 1: w/ Rhy. Fig. 1

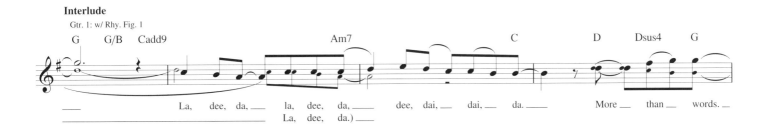

La, dee, da, la, dee, da, dee, dai, dai, da. More than words.
La, dee, da.) You.

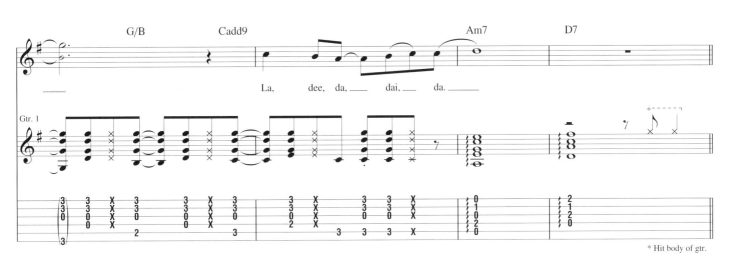

La, dee, da, dai, da.

Gtr. 1

* Hit body of gtr.

Verse

Gtr. 1: w/ Rhy. Fig. 1

2. Now that I've tried to talk to you and make you un - der - stand,

Gtr. 1: w/ Rhy. Fig. 3

all you have to do is close your eyes and just

reach out your hands and touch me.

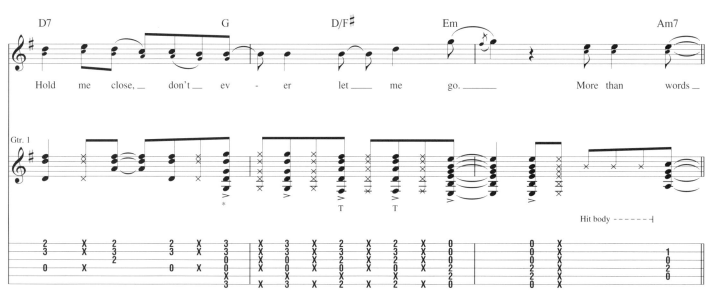

* Strum accented chords w/ nails (all downstrokes);
hit muted strings w/ R.H. as before.

Chorus

Gtr. 1: w/ Rhy. Fig. 4

is all I ev - er need - ed you to show.

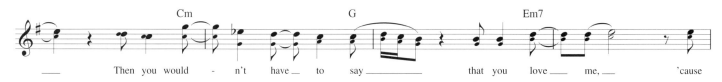

Then you would - n't have to say that you love me, 'cause

200

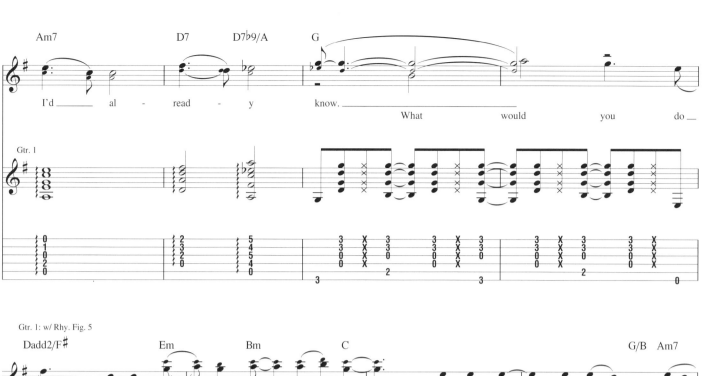

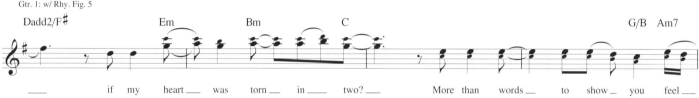

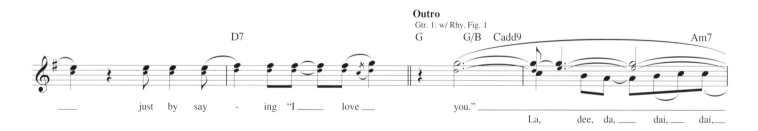

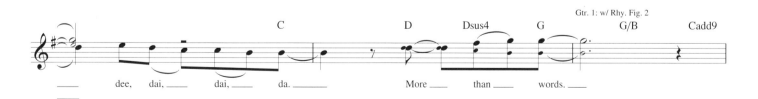

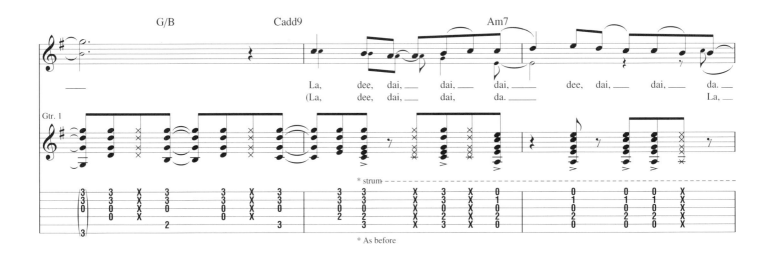

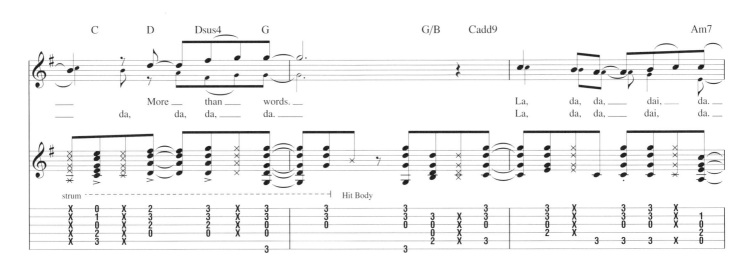

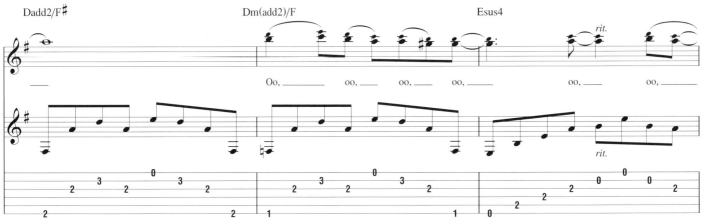

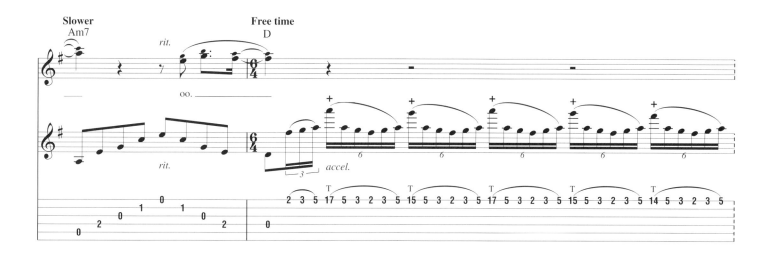

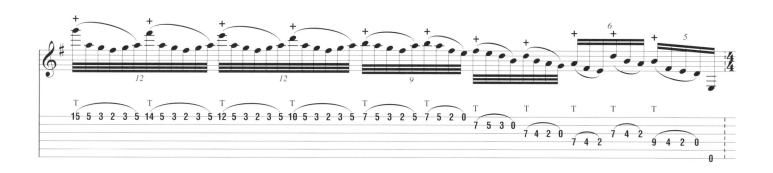

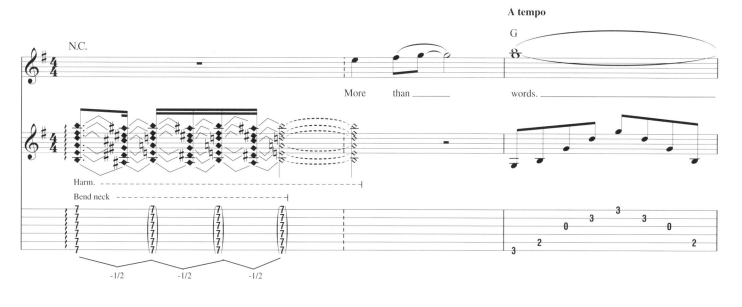

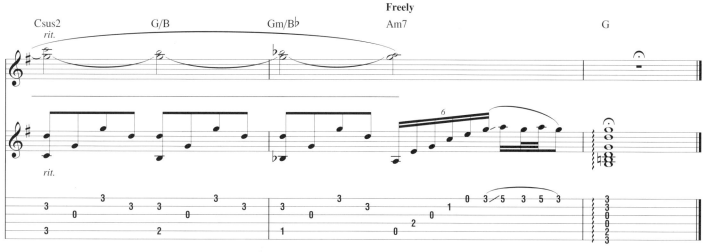

New Kid in Town

Words and Music by John David Souther, Don Henley and Glenn Frey

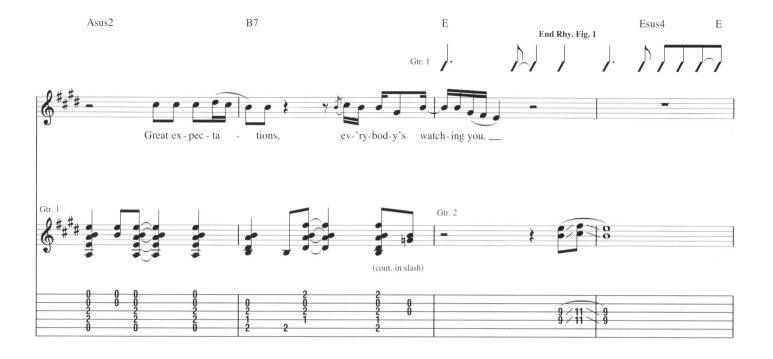

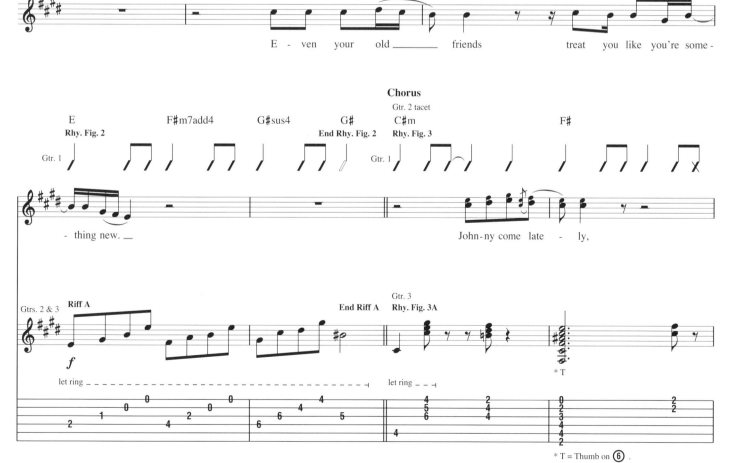

* T = Thumb on ⑥.

Guitar Solo

Gtr. 1: w/ Rhy. Fig. 1, simile
Gtr. 2 tacet

Interlude

There's so man - y

* next 6 meas.

things you should have told _____ her, but night af - ter

night you're wil - lin' to hold _____ her, just hold _____ her. Tears _____ on your

shoul - der.
(Oo. _____)

There's talk on the street _____ it's there to re - mind _

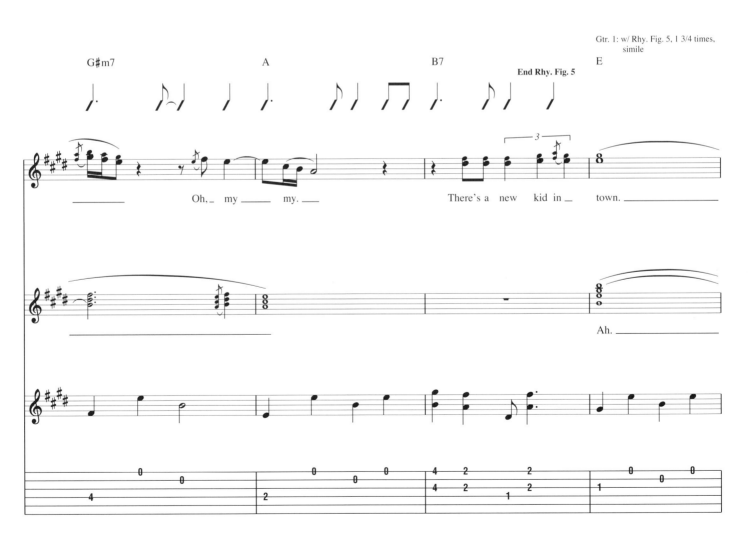

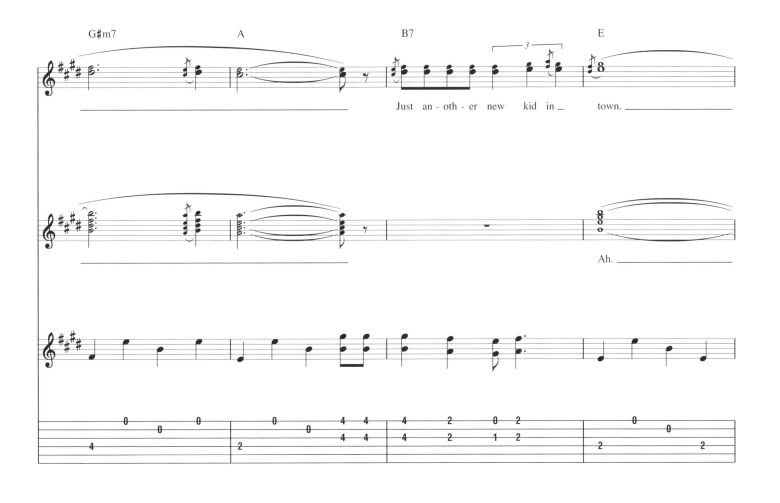

Just an-oth-er new kid in ___ town. ___

Ah. ___

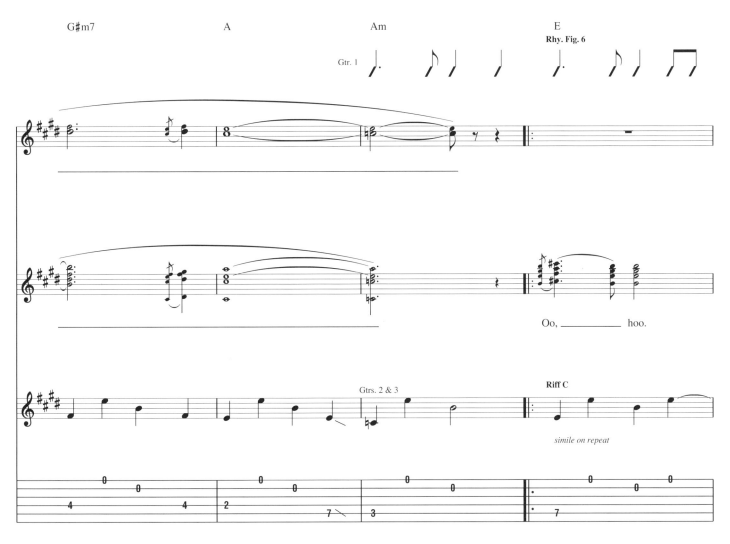

Oo, ___ hoo.

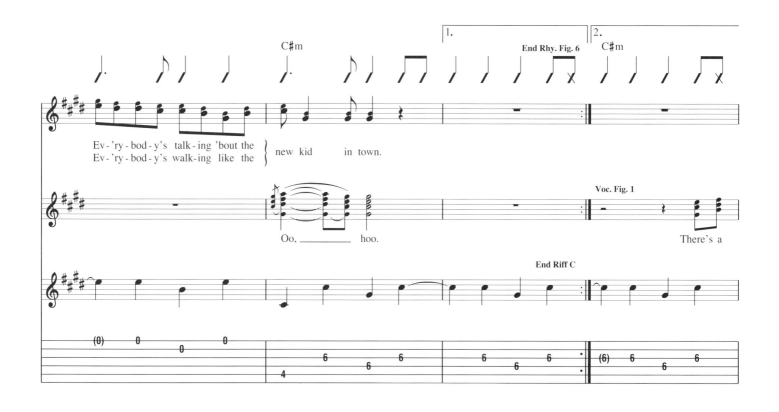

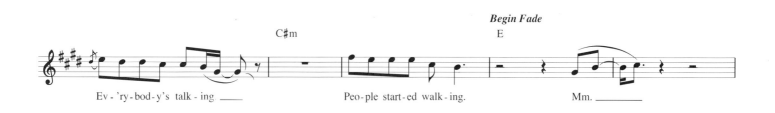

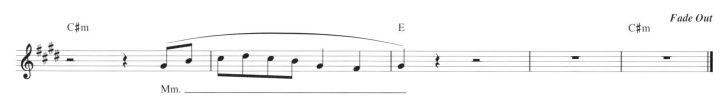

Oye Como Va

Words and Music by Tito Puente

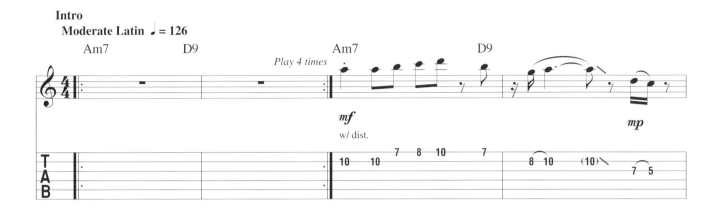

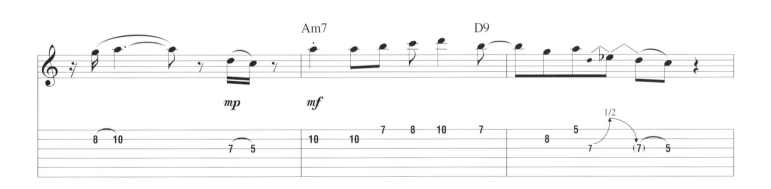

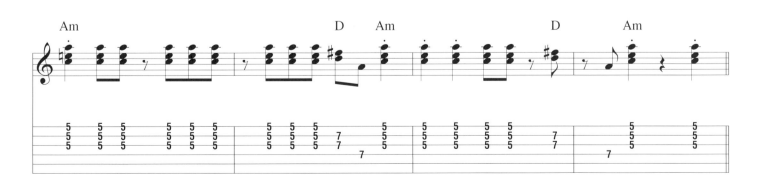

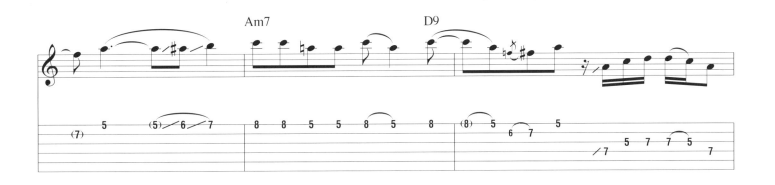

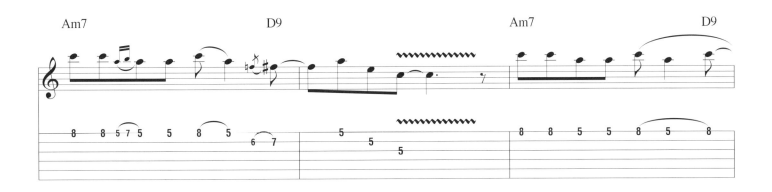

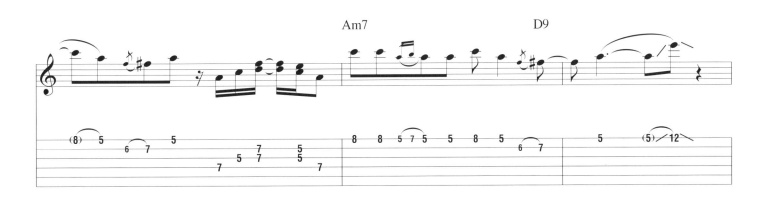

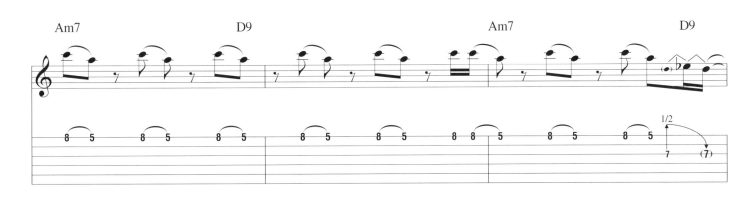

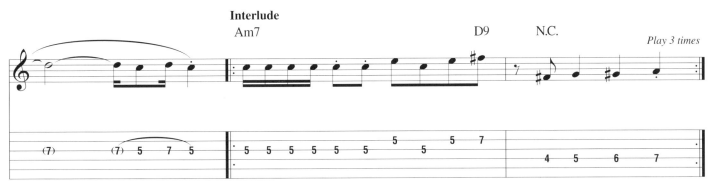

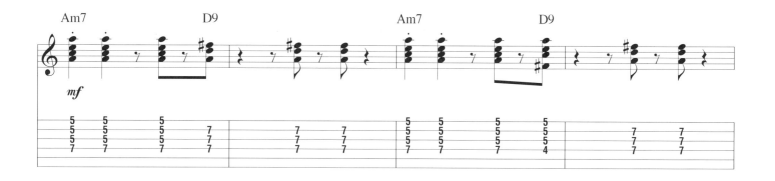

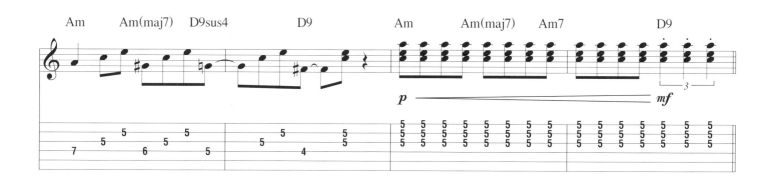

Organ Solo

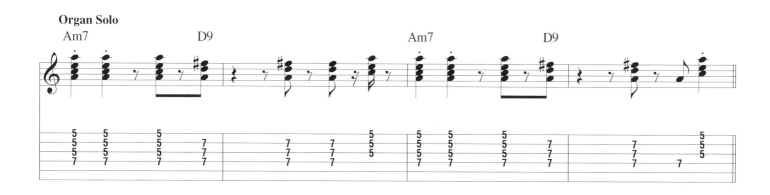

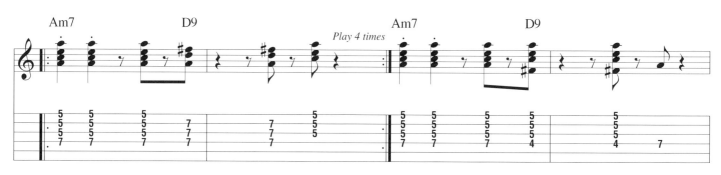

Bridge

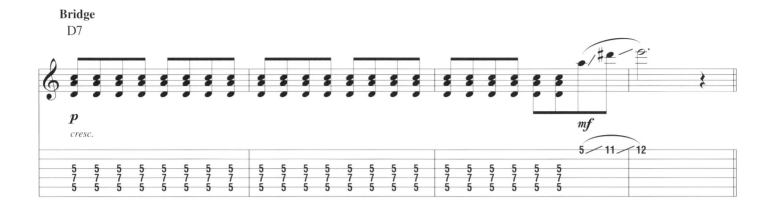

Guitar Solo

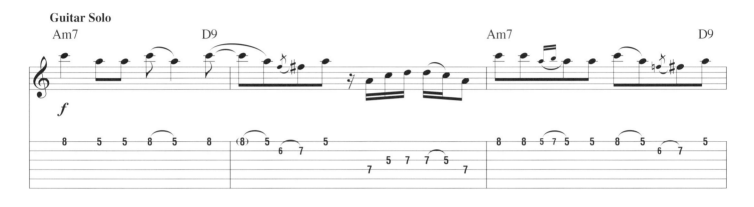

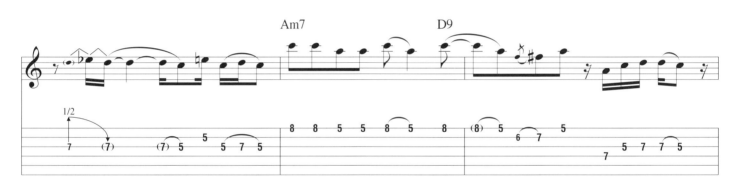

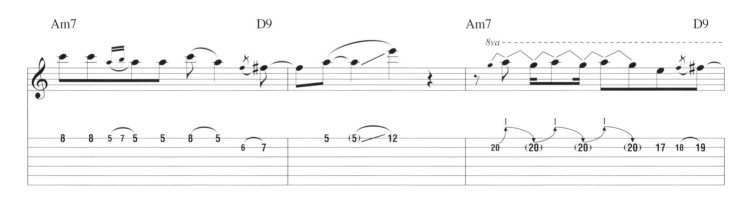

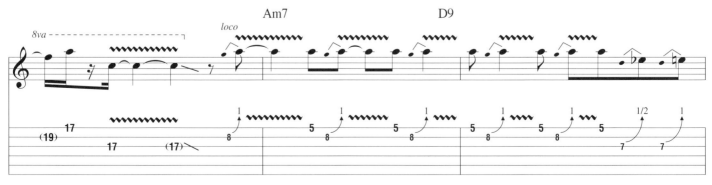

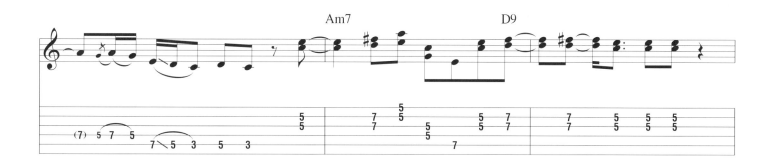

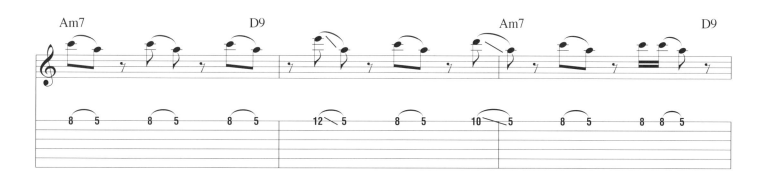

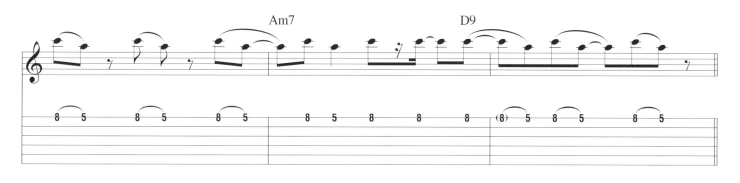

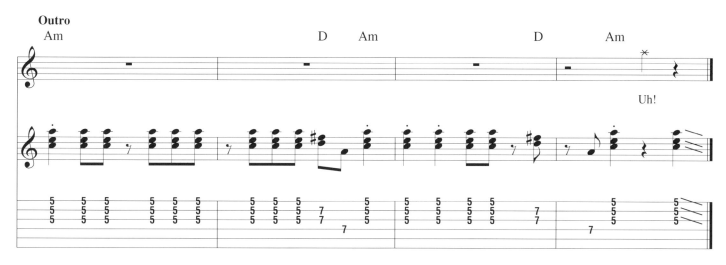

Pink Houses

Words and Music by John Mellencamp

Open G tuning:
(low to high) D-G-D-G-B-D

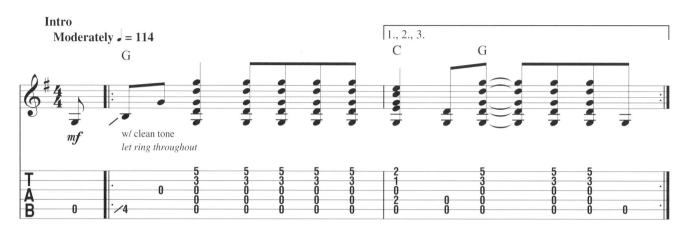

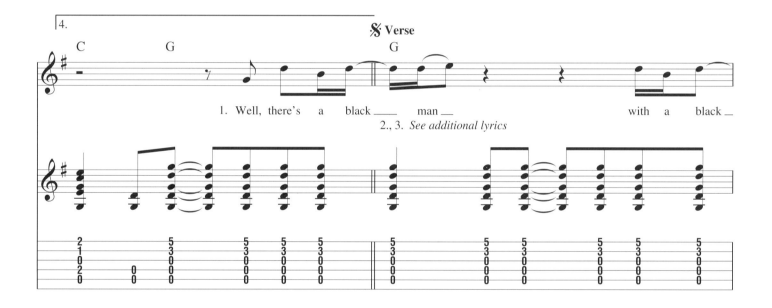

1. Well, there's a black ___ man ___ with a black ___
2., 3. *See additional lyrics*

___ cat, liv-in' in a black ___ neigh-bor-hood. ___ He's got an

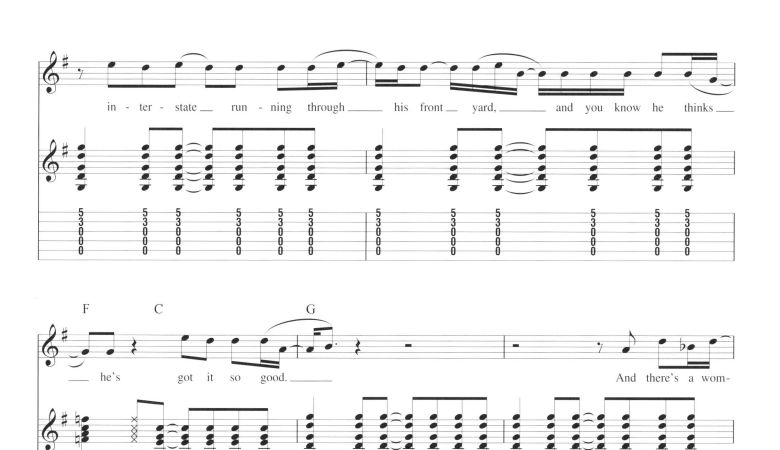

in - ter - state __ run - ning through _____ his front __ yard, _____ and you know he thinks ___

F   C   G

___ he's   got it so good. _____   And there's a wom-

- an __   in the kitch - en, __   clean - ing up the eve - ning __ slop. __

To Coda 1
To Coda 2

F   C

___   And he looks __ at her and __ says, "Hey dar - lin',   I can re - mem - ber when __ you could __

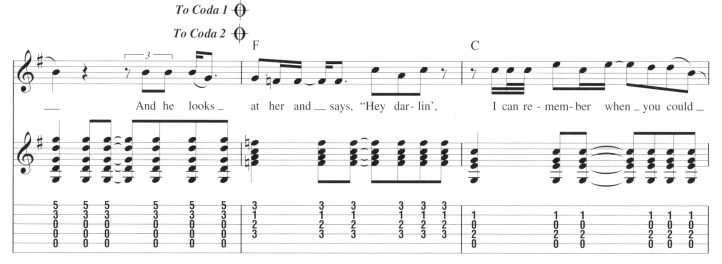

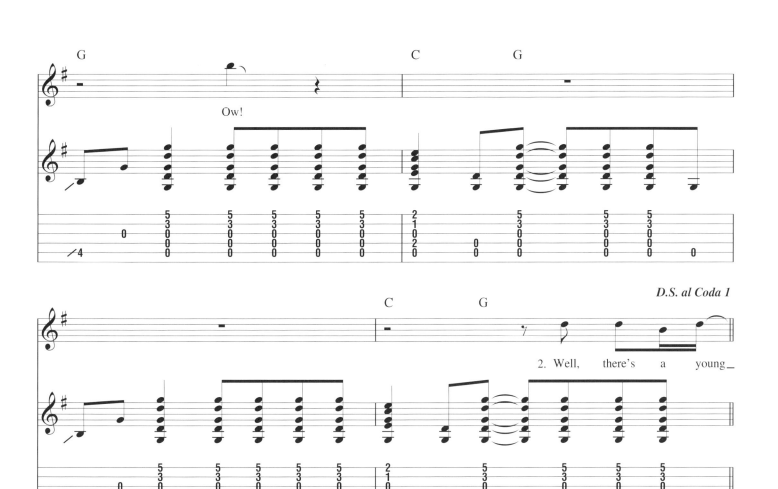

D.S. al Coda 1

2. Well, there's a young_

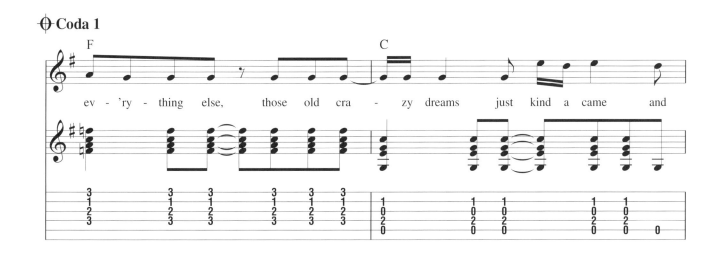

⊕ Coda 1

ev - 'ry - thing else, those old cra - zy dreams just kind a came and

went._____ Oh, but ain't that A - mer -

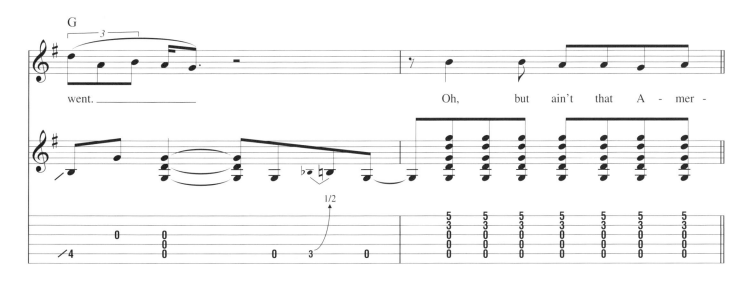

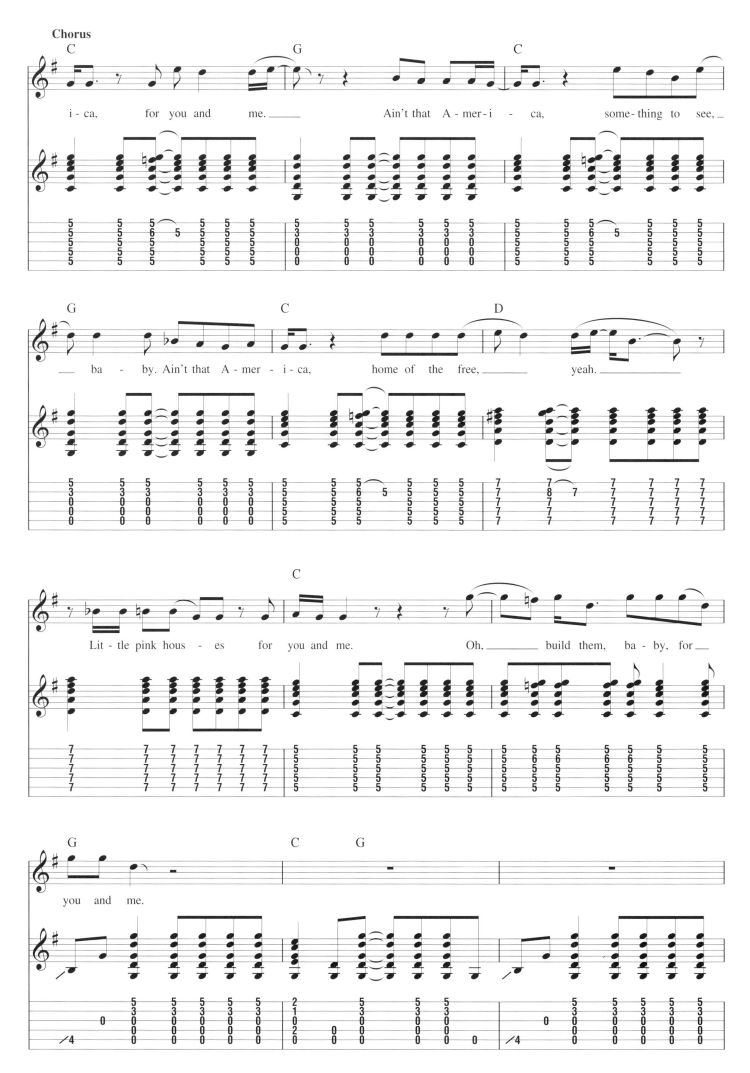

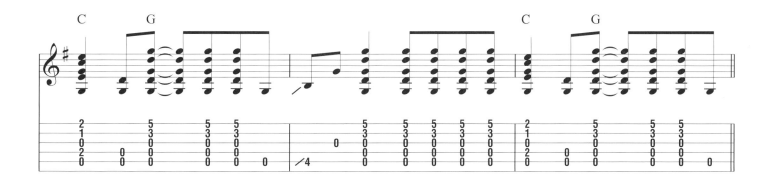

Interlude

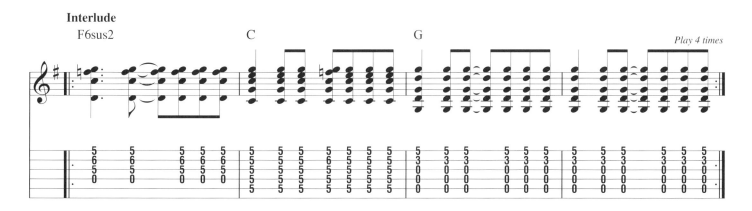

Play 4 times

D.S. al Coda 2

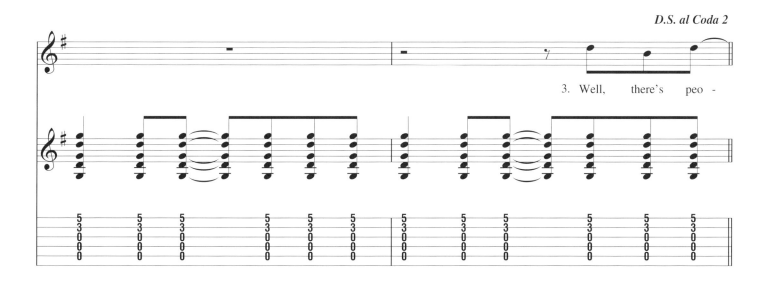

3. Well, there's peo -

Coda 2

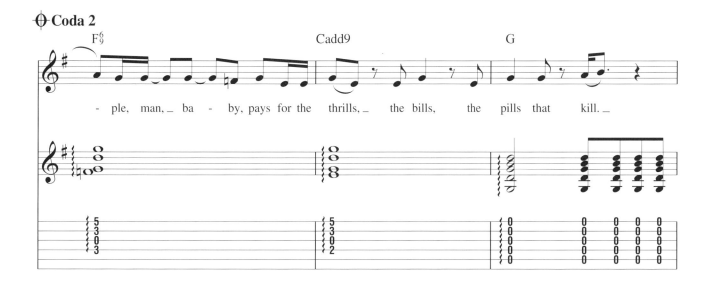

- ple, man,_ ba - by, pays for the thrills,_ the bills, the pills that kill._

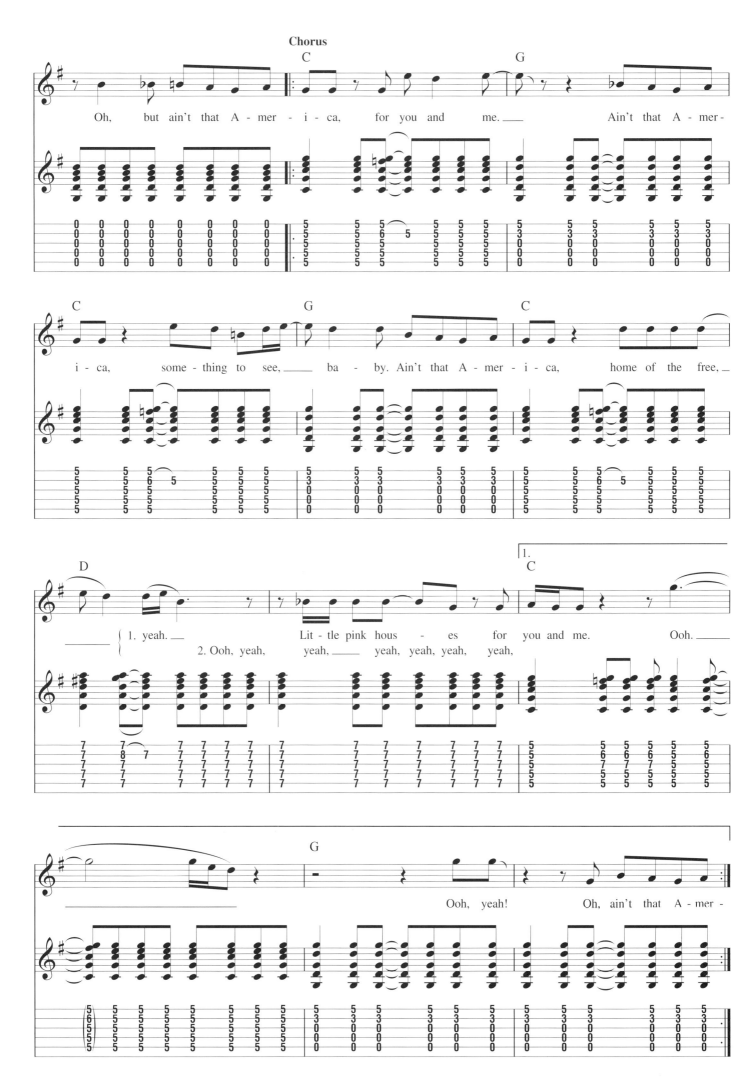

yeah. ___ Lit - tle pink hous - es, babe, for you and me. ___

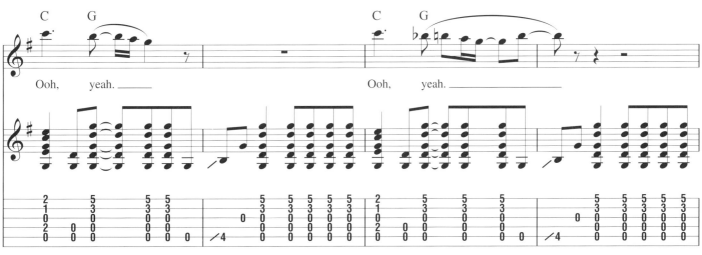

Ooh, yeah. ___ Ooh, yeah. ___

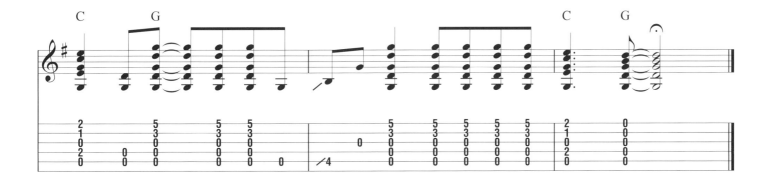

Additional Lyrics

2. Well, there's a young man in a tee-shirt,
   List'nin' to a rock 'n' roller station.
   He's got a greasy hair and a greasy smile.
   He says, "Lord, this must be my destination."
   'Cause they told me when I was younger,
   Sayin', "Boy, you're gonna be president."
   But just like ev'rything else, those old crazy dreams
   Just kinda came and went.

3. Well, there's people, and more people.
   What do they know, know, know?
   Go to work in some high rise
   And vacation down at the Gulf of Mexico, ooh, yeah.
   And there's winners and there's losers,
   But they ain't no big deal.
   'Cause the simple, man, baby, pays for the thrills,
   The bills, the pills that kill.

The Pretender

Words and Music by Dave Grohl, Taylor Hawkins, Christopher Shiflett and Nate Mendel

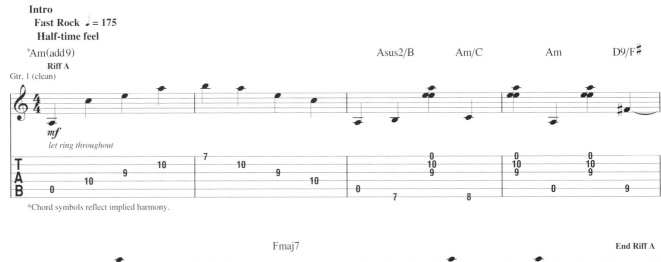

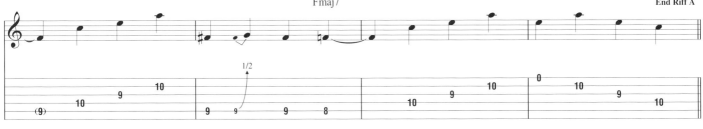

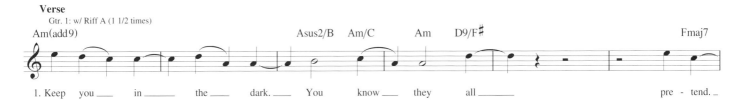

Interlude
Gtr. 1 tacet
A5

Verse
Gtr. 2: w/ Riff B (16 times)
Am

2. Send in ___ your skel - e - tons. ___ Sing as ___ their bones ___

Riff B
*Gtr. 2 (dist.)

End Riff B Rhy. Fig. 1
**Gtr. 3
(dist.)

*Doubled throughout

**Doubled throughout

D/F♯   F   Fsus2

___ come march-ing in ___   a - gain. ___

End Rhy. Fig. 1

Gtr. 3: w/ Rhy. Fig. 1
Am

The need ___ you bur - ied deep, ___   the se - crets that ___ you keep ___ are

D/F♯   F   Fsus2   G5

at ___ the read - y.   Are ___ you read - y?

Gtr. 3 **Rhy. Fig. 2**   **End Rhy. Fig. 2**

Gtr. 3: w/ Rhy. Fig. 1
Am

I'm fin - ished mak - ing sense, ___   done plead-ing ig - no - rance, ___ that old ___

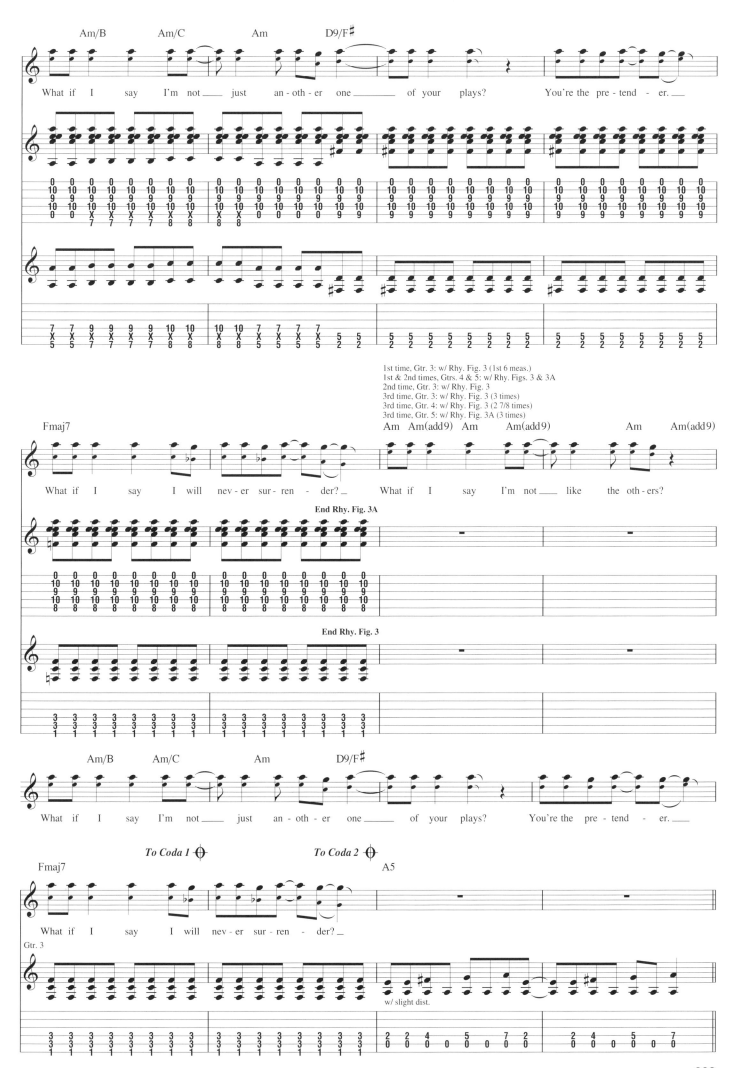

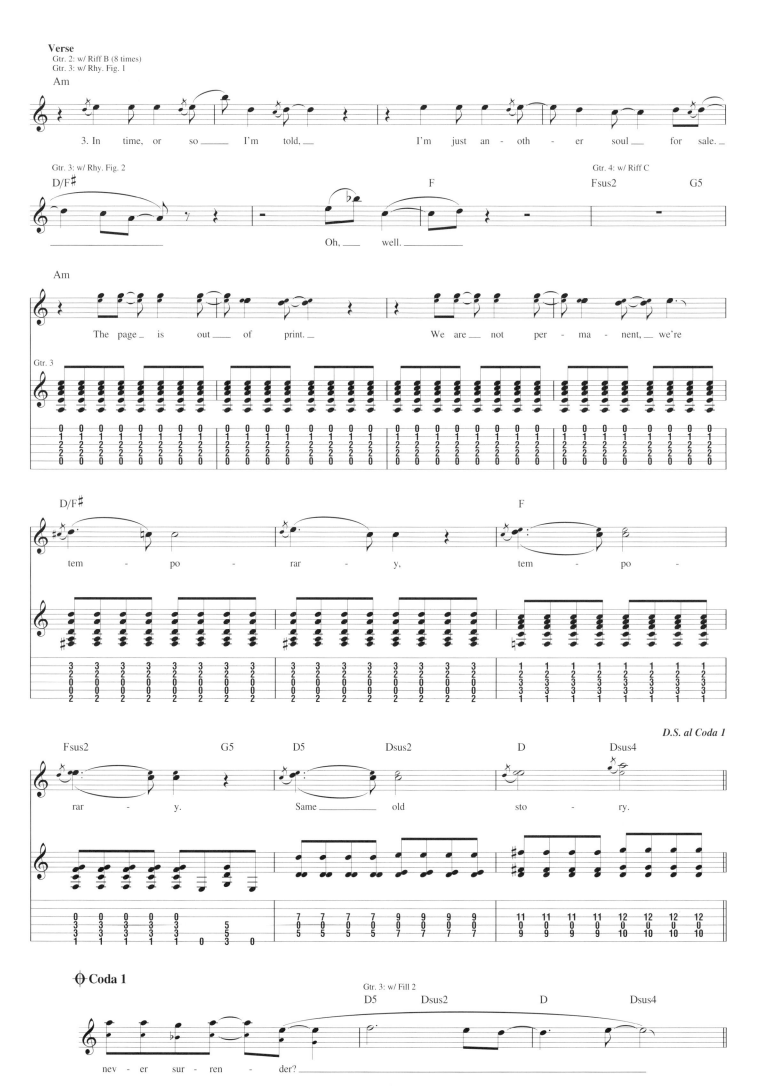

237

Raining Blood

Words and Music by Jeff Hanneman and Kerry King

Tune down 1/2 step:
(low to high) E♭-A♭-D♭-G♭-B♭-E♭

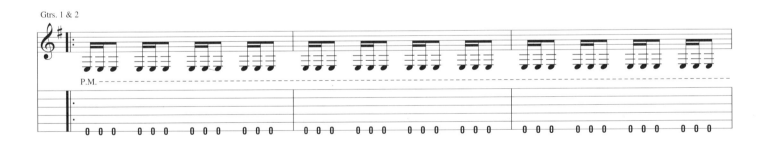

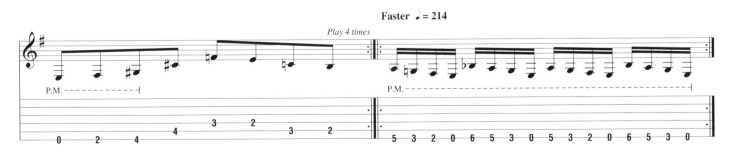

Interlude

Slower ♩ = 188

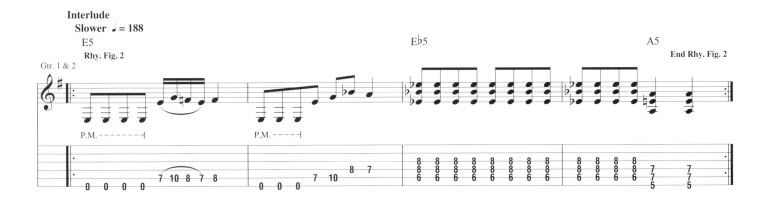

Verse

Gtrs. 1 & 2: w/ Rhy. Fig. 2 (2 times)

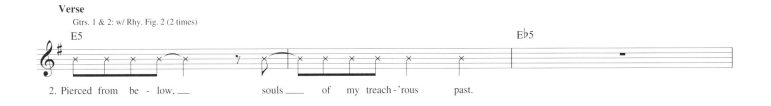

2. Pierced from be - low, __ souls __ of my treach - 'rous past.

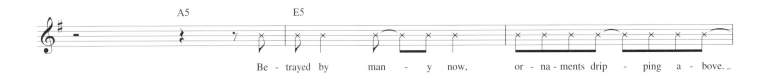

Be - trayed by man - y now, or - na - ments drip - ping a - bove. __

Bridge

Gtrs. 1 & 2: w/ Riff A (2 times)

Half-time feel

Gtr. 1: w/ Riff A (2 times)

A - wait - ing the hour of re - pris - al, your time _____

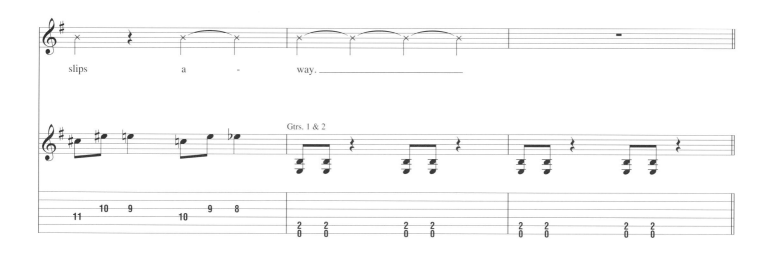

slips a - way. _____

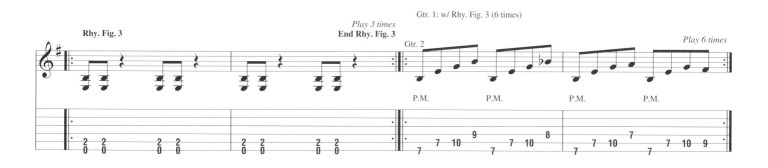

Gtr. 1: w/ Rhy. Fig. 3 (6 times)

Rhy. Fig. 3

Play 3 times
End Rhy. Fig. 3

Gtr. 2

Play 6 times

P.M.   P.M.   P.M.   P.M.

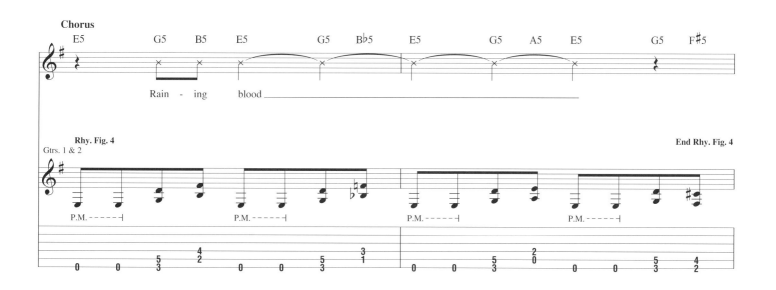

Chorus

E5   G5   B5   E5   G5   Bb5   E5   G5   A5   E5   G5   F#5

Rain - ing blood _____

Rhy. Fig. 4

Gtrs. 1 & 2

End Rhy. Fig. 4

P.M. - - - - - - | P.M. - - - - - | P.M. - - - - - | P.M. - - - - - |

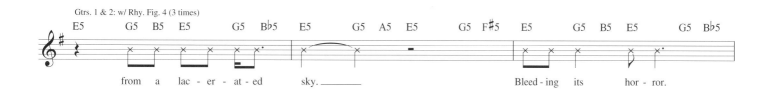

Gtrs. 1 & 2: w/ Rhy. Fig. 4 (3 times)

E5   G5   B5   E5   G5   Bb5   E5   G5   A5   E5   G5   F#5   E5   G5   B5   E5   G5   Bb5

from a lac - er - at - ed sky. ____ Bleed - ing its hor - ror.

End half-time feel

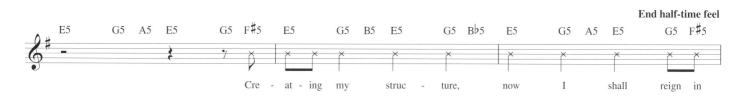

E5   G5   A5   E5   G5   F#5   E5   G5   B5   E5   G5   Bb5   E5   G5   A5   E5   G5   F#5

Cre - at - ing my struc - ture, now I shall reign in

E5

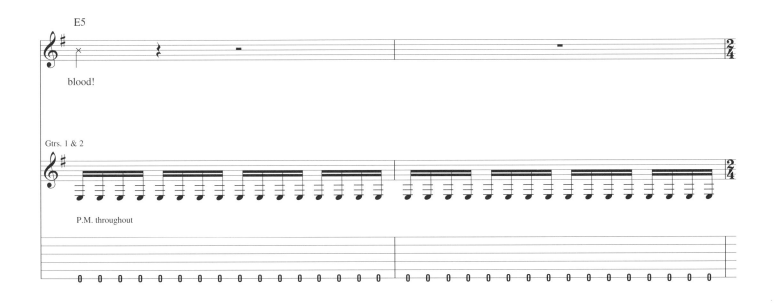

blood!

Gtrs. 1 & 2

P.M. throughout

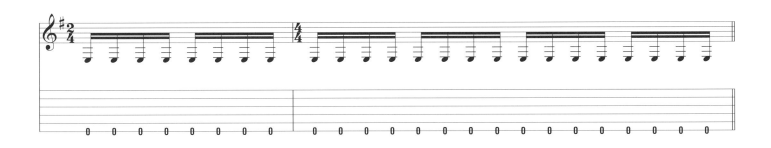

Outro
Faster ♩ = 247
Double-time feel

*Gtrs. 3 & 4 (dist.): w/ misc. whammy bar effects

Gtr. 2

Play 4 times

Gtr. 1

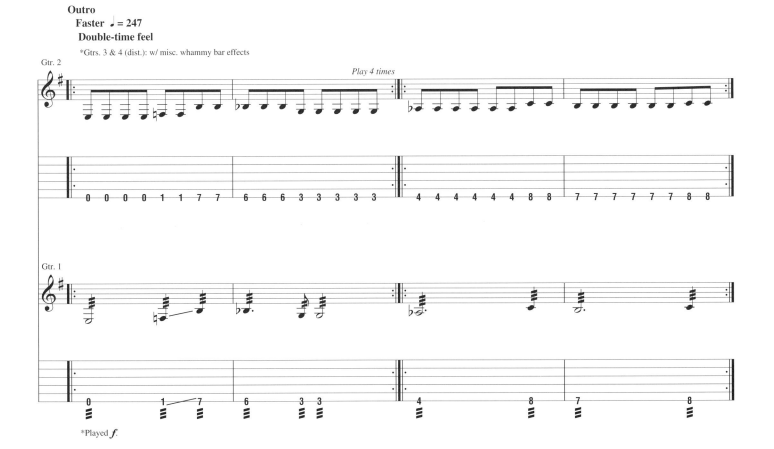

*Played **f**.

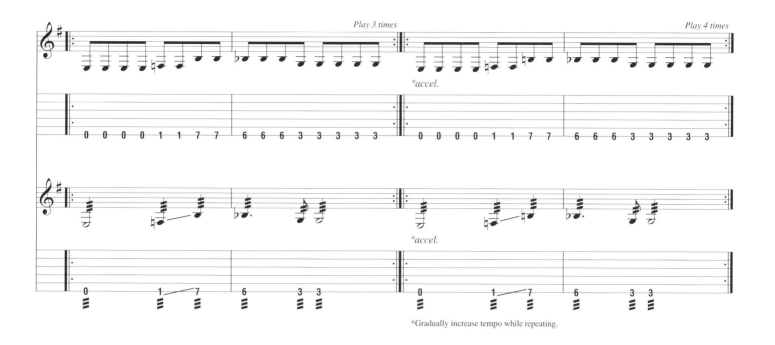

*Gradually increase tempo while repeating.

Redemption Song

Words and Music by Bob Marley

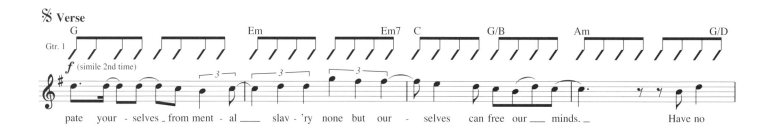

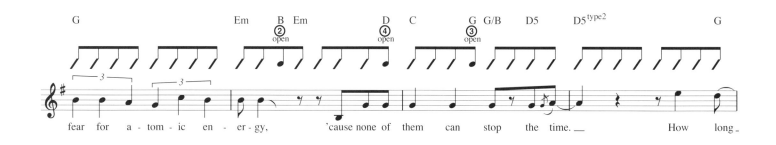

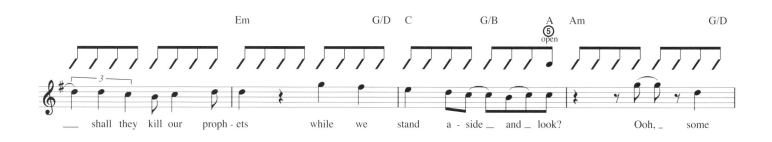

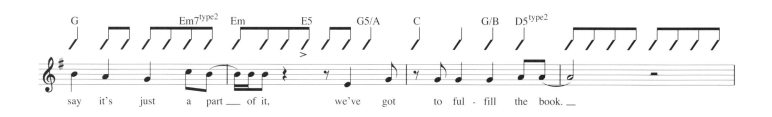

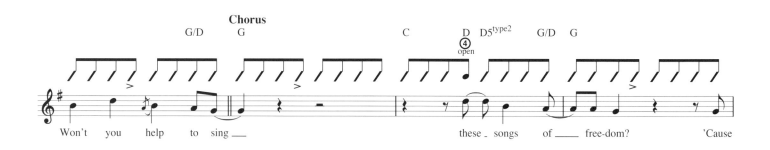

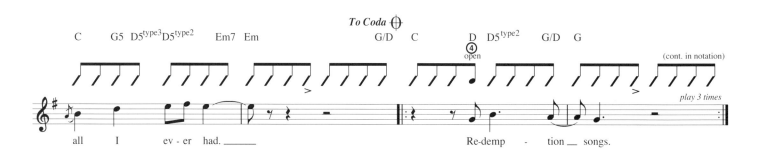

Rock Lobster

Words and Music by Kate Pierson, Fred Schneider, Keith Strickland, Cindy Wilson and Ricky Wilson

253

Interlude

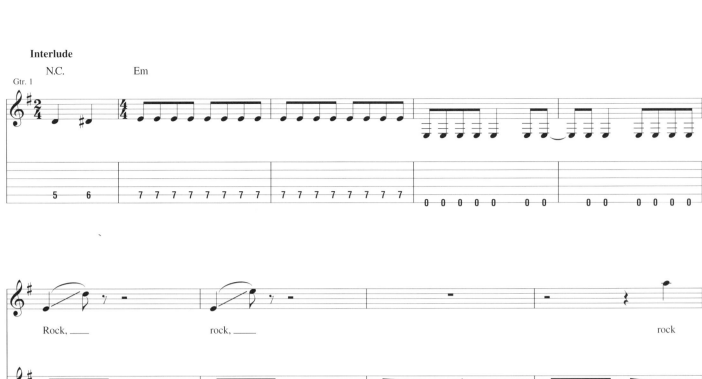

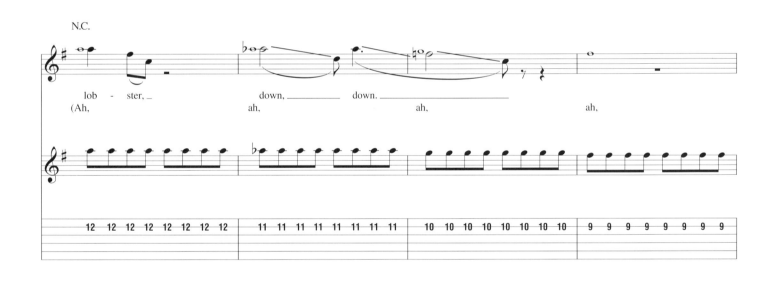

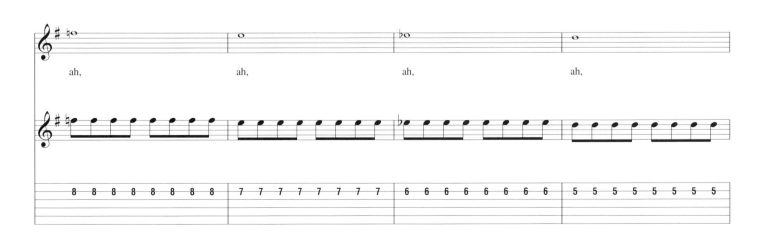

254

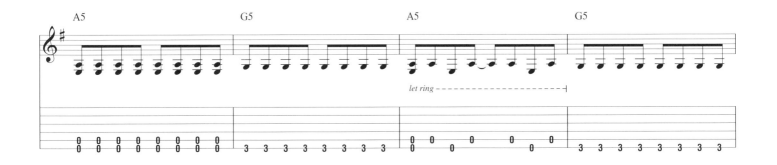

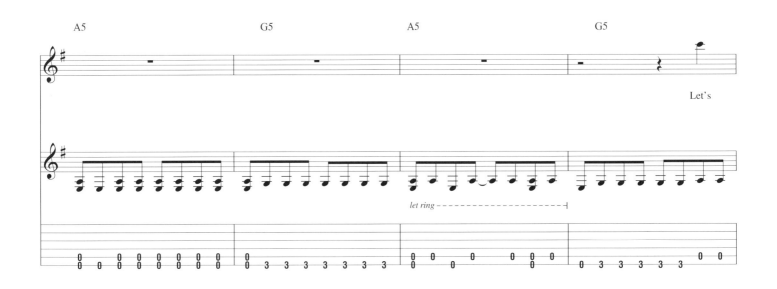

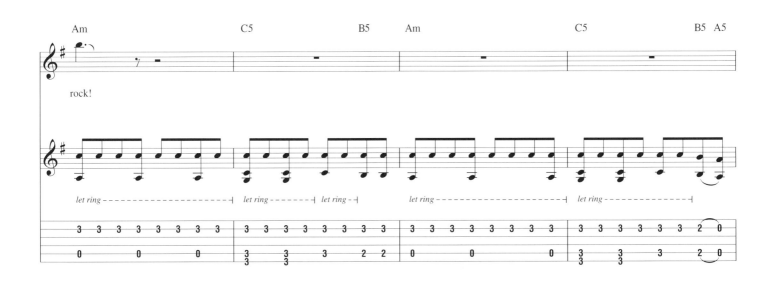

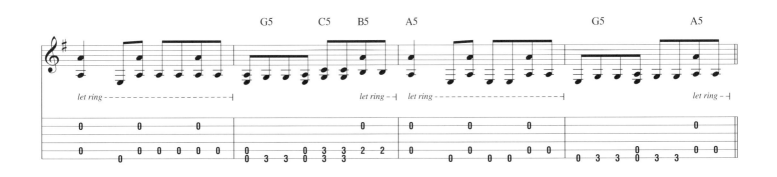

Santeria

Words and Music by Brad Nowell, Eric Wilson and Floyd Gaugh

To Coda

Guitar Solo

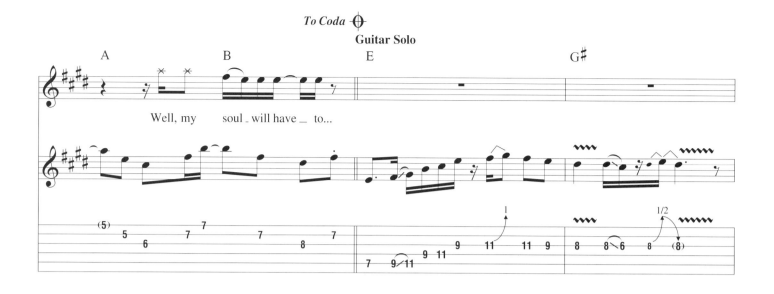

Well, my   soul ⌣ will have ⌣ to...

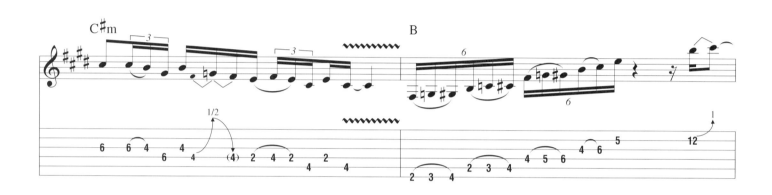

Chorus

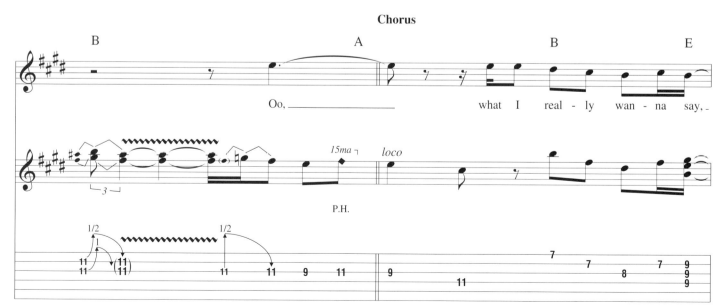

Oo, _____   what I real - ly wan - na say, ⌣

Additional Lyrics

3. Tell Sanchito that if he knows what is good for him
   He best go run and hide.
   Daddy's got a new .45
   And I won't think twice to stick that barrel
   Straight down Sancho's throat.
   Believe me when I say that I
   Got something for his punk ass.

Chorus What I really wanna know, my baby.
   Oo, what I really wanna say is there's just
   One way back and I'll make it.
   Yeah, my soul will have to wait. Yeah, yeah, yeah.

The Sky Is Crying

Words and Music by Elmore James

Tune down 1/2 step:
(low to high) E♭-A♭-D♭-G♭-B♭-E♭

Verse

Slow Blues ♩. = 55

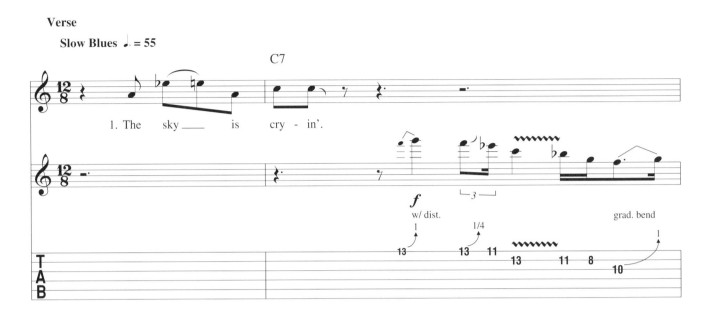

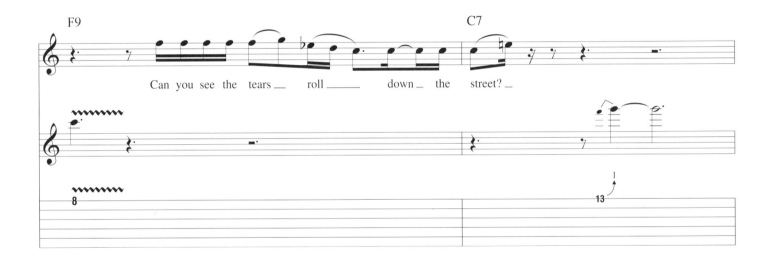

Can you see the tears __ roll __ down __ the street? __

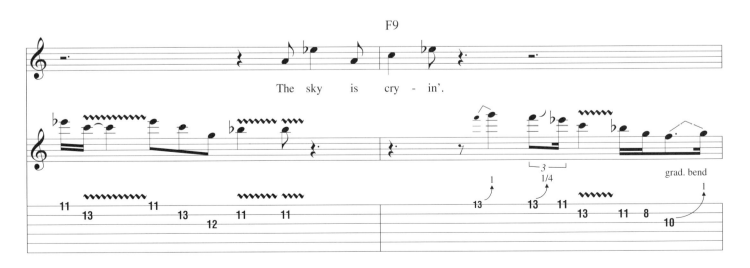

The sky is cry - in'.

made my poor heart, uh, skip a beat.____

Guitar Solo

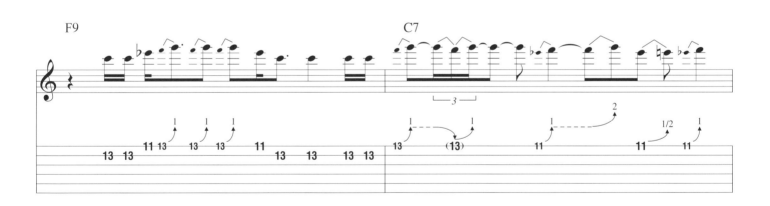

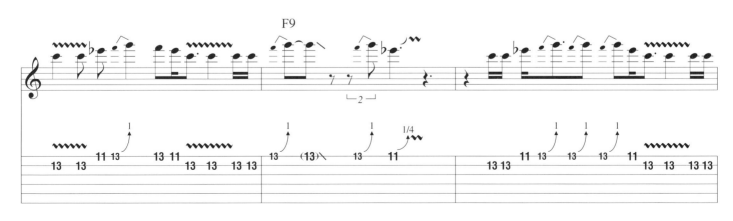

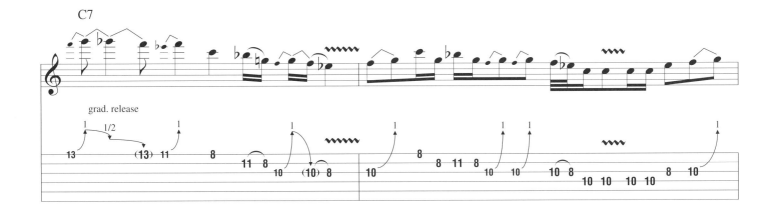

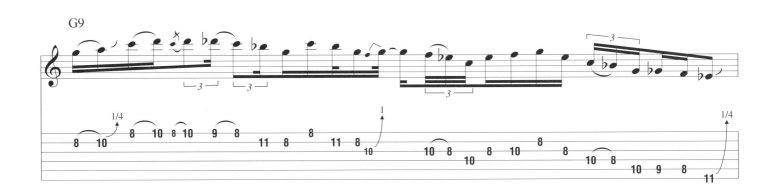

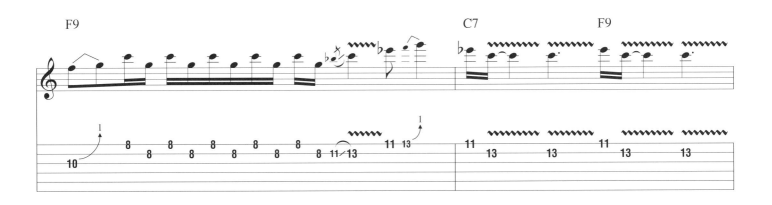

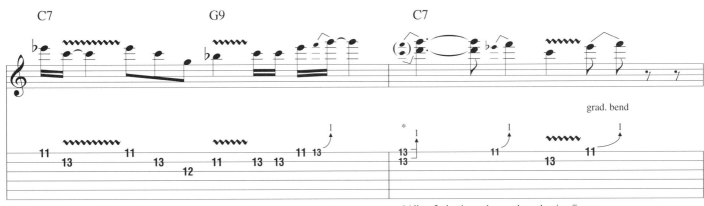

*Allow 2nd string to be caught under ring finger.

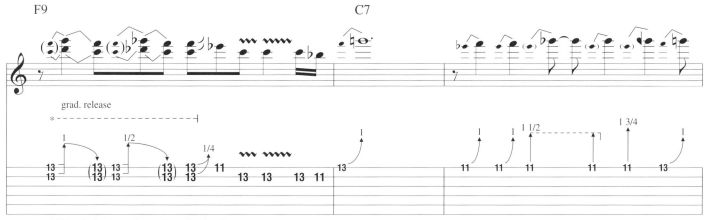

*Allow 2nd string to be caught under ring finger.

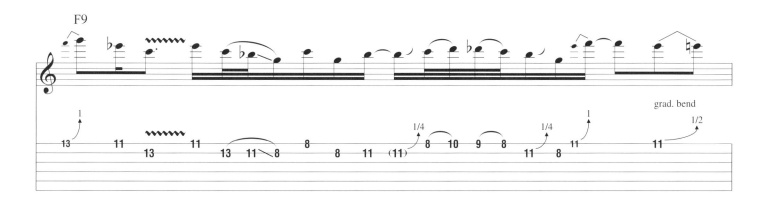

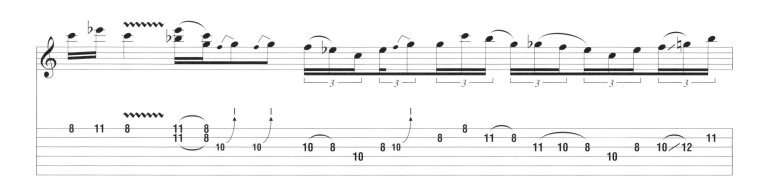

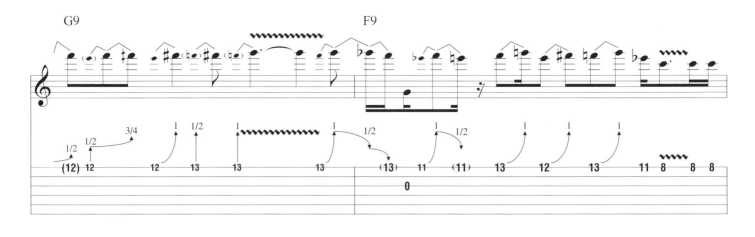

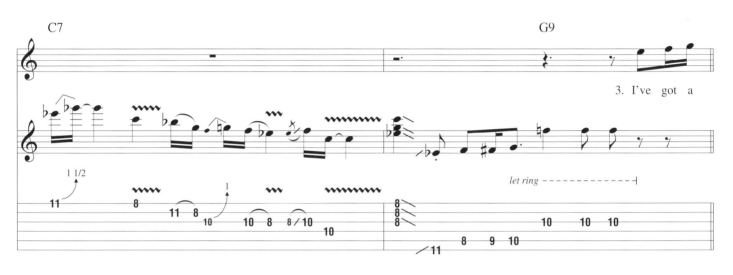

Verse

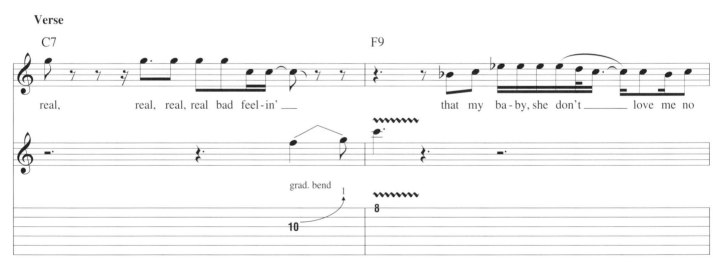

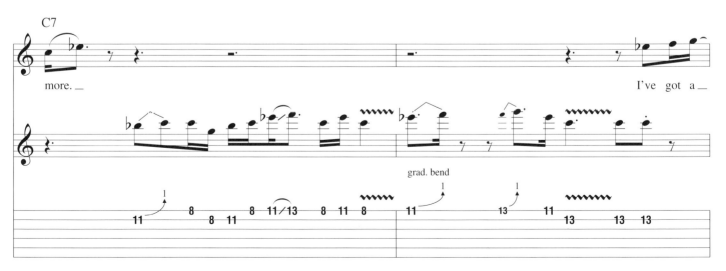

real,   real bad feel-in'   that my ba-by don't __ love me no more.

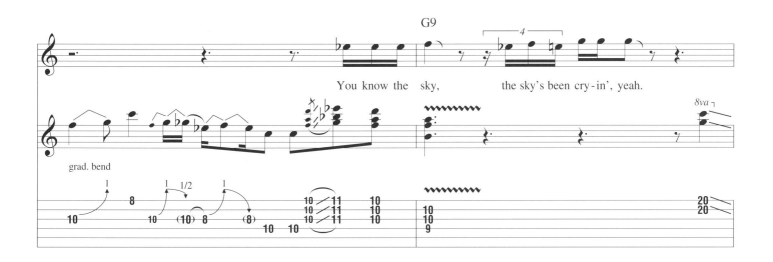

You know the   sky,   the sky's been cry-in', yeah.

Can you see the tears __ roll down my   nose?

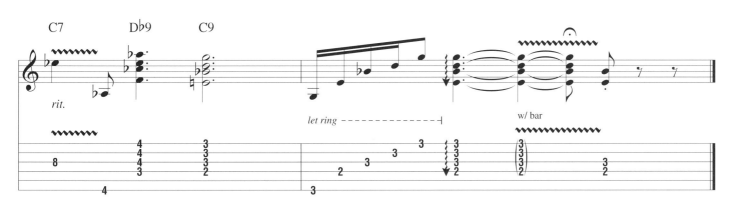

Smells Like Teen Spirit

Words and Music by Kurt Cobain, Krist Novoselic and Dave Grohl

277

Smoke on the Water

Words and Music by Ritchie Blackmore, Ian Gillan, Roger Glover, Jon Lord and Ian Paice

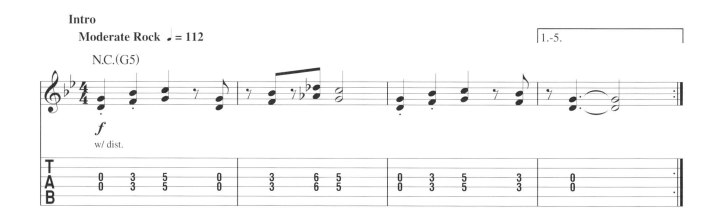

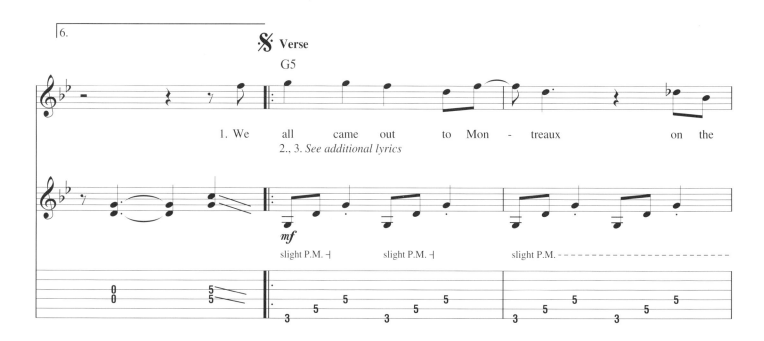

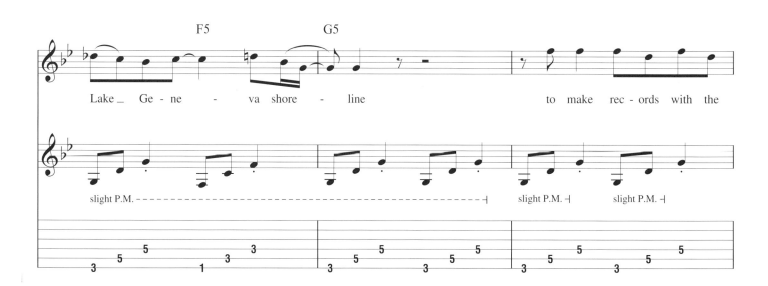

wa - ter, a fire in the sky.

To Coda ⊕

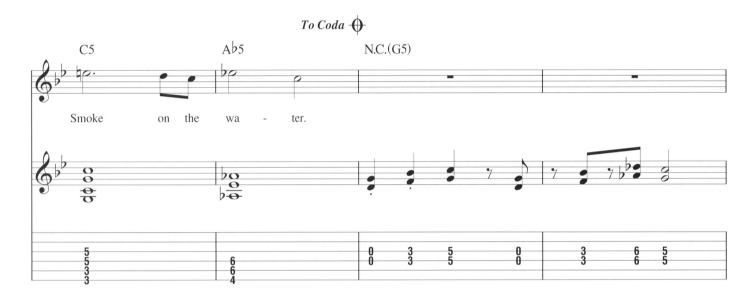

Smoke on the wa - ter.

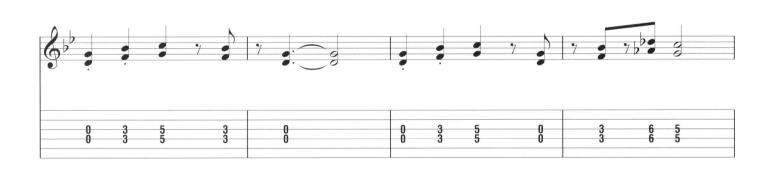

1. 2.

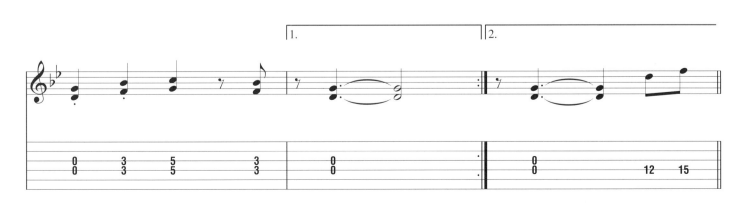

Guitar Solo

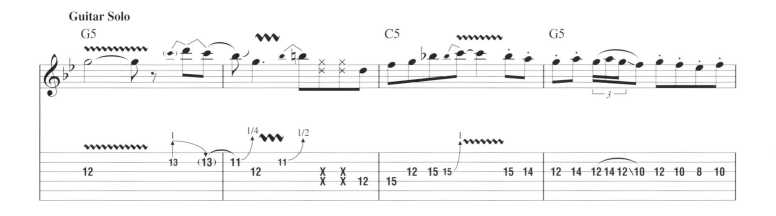

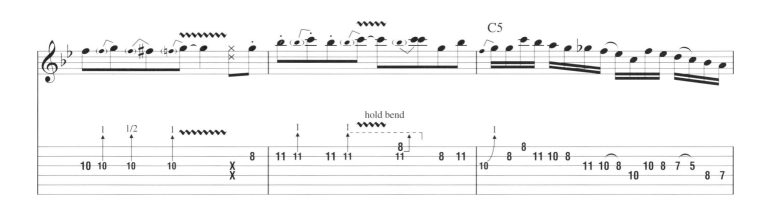

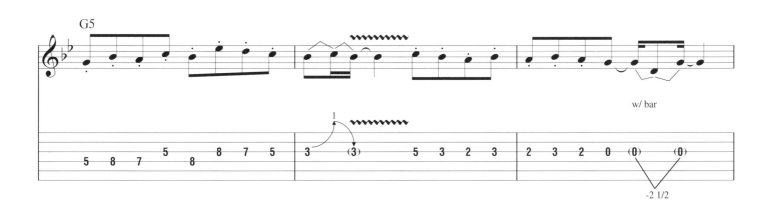

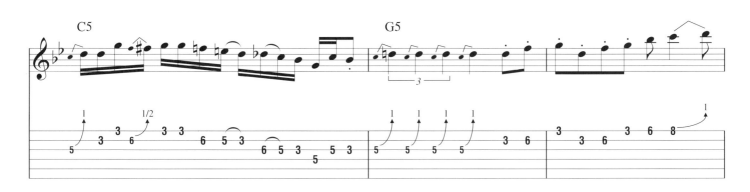

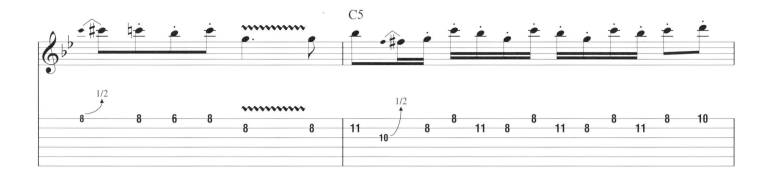

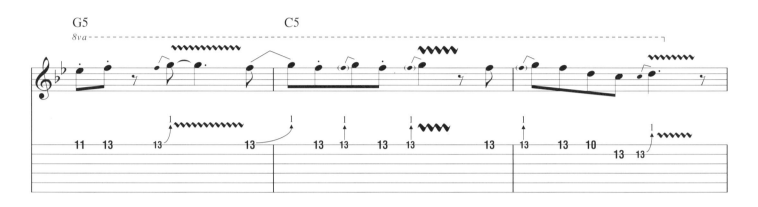

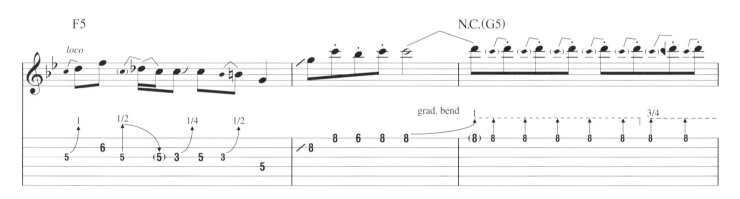

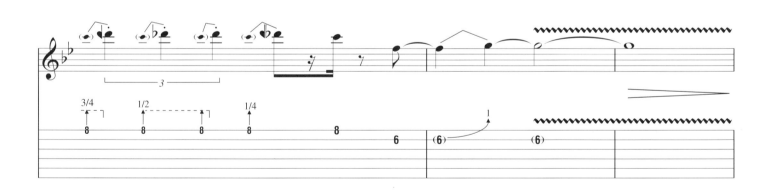

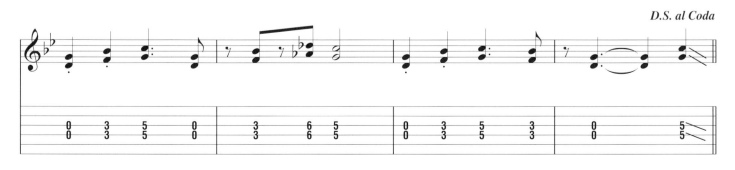

Coda

Outro-Organ Solo

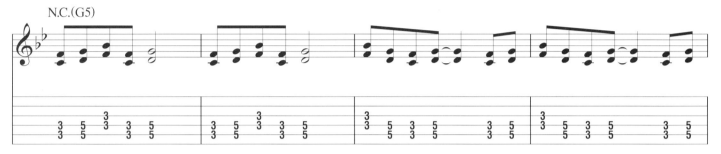

Begin fade

Fade out

Additional Lyrics

2. They burned down the gambling house,
   It died with an awful sound.
   A Funky Claude was running in and out,
   Pulling kids out the ground.
   When it all was over, we had to find another place.
   But Swiss time was running out;
   It seemed we would lose the race.

3. We ended up at the Grand Hotel,
   It was empty, cold and bare.
   But with the Rolling truck Stones thing just outside,
   Making our music there.
   With a few red lights, a few old beds
   We made a place to sweat.
   No matter what we get out of this,
   I know, I know we'll never forget.

So Far Away

Words and Music by Matthew Sanders, Jonathan Seward, James Sullivan, Brian Haner, Jr. and Zachary Baker

*Two gtrs. arr. for one.
**Chord symbols reflect basic harmony.
***Omit arpeggiation when figure is recalled.

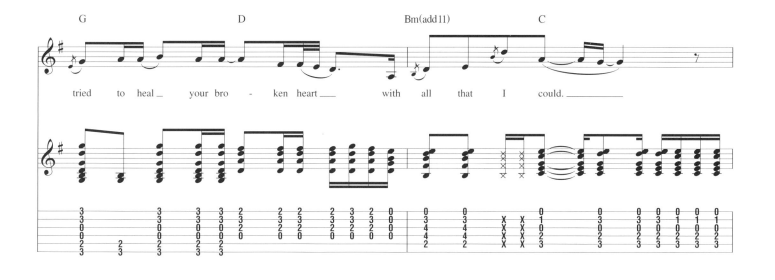

tried to heal __ your bro - ken heart __ with all that I could. __

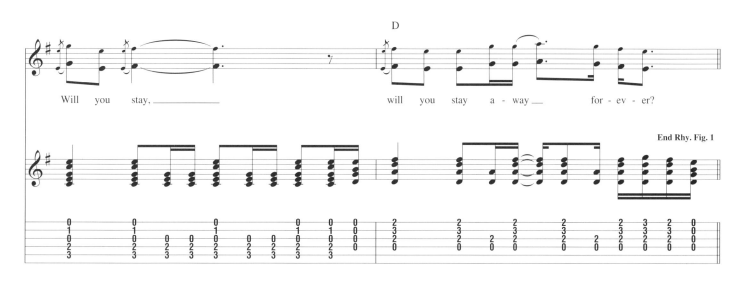

Will you stay, __ will you stay a - way __ for - ev - er?

End Rhy. Fig. 1

Chorus

How do I live with - out the ones I __ love? __ Time __

Gtr. 2 (elec.)

mf
w/ dist.

Rhy. Fig. 2

Gtr. 1

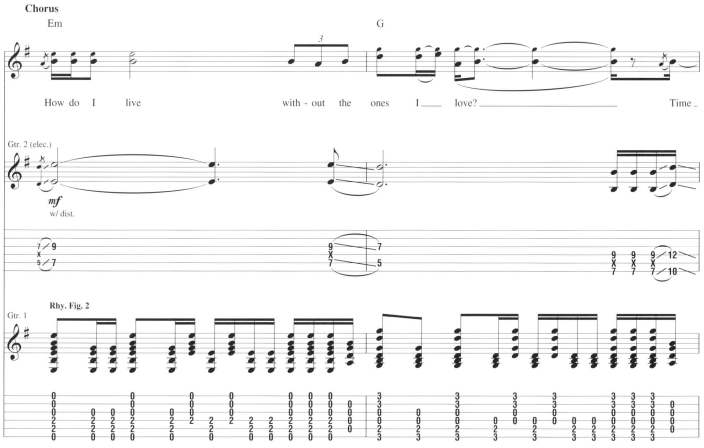

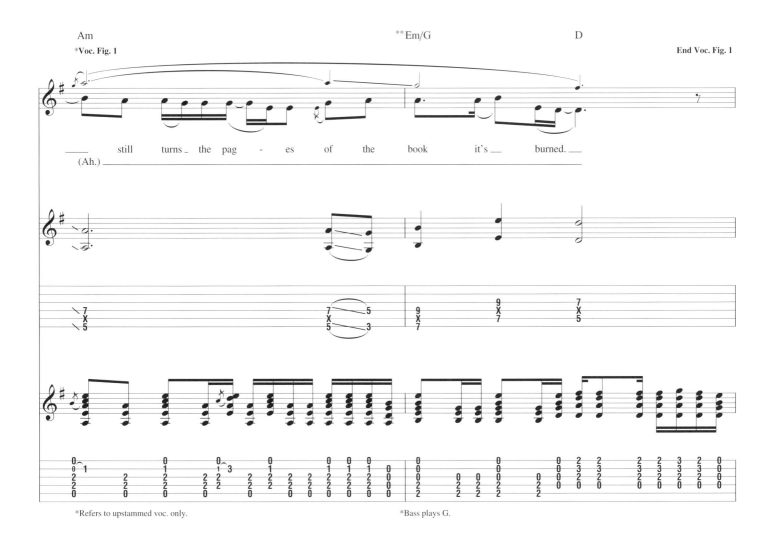

*Refers to upstammed voc. only.

*Bass plays G.

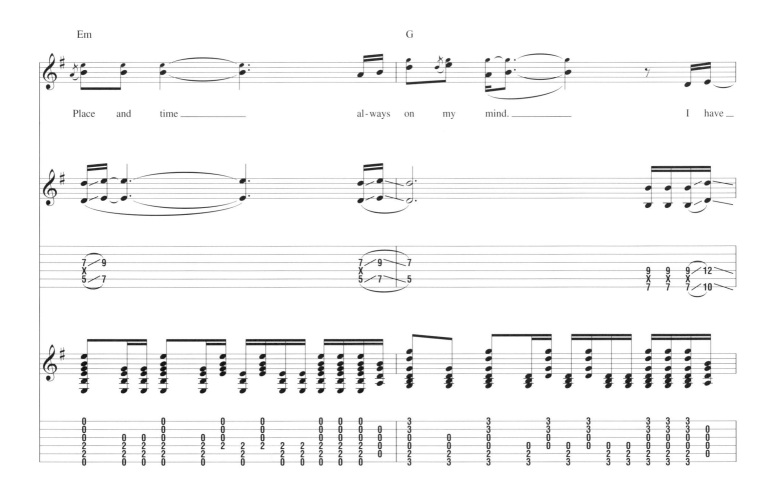

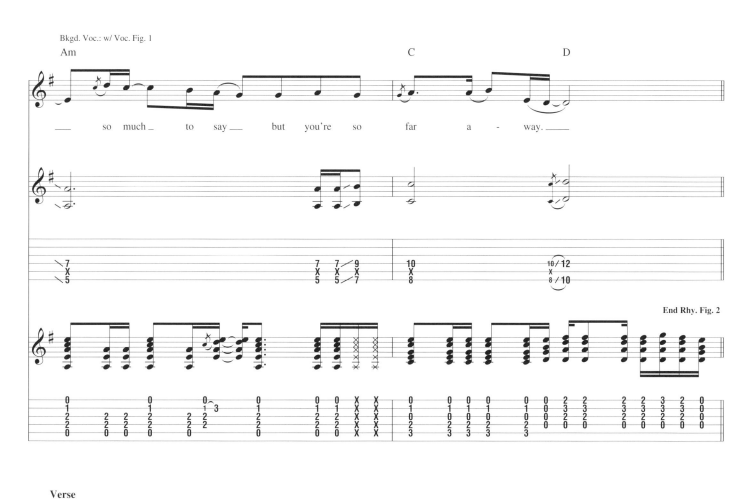

so much to say but you're so far a - way.

Verse

Gtr. 1: w/ Rhy. Fig. 1
Gtr. 2 tacet

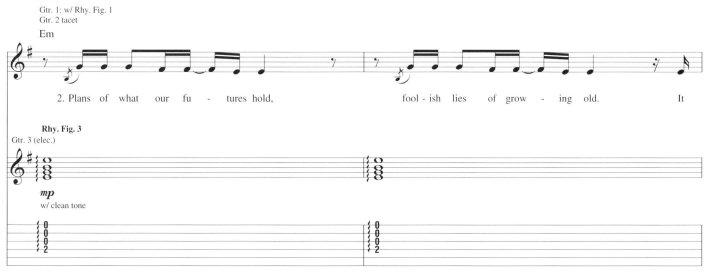

2. Plans of what our fu - tures hold, fool - ish lies of grow - ing old. It

Rhy. Fig. 3

Gtr. 3 (elec.)

mp
w/ clean tone

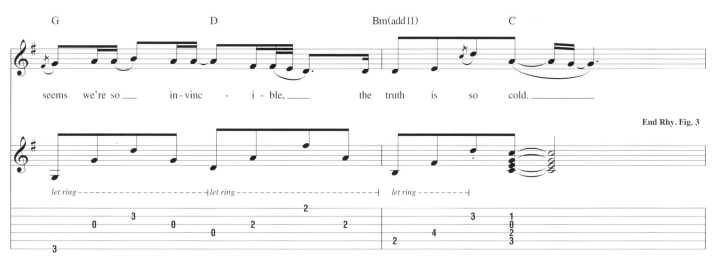

seems we're so in - vinc - i - ble, the truth is so cold.

End Rhy. Fig. 3

Guitar Solo

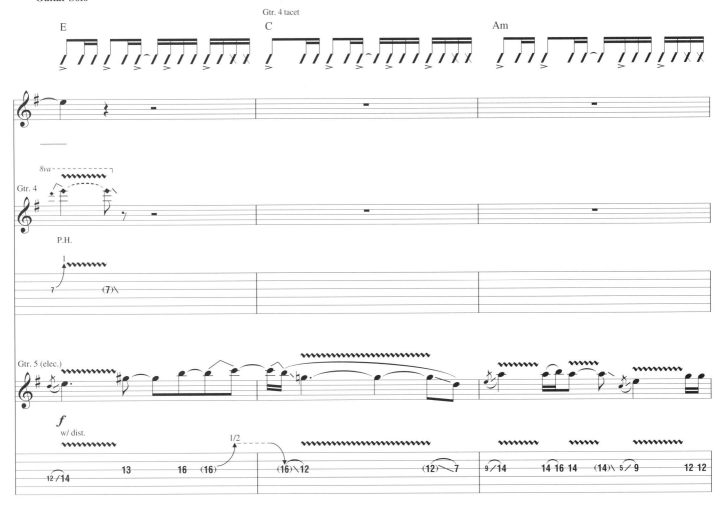

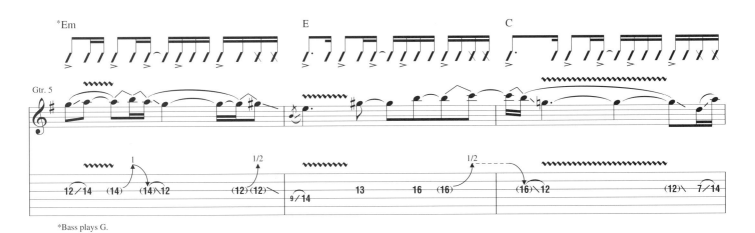

*Bass plays G.

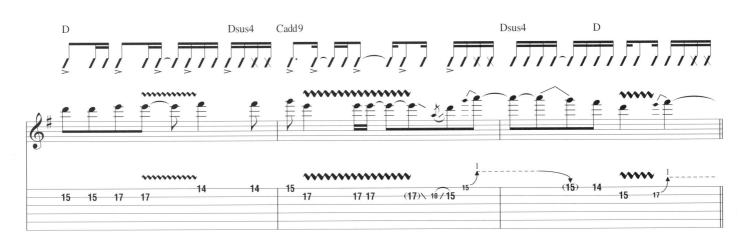

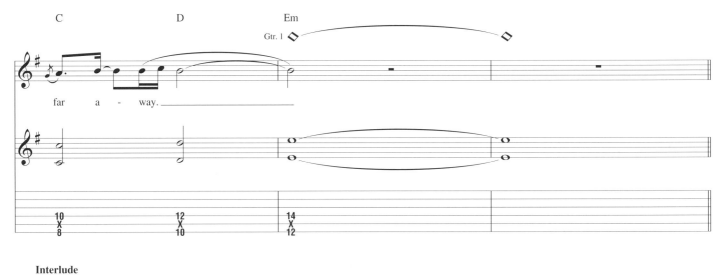

Interlude

Gtrs. 1 & 2 tacet

*Doubled throughout

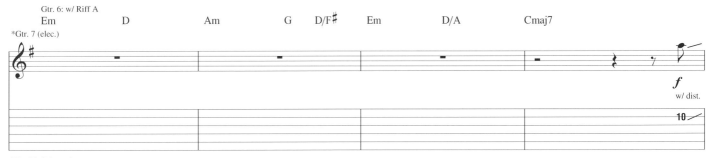

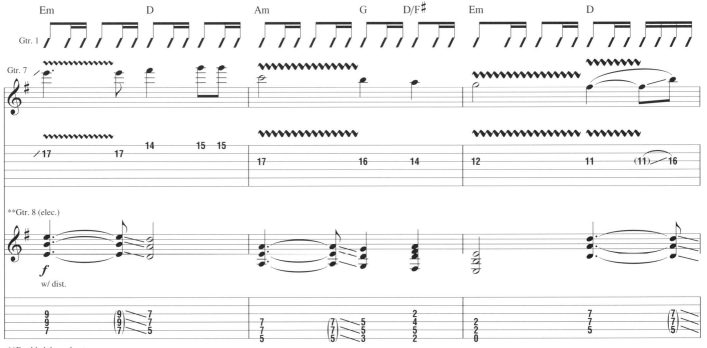

**Doubled throughout

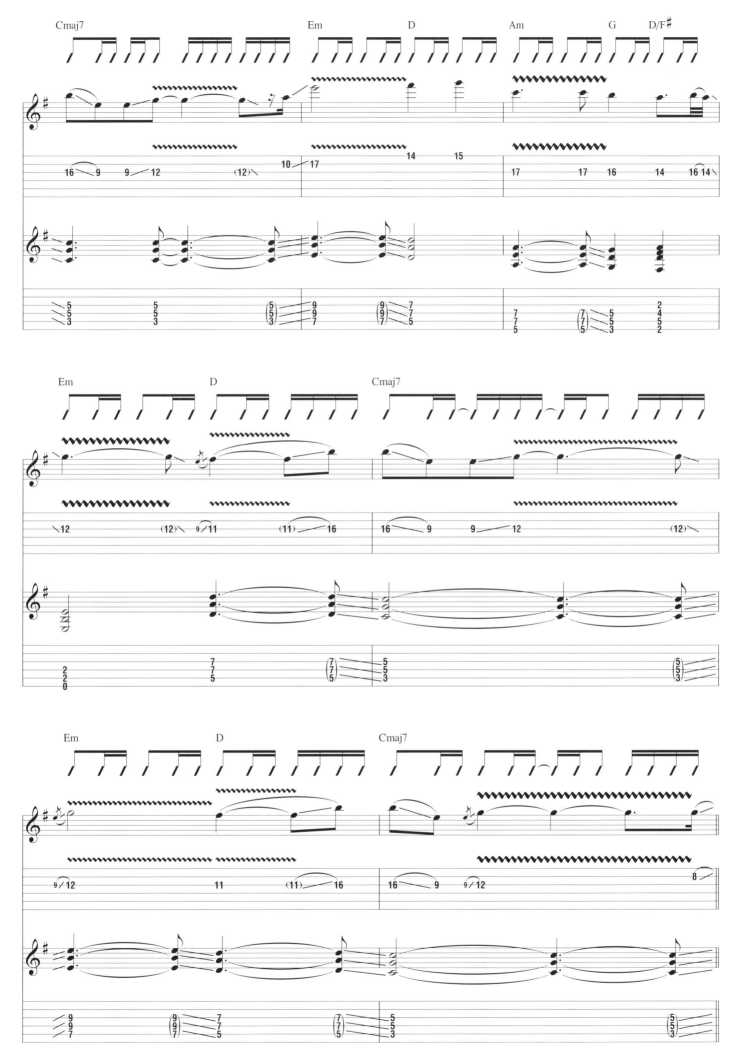

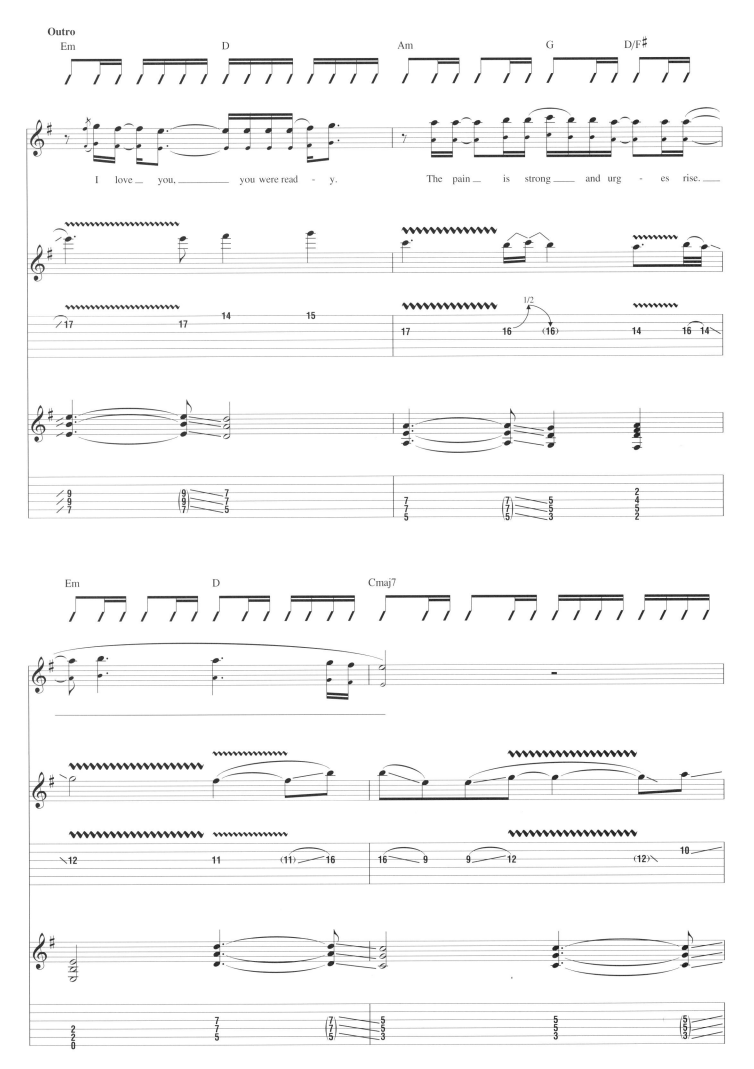

But I see __ you __ when it lets __ me. Your pain __ is gone, __ your hands __ un - tied. __

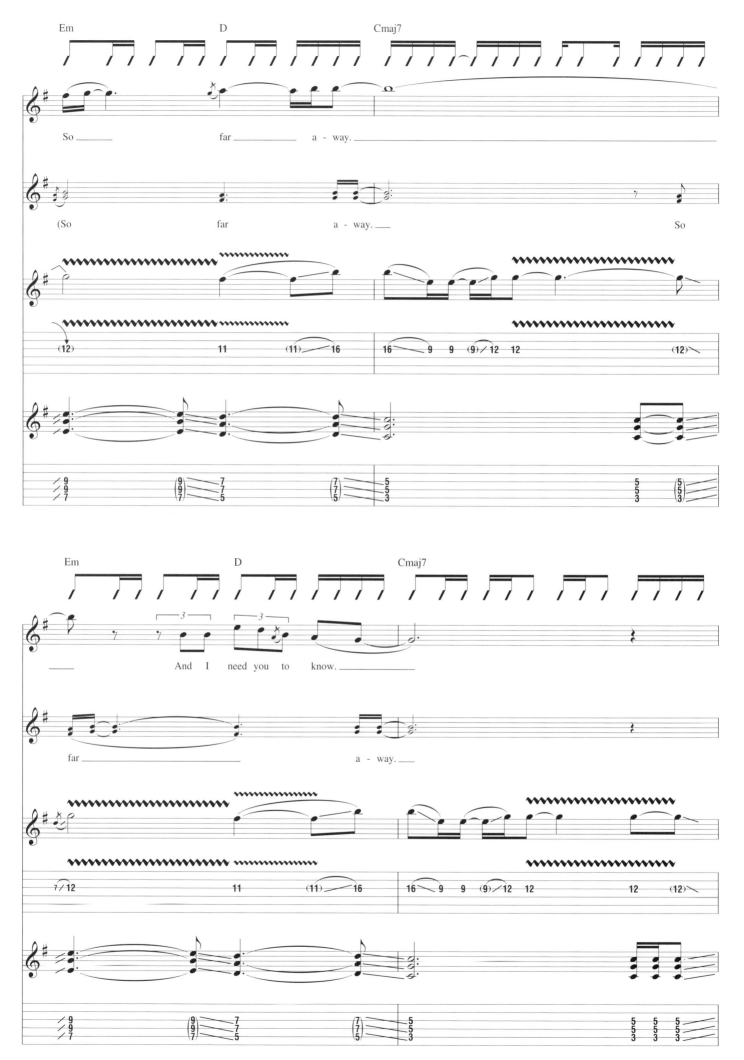

So _____ far _____ a - way. _____

So _____ far a - way. _____ So

_____ And I need you to, need you to know. _____

far.) _____

Still Got the Blues

Words and Music by Gary Moore

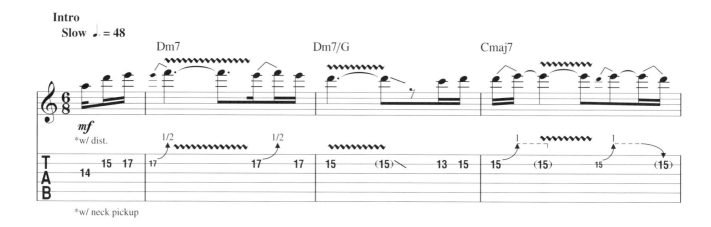

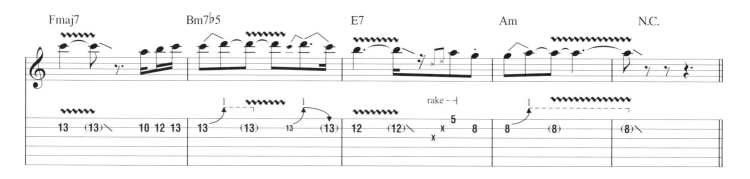

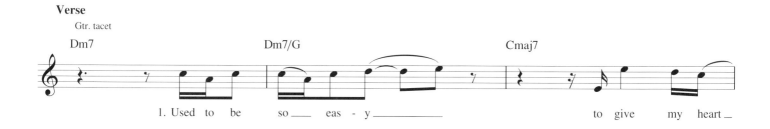

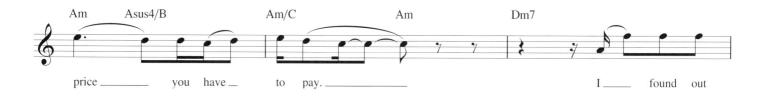

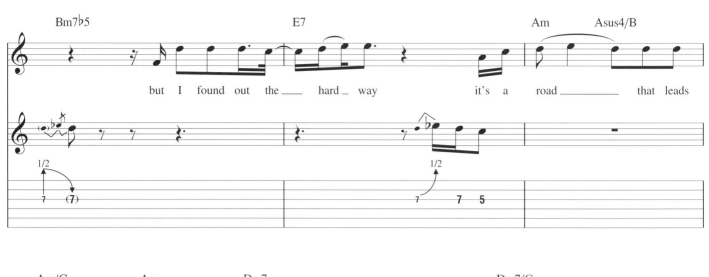

but I found out the ___ hard ___ way   it's a   road _____ that leads

to   pain. ___   Well, I   found ___ that love _____

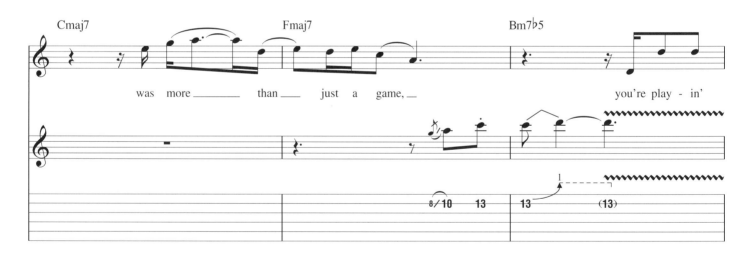

was   more _____ than ___ just   a   game, ___   you're play - in'

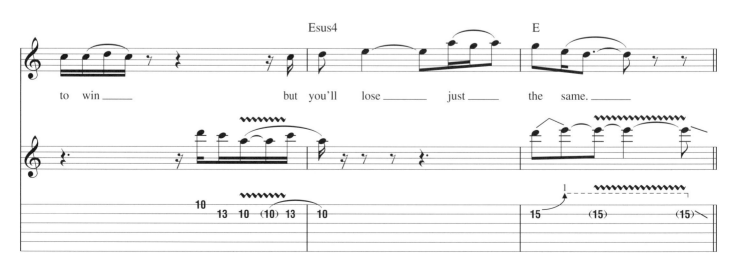

to   win _____   but you'll   lose _____ just _____   the   same.

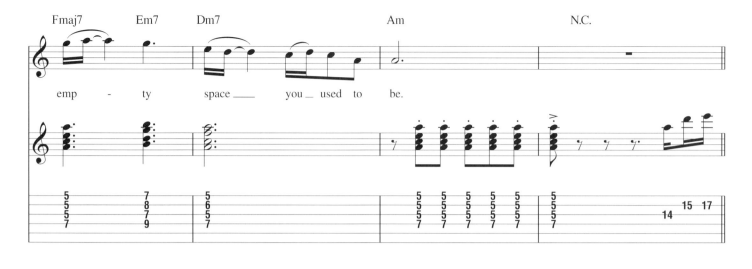

emp - ty space ___ you ___ used to be.

Guitar Solo

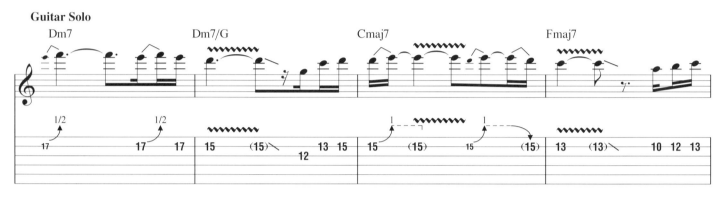

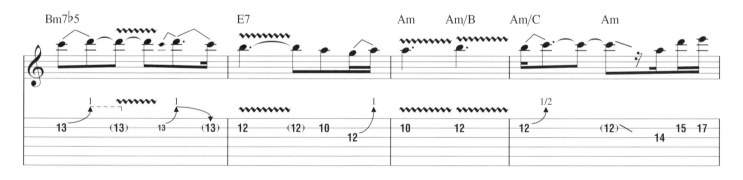

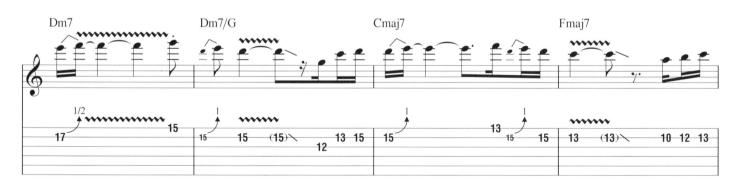

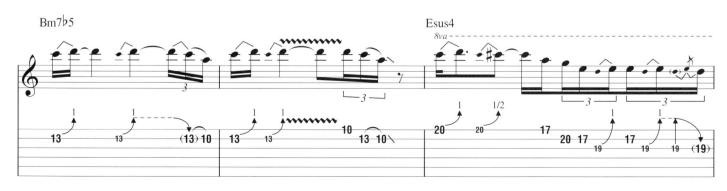

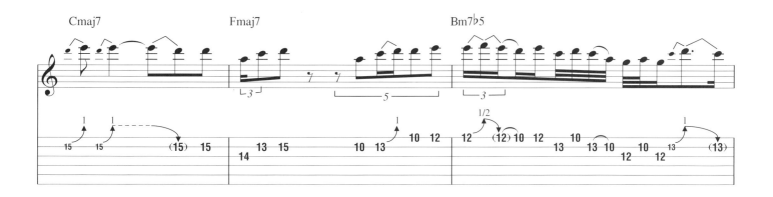

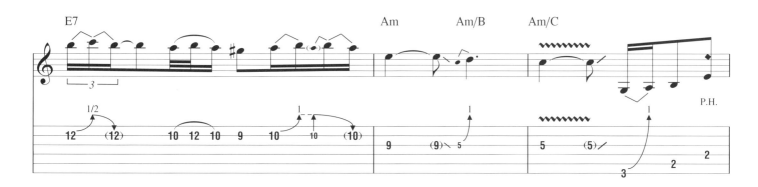

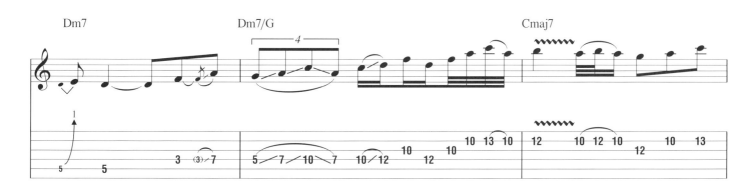

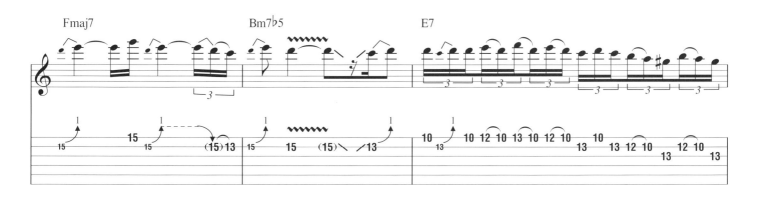

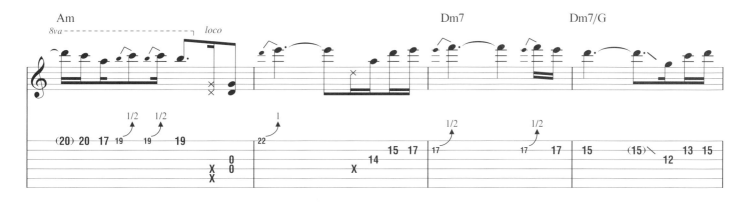

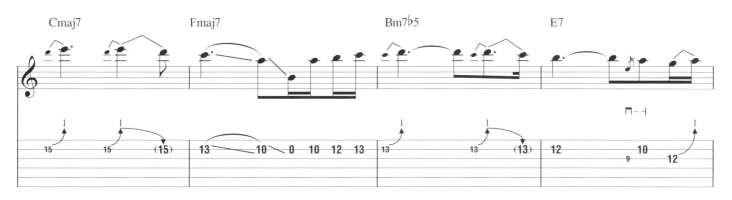

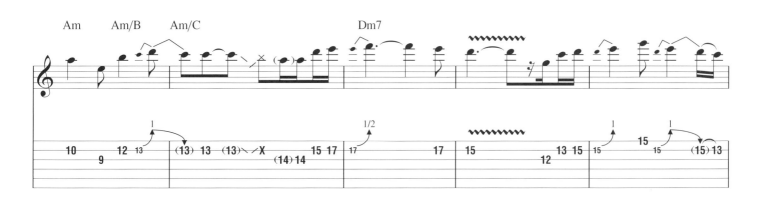

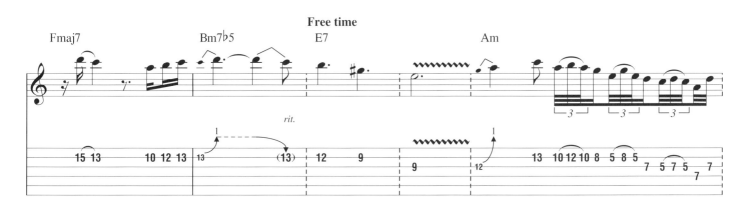

Sweet Child O' Mine

Words and Music by W. Axl Rose, Slash, Izzy Stradlin', Duff McKagan and Steven Adler

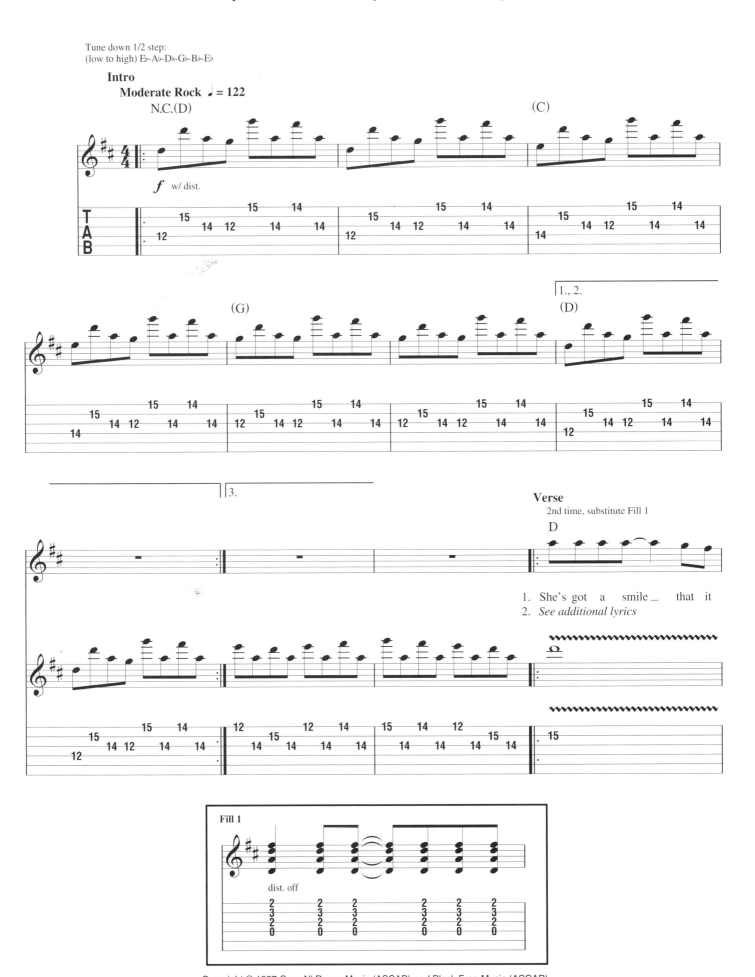

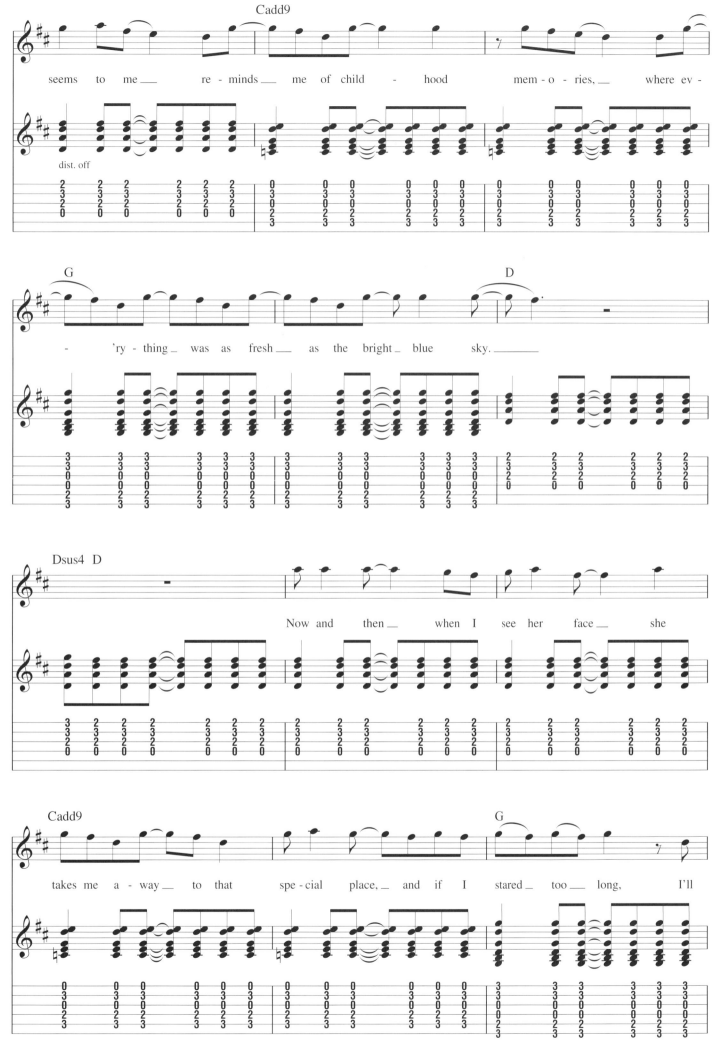

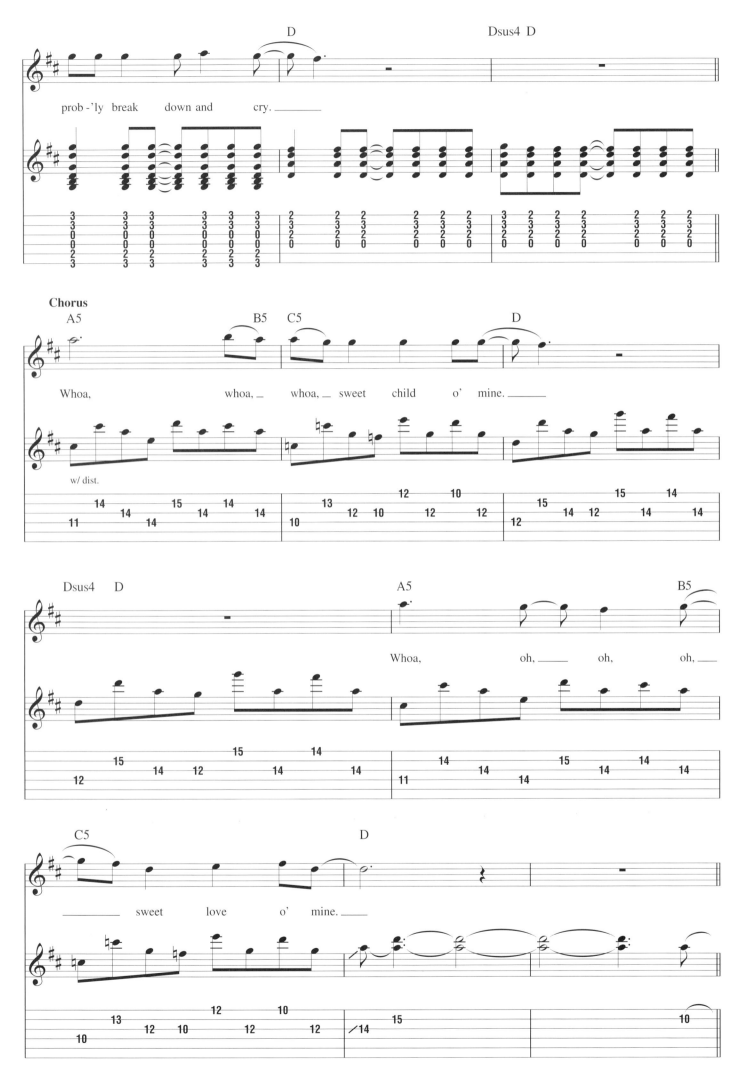

Guitar Solo

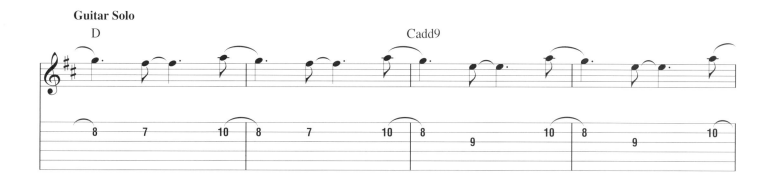

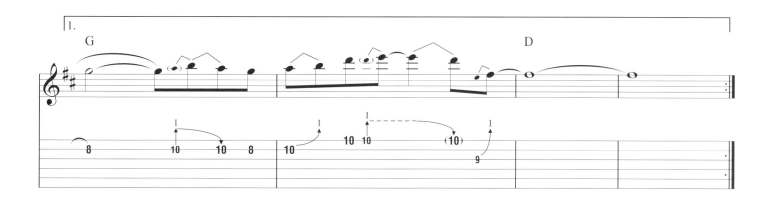

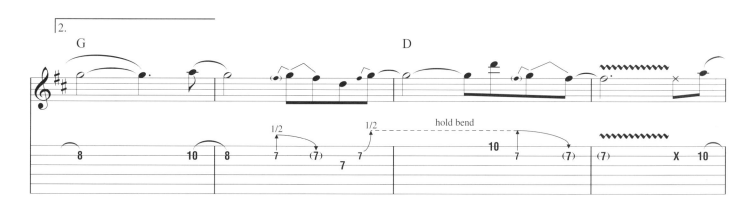

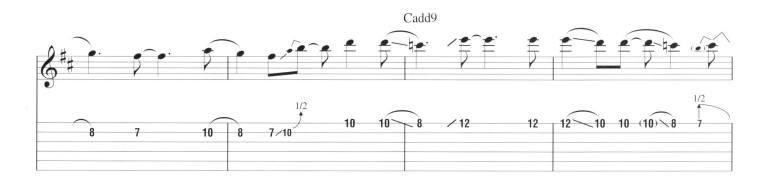

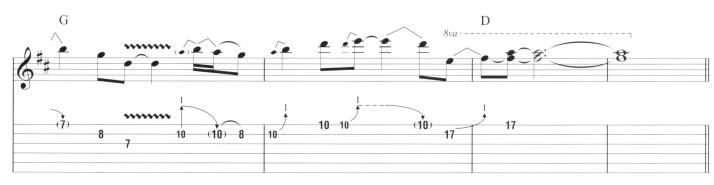

sweet   love   o'   mine.

Guitar Solo

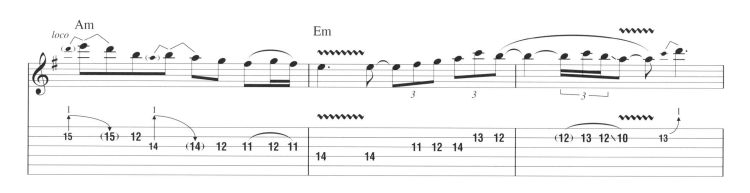

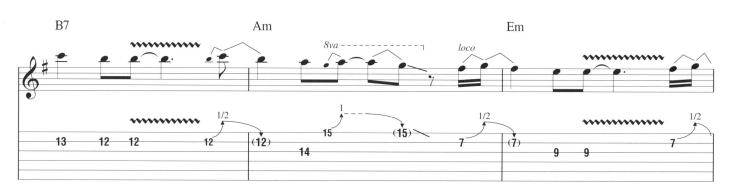

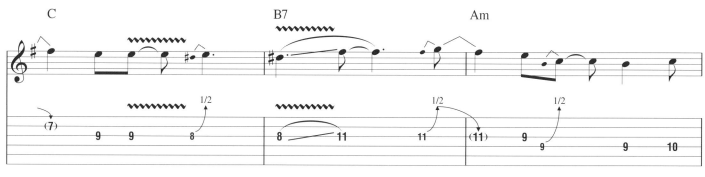

314

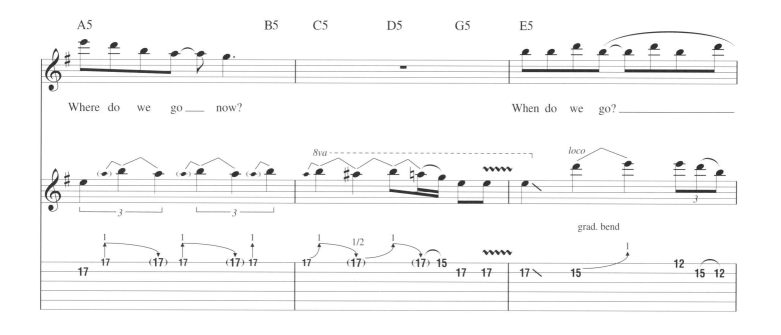

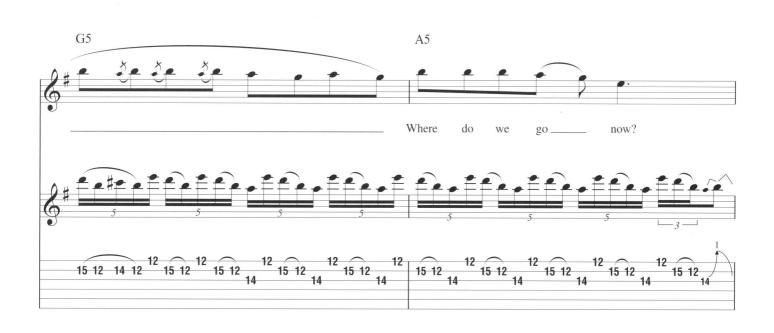

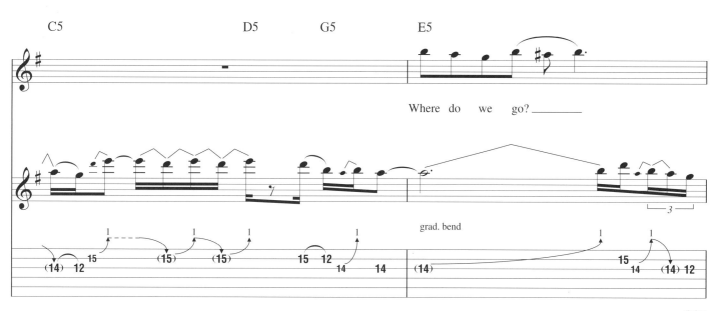

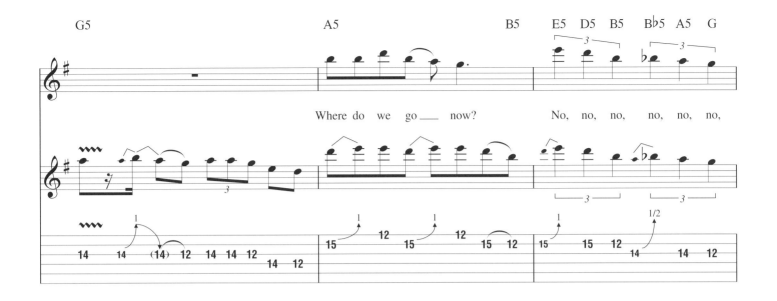

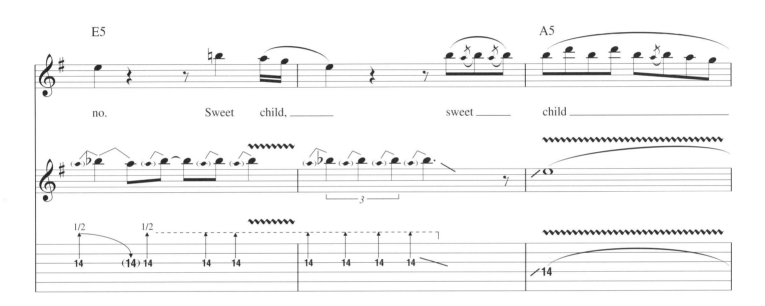

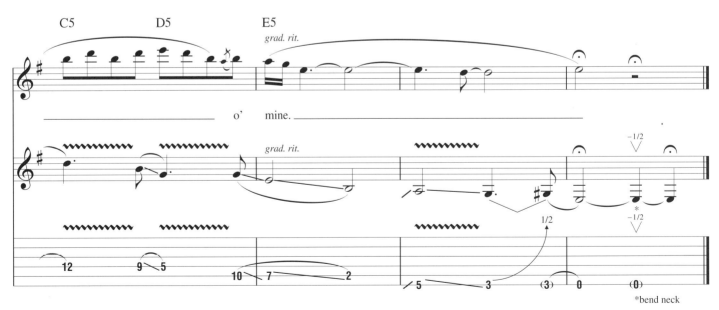

*bend neck

Additional Lyrics

2. She's got eyes of the bluest skies,
As if they thought of rain.
I'd hate to look into those eyes and see an ounce of pain.
Her hair reminds me of a warm safe place
Where as a child I'd hide,
And pray for the thunder and the rain to quietly pass me by.

Sweet Home Alabama

Words and Music by Ronnie Van Zant, Ed King and Gary Rossington

Intro
Moderate Rock ♩ = 100

*Key signature denotes D Mixolydian.

Verse

1. Big wheels keep on turn-

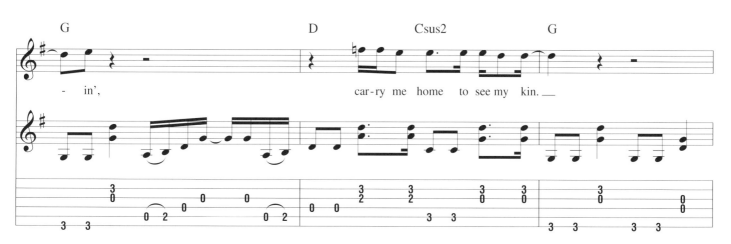

- in', car-ry me home to see my kin.

Singin' songs a-bout __ the south - land.   I miss ole 'Bam - ee once a-gain __

Interlude

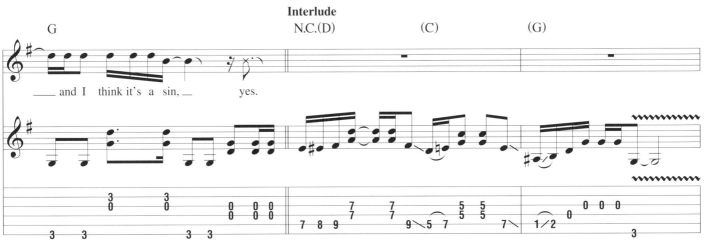

__ and I think it's a sin, __   yes.

Verse

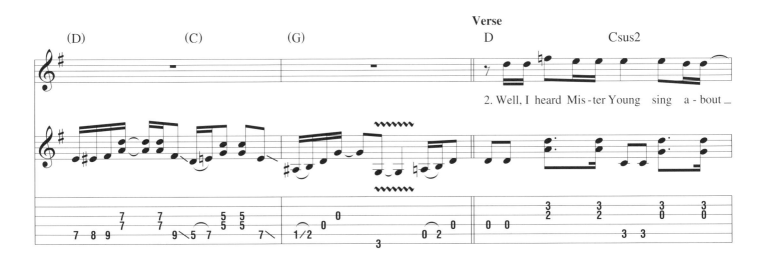

2. Well, I heard Mis-ter Young sing a-bout __

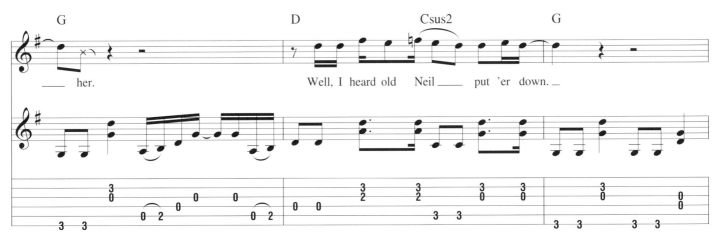

__ her.   Well, I heard old Neil __ put 'er down. __

Well, I hope Neil Young will re-mem - ber, a south-ern man _ don't need him a-

Chorus

round, an - y-how. Sweet _ home Al - a-bam-a,

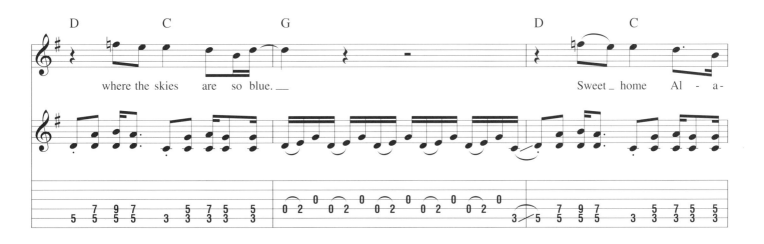

where the skies are so blue. _ Sweet _ home Al - a-

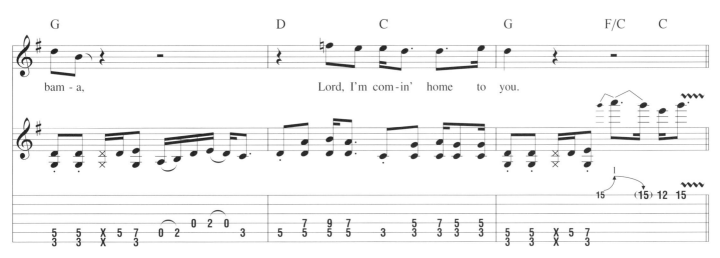

bam - a, Lord, I'm com-in' home to you.

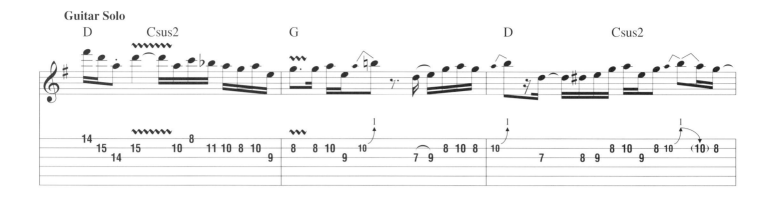

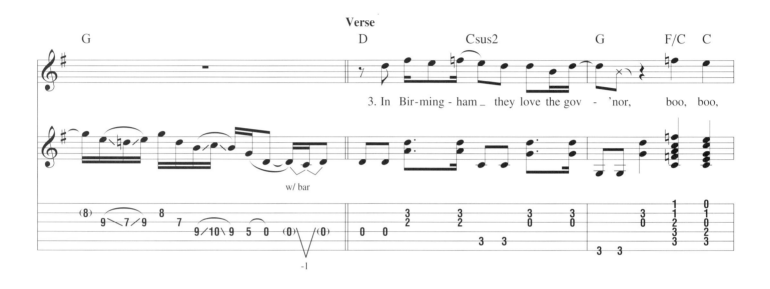

3. In Bir-ming-ham _ they love the gov - 'nor, boo, boo,

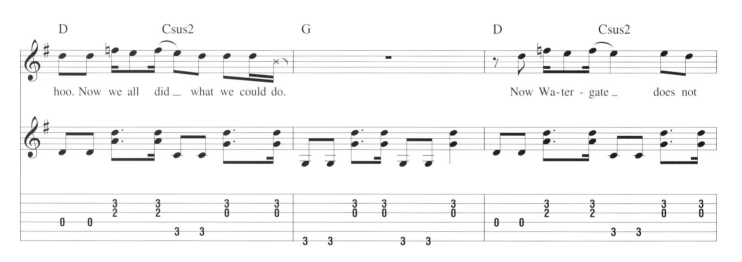

hoo. Now we all did _ what we could do. Now Wa-ter-gate _ does not

both - er me, does your con-science both-er you? _ Tell the truth.

Chorus

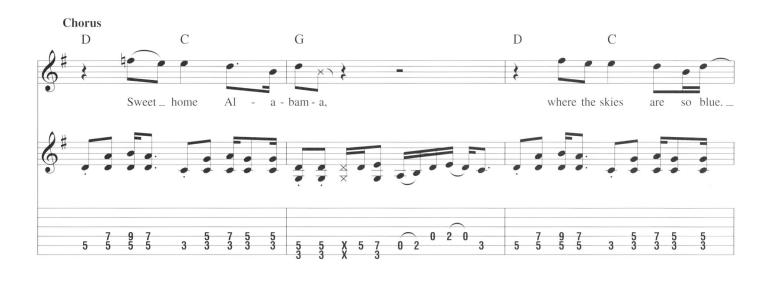

Sweet _ home Al - a-bam-a, where the skies are so blue. _

_ Sweet _ home Al - a-bam-a, yeah.

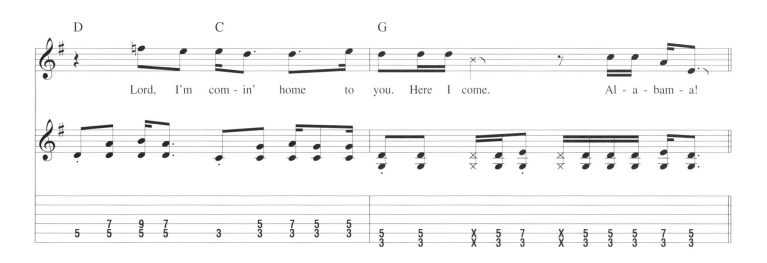

Lord, I'm com-in' home to you. Here I come. Al - a - bam - a!

Guitar Solo

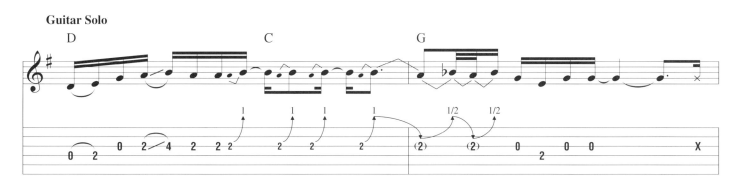

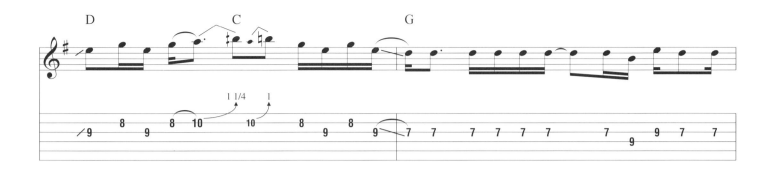

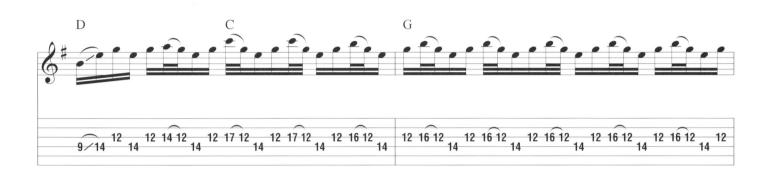

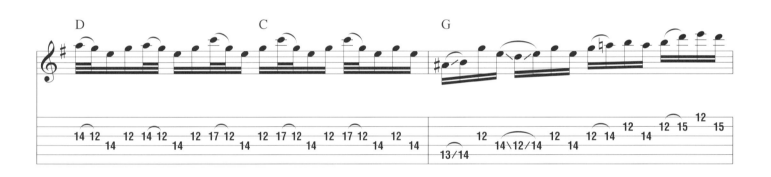

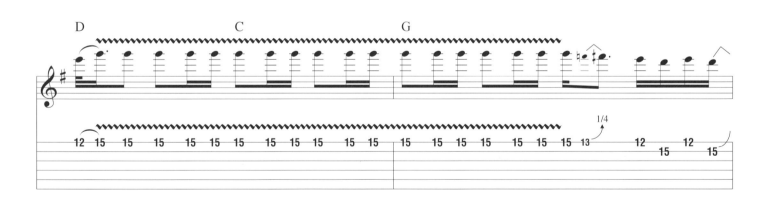

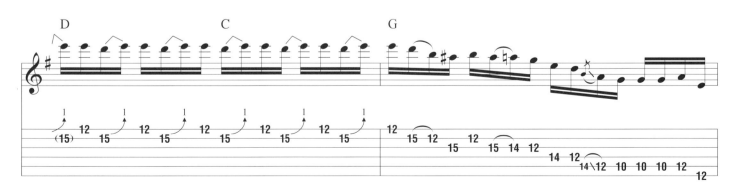

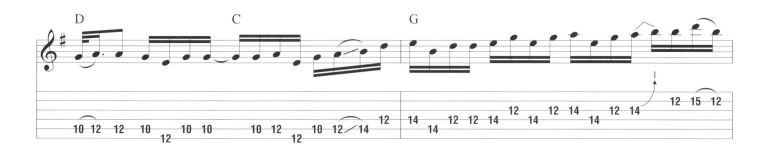

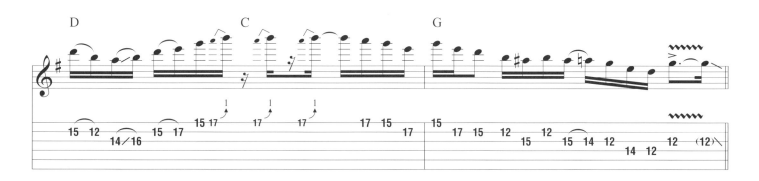

Interlude

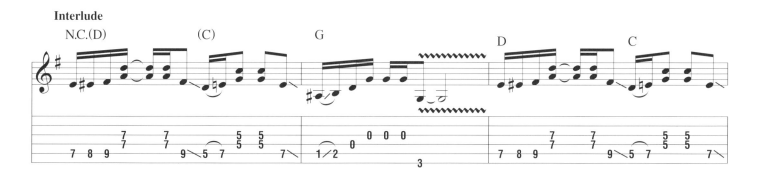

Verse

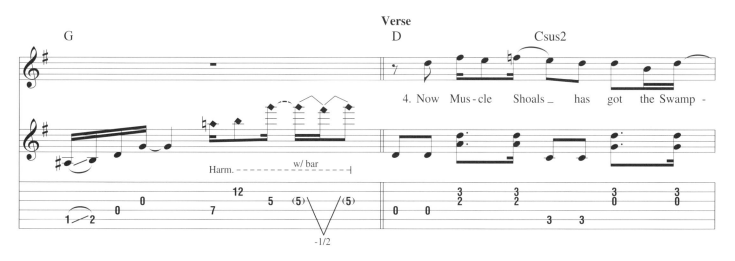

4. Now Mus-cle Shoals _ has got the Swamp-

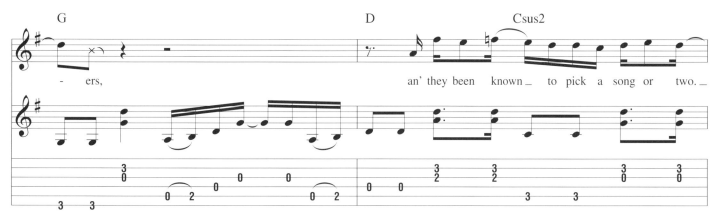

-ers, an' they been known _ to pick a song or two. _

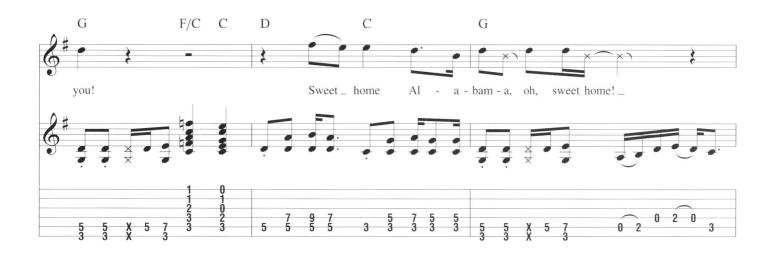

you!   Sweet _ home   Al - a - bam - a,   oh,   sweet home! _

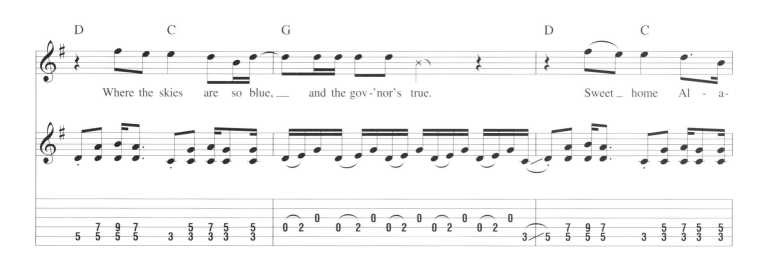

Where the skies   are   so blue, __   and the gov -'nor's true.   Sweet _ home   Al - a-

bam - a,   oh, __   yeah.   Lord, I'm com -in' home   to   you.   Yeah. _____

Outro   *Repeat and fade*

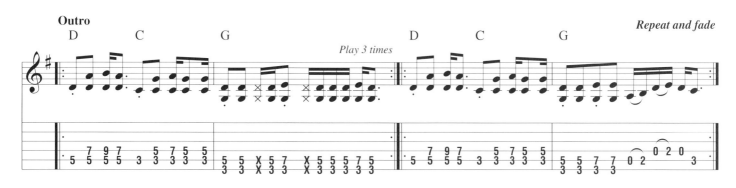

Play 3 times

Symphony of Destruction

Words and Music by Dave Mustaine

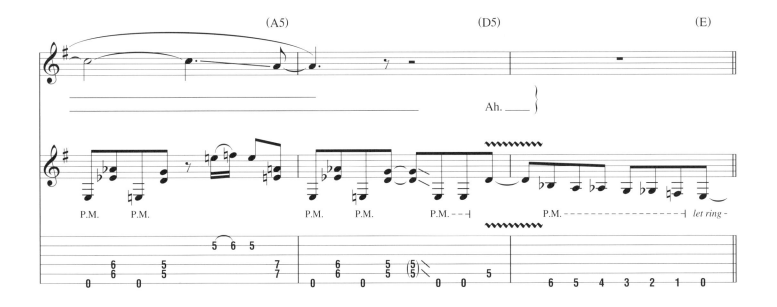

Chorus

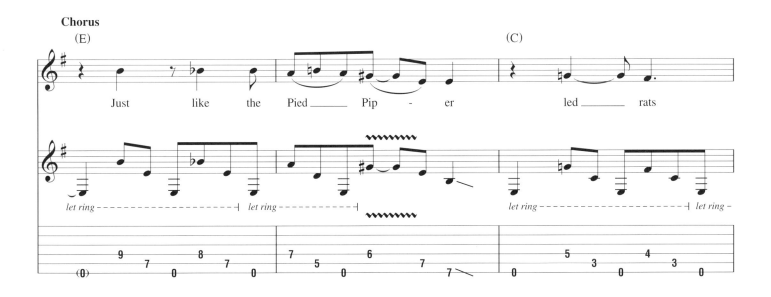

Just like the Pied ___ Pip - er led ___ rats

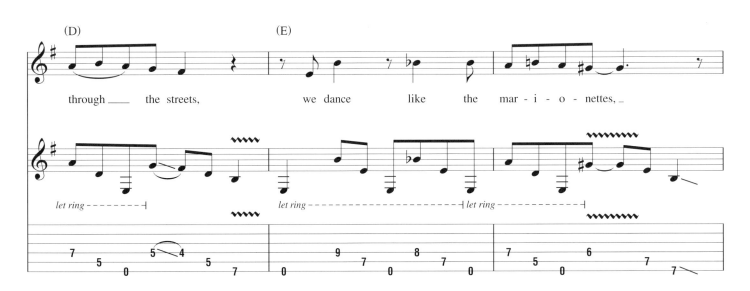

through ___ the streets, we dance like the mar - i - o - nettes, _ sway-in' ___ to the Sym-pho-ny of ___ De - struc - tion. ___

let ring - - - - - - - - - - - - - - -| P.M. - - - - - - - - - - - - -|

2. Mm, ___ act - in' like a ___ ro - bot,

P.M. - - - - -|

its ___ met - al brain cor - rodes. ___

P.M. - - - - -|

You try to take ___ its pulse _____

P.M. - - - - -|

331

Coda 1

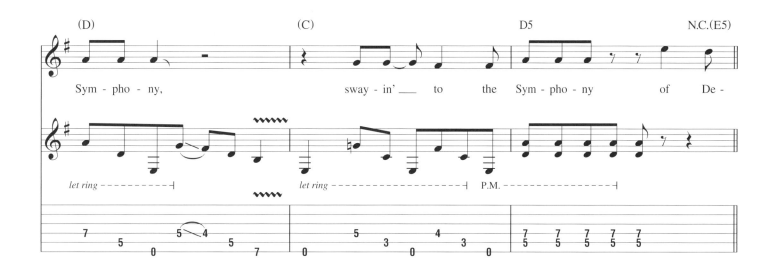

Sym - pho - ny, sway - in' ___ to the Sym - pho - ny of De -

Guitar Solo

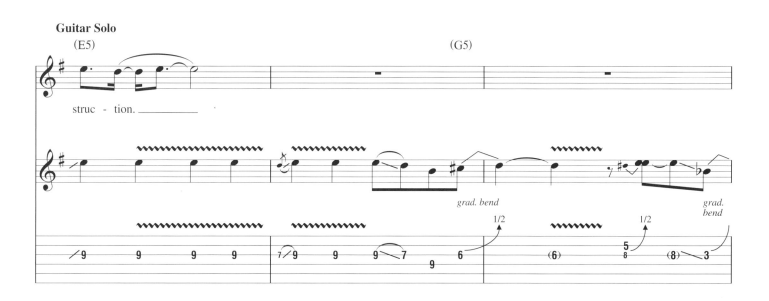

struc - tion. _____

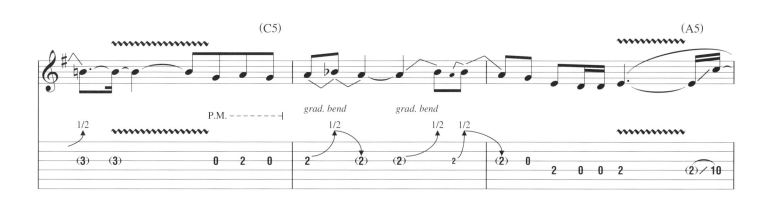

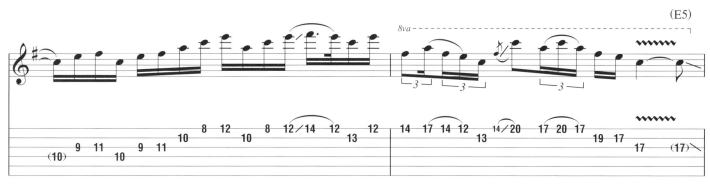

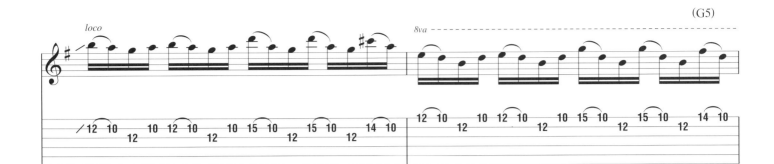

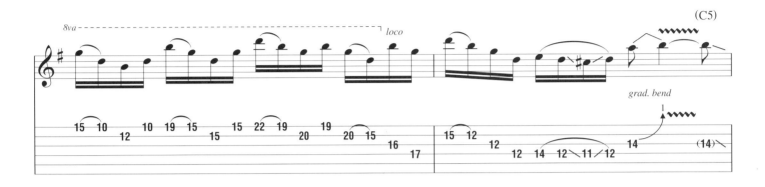

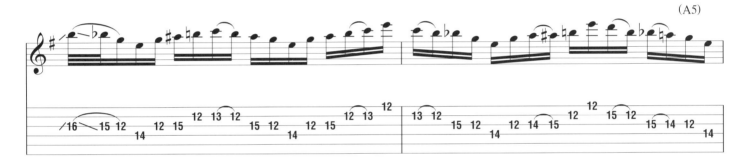

D.S.S. al Coda 2

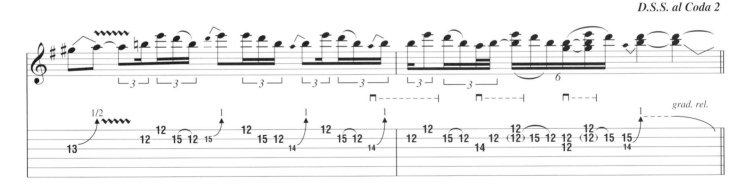

Coda 2

Sym-pho-ny... Just like the Pied _____ Pip - er

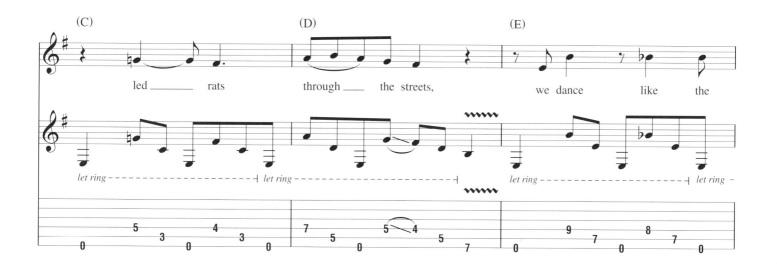

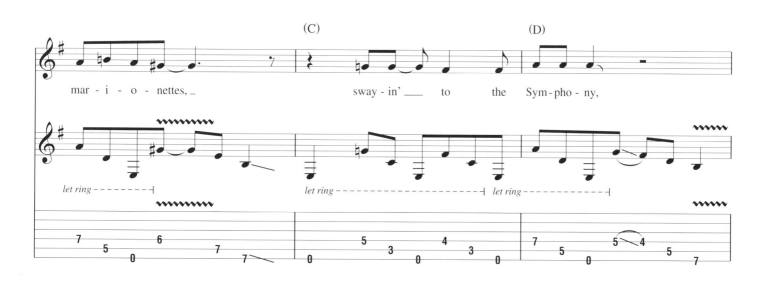

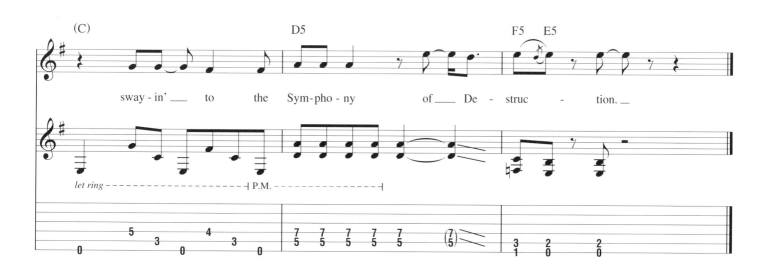

Additional Lyrics

3. The earth starts to rumble.
World powers fall.
A, warring for the heavens,
A peaceful man stands tall, a, tall, a, tall.

21 Guns

Words and Music by David Bowie, John Phillips, Billie Joe Armstrong, Mike Pritchard and Frank Wright

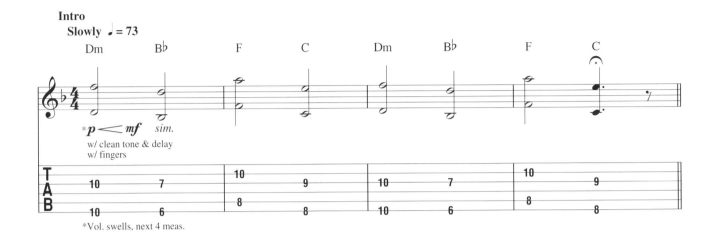

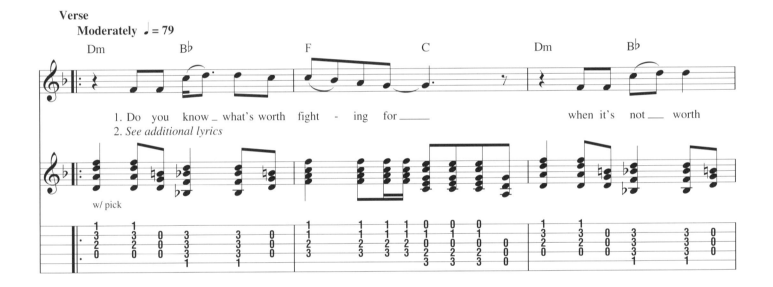

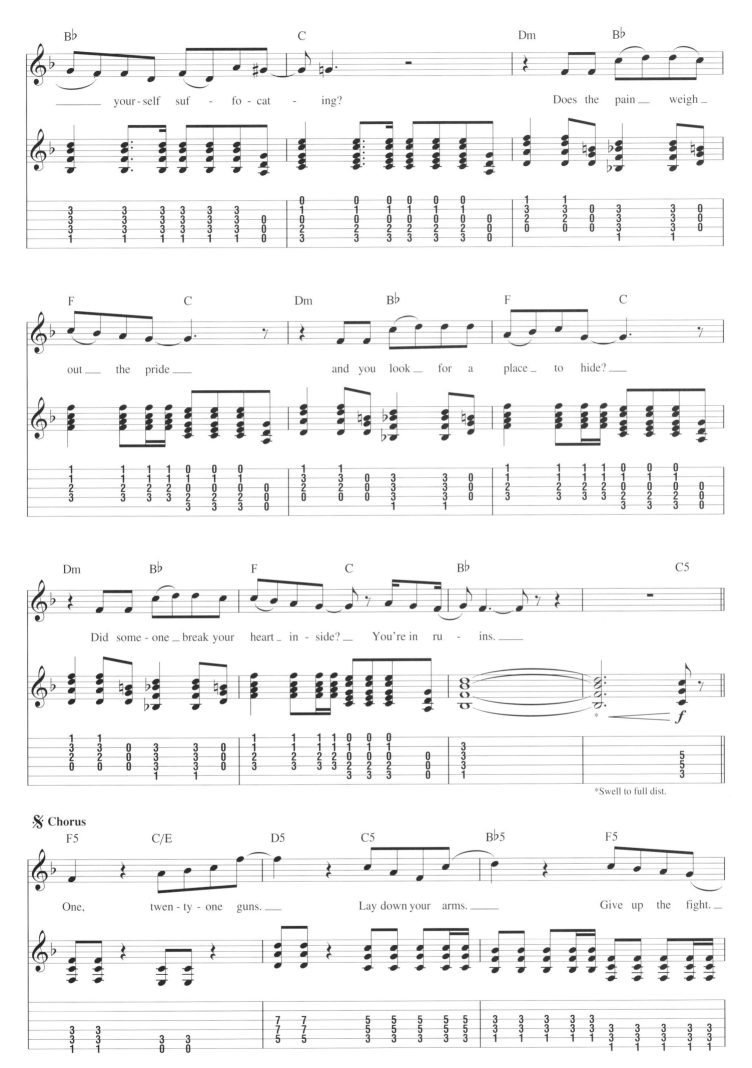

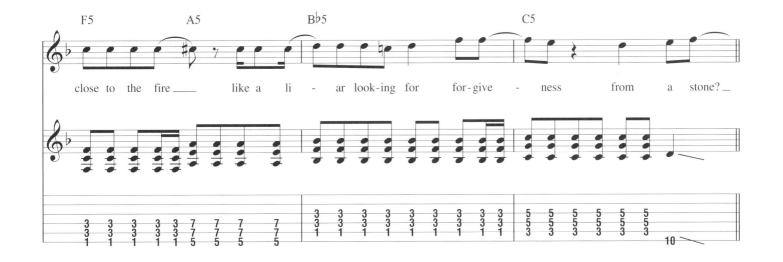

close to the fire____ like a li - ar look-ing for for-give - ness from a stone?__

Interlude

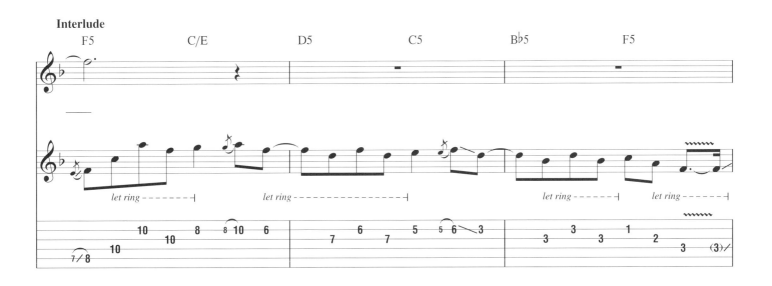

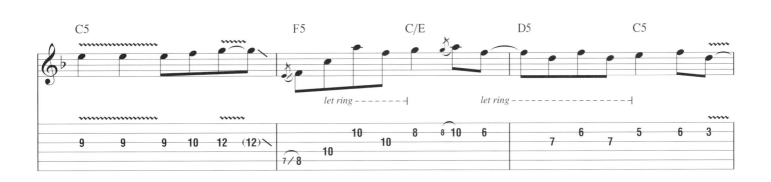

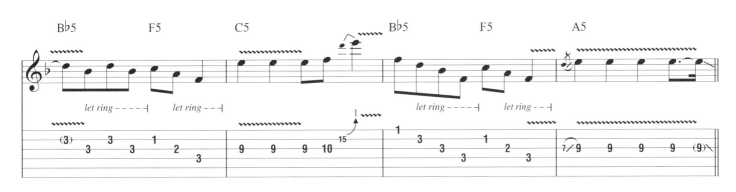

Interlude

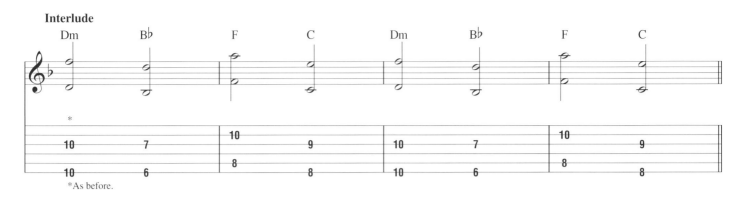

*As before.

Verse

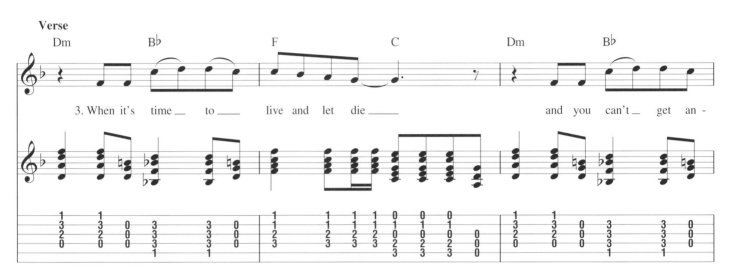

3. When it's time ___ to ___ live and let die ___ and you can't ___ get an-

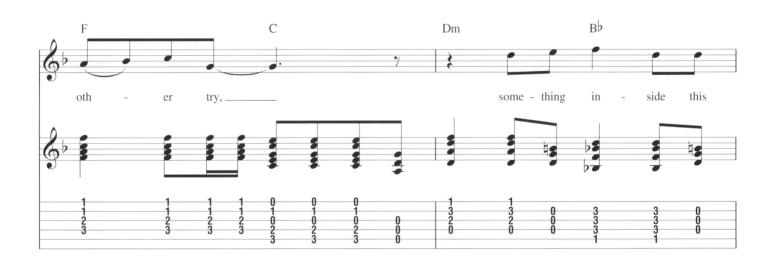

oth - er try, ___ some - thing in - side this

D.S. al Coda

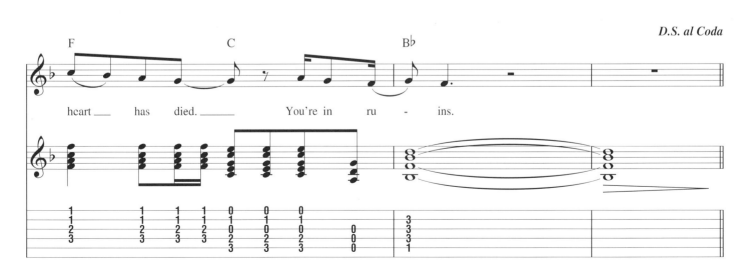

heart ___ has died. ___ You're in ru - ins.

340

⊕ Coda

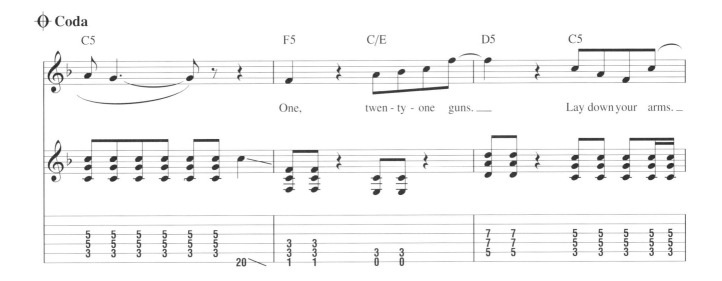

One, twen-ty-one guns.___ Lay down your arms.___

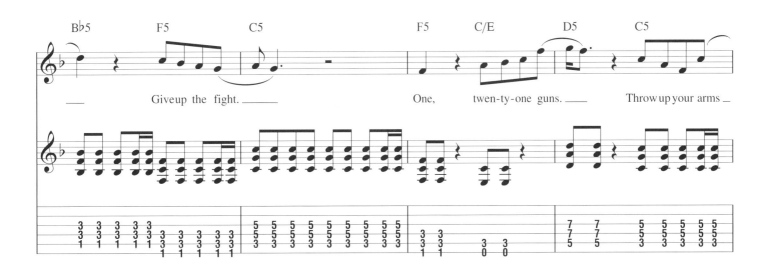

___ Give up the fight._____ One, twen-ty-one guns.___ Throw up your arms___

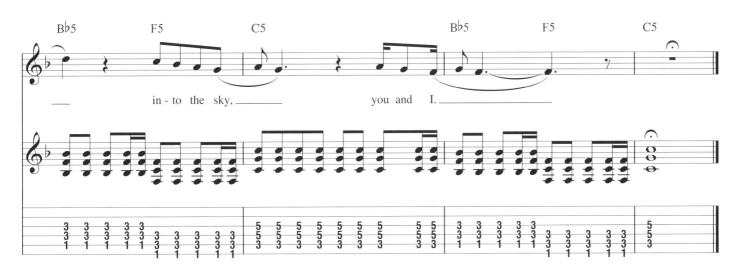

___ in - to the sky,_____ you and I._____

Additional Lyrics

2. When you're at the end of the road
   And you lost all sense of control.
   And your thoughts have taken their toll
   When your mind breaks the spirit of your soul.
   Your faith walks on broken glass
   And the hangover doesn't pass.
   Nothing's ever built to last.
   You're in ruins.

Under the Bridge

Words and Music by Anthony Kiedis, Flea, John Frusciante and Chad Smith

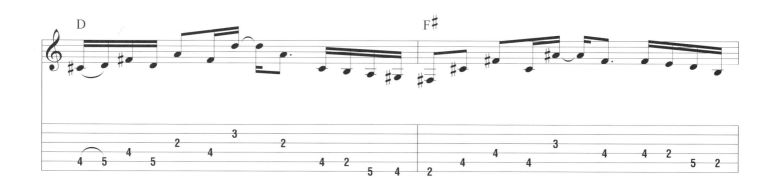

2. I drive on her streets _ 'cause
3. *See additional lyrics*

she's my com-pan-ion. I walk through her hills _ 'cause she

knows who I am. _ She sees my good deeds, _ and she

kiss-es me wind-y. I nev-er wor - ry, now,

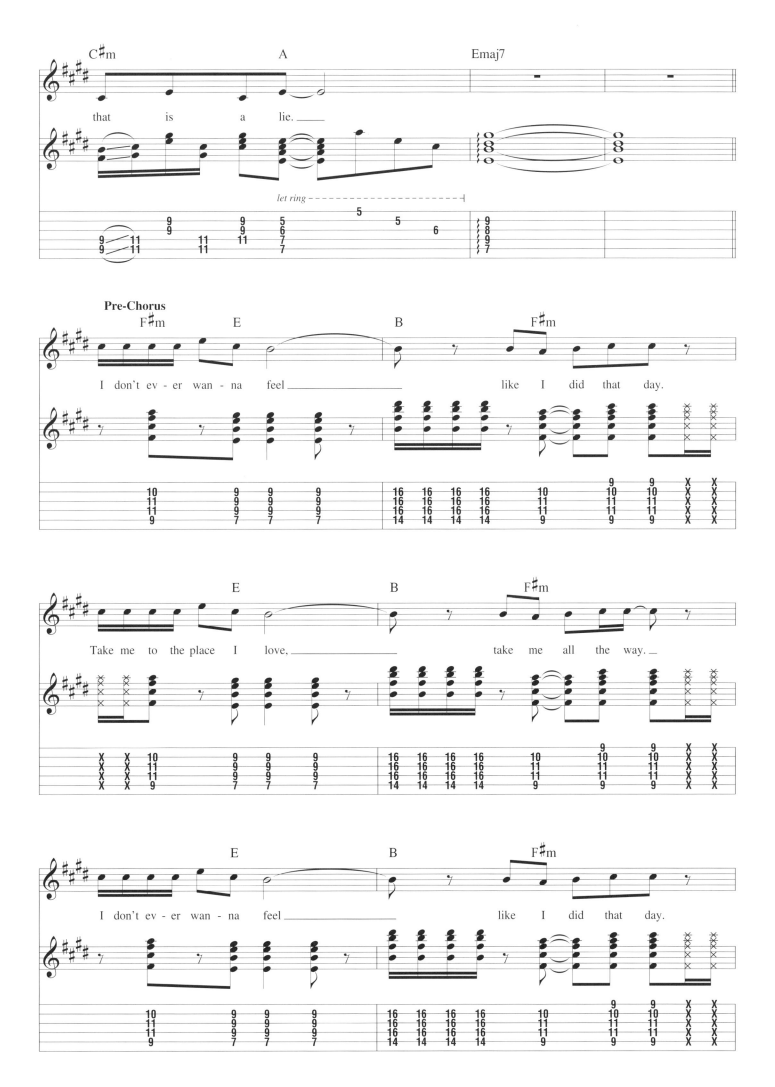

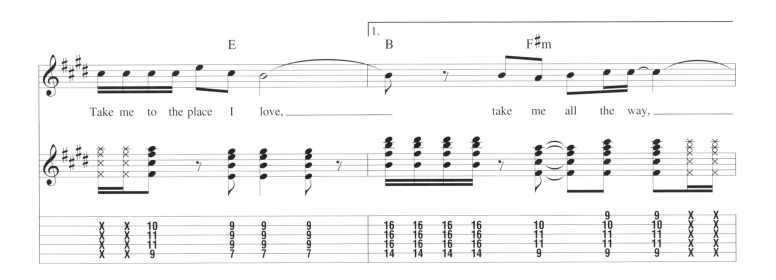

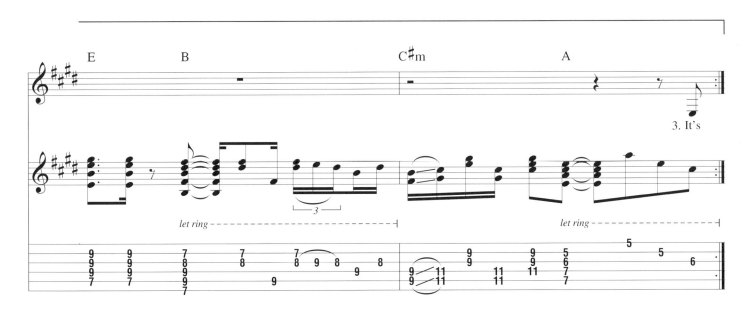

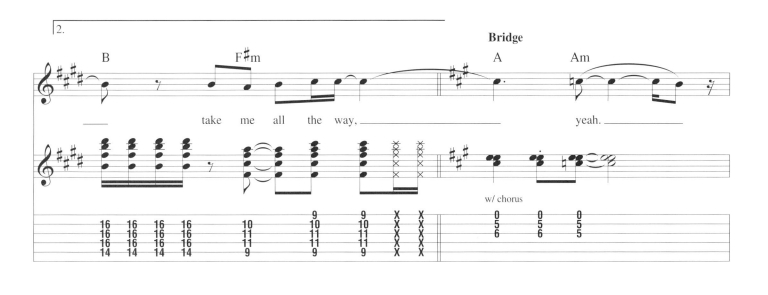

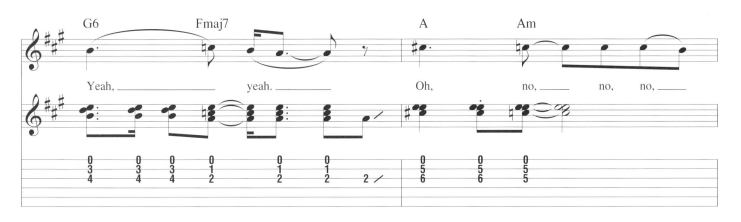

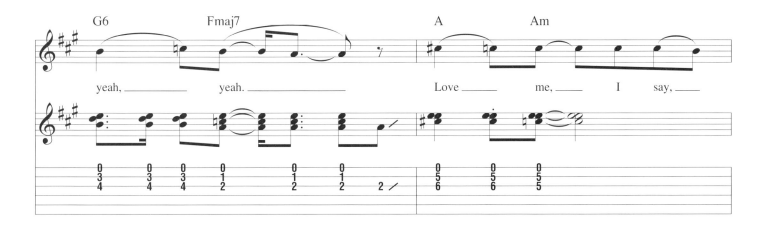

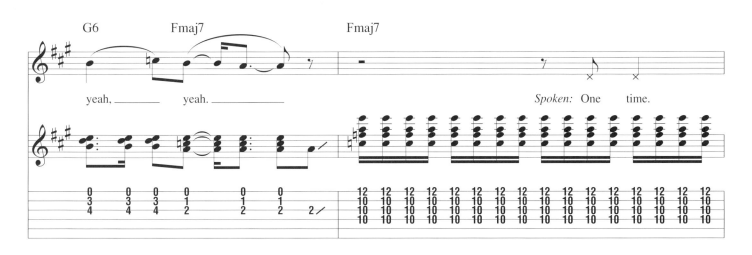

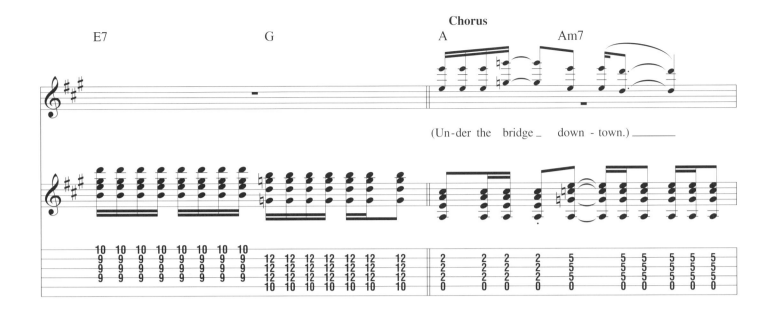

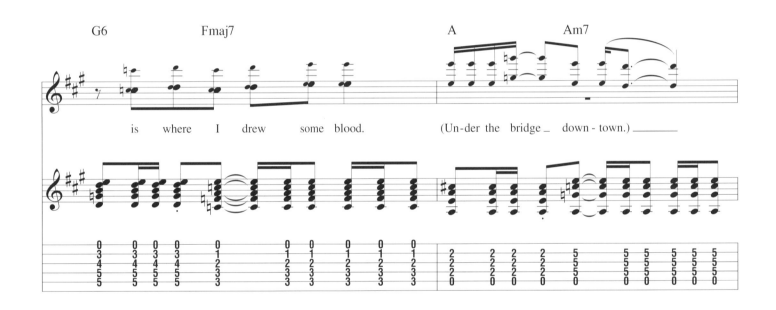

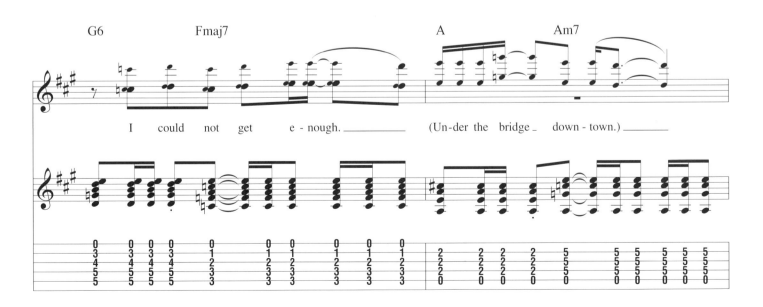

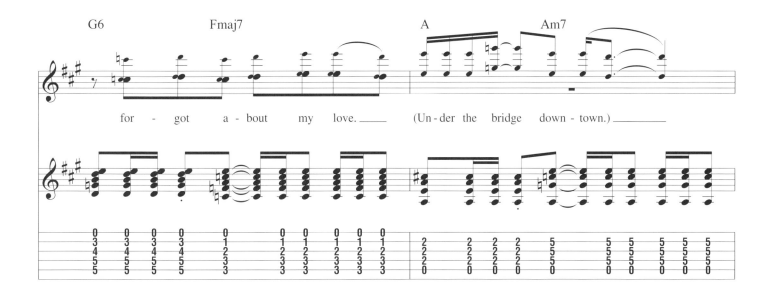

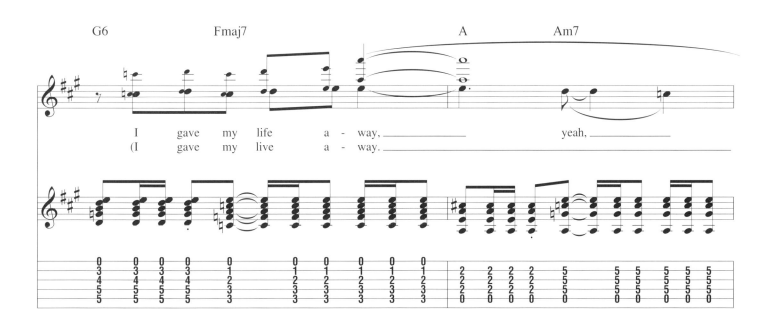

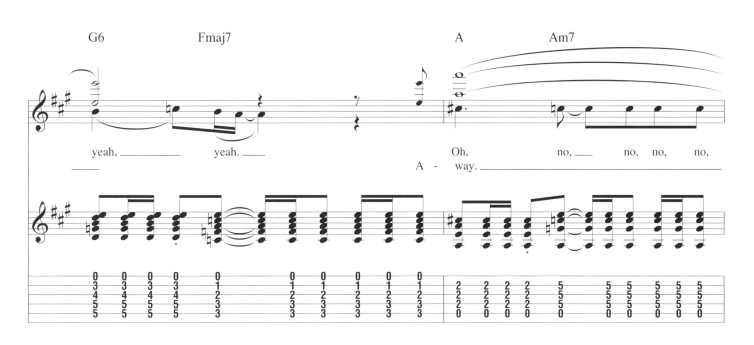

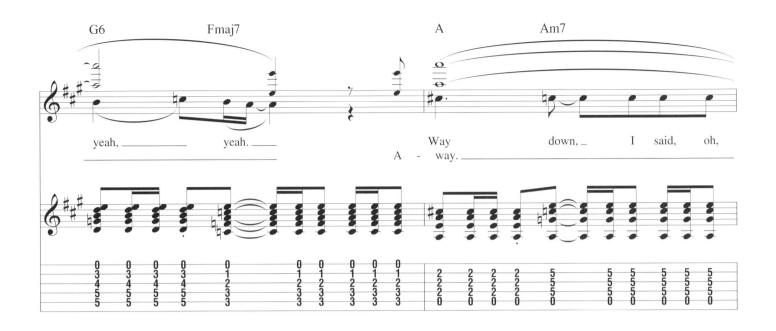

yeah, _____ yeah. _____

A - way. _____

Way down, _ I said, oh,

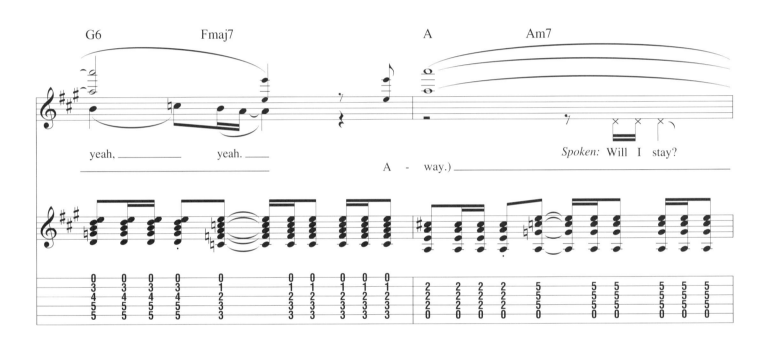

yeah, _____ yeah. _____

A - way.) _____

Spoken: Will I stay?

Outro

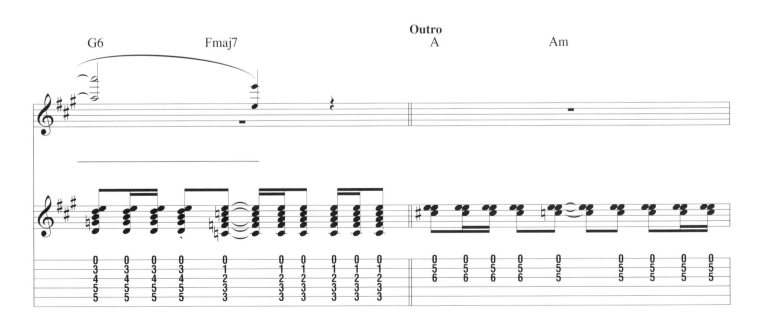

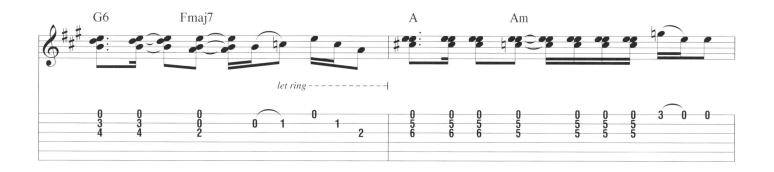

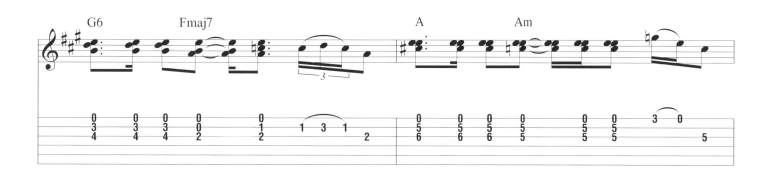

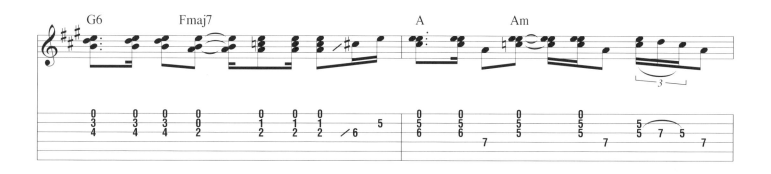

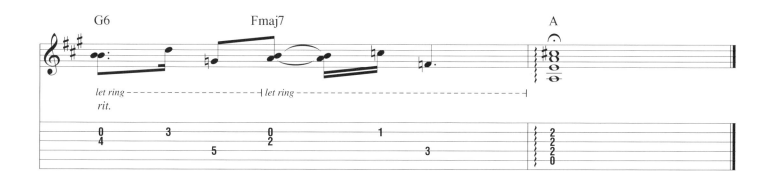

Additional Lyrics

3. It's hard to believe that there's nobody out there.
It's hard to believe that I'm all alone.
At least I have her love, the city, she loves me.
Lonely as I am, together we cry.

Welcome Home

Words and Music by Claudio Sanchez, Michael Todd, Joshua Eppard and Travis Stever

Tune down 1/2 step:
(low to high) E♭-A♭-D♭-G♭-B♭-E♭

Intro
Moderately ♩ = 78

*Chord symbols reflect implied harmony.

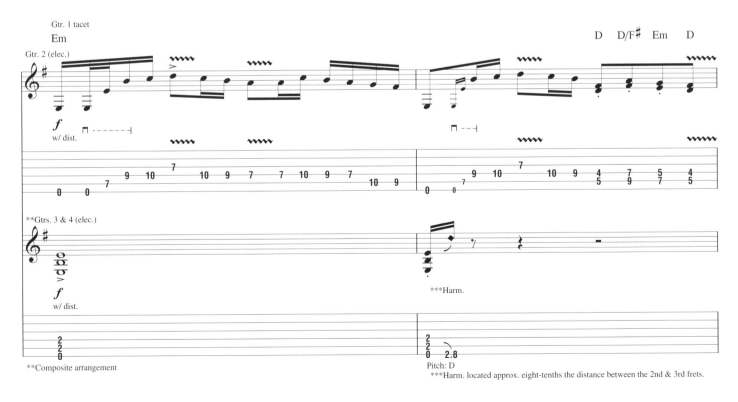

**Composite arrangement

***Harm.

Pitch: D

***Harm. located approx. eight-tenths the distance between the 2nd & 3rd frets.

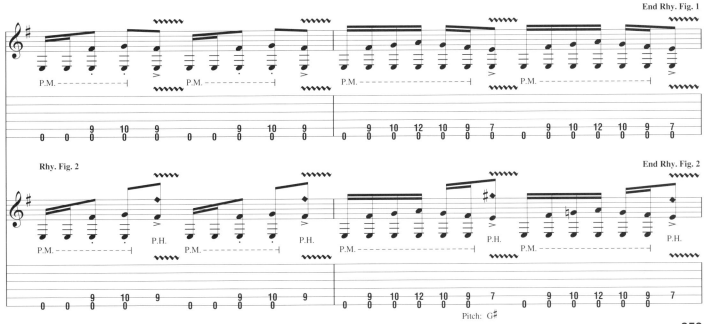

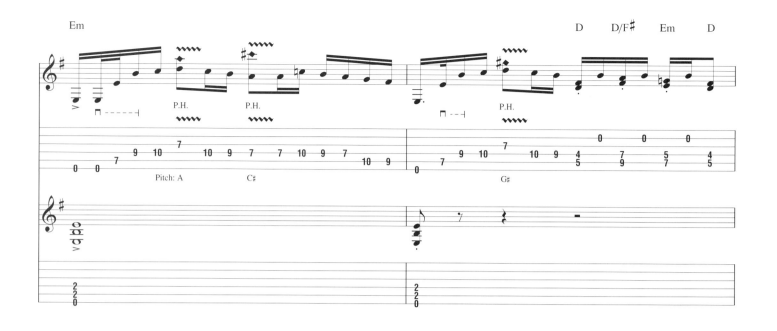

Gtr. 4: w/ Rhy. Fill 1

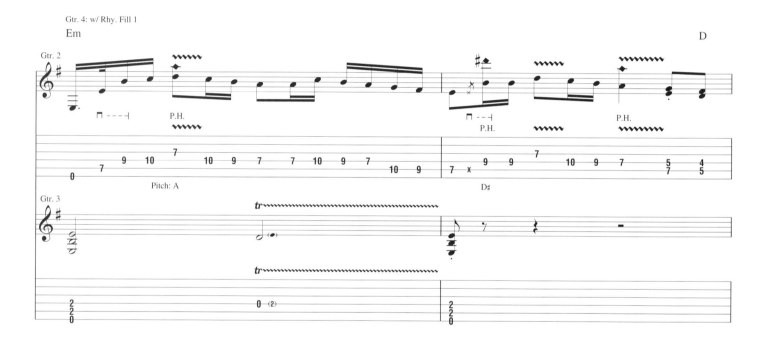

Gtr. 2: w/ Rhy. Fig. 1
Gtrs. 3 & 4: w/ Rhy. Fig. 2 (2 times)

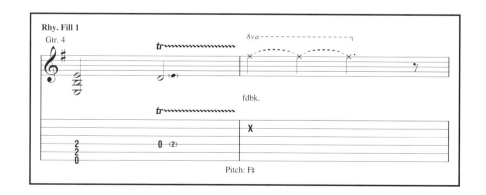

𝄋 Verse

2nd time, Lead Voc.: w/ Voc. Fill 1
2nd time, Gtrs. 1 & 4 tacet

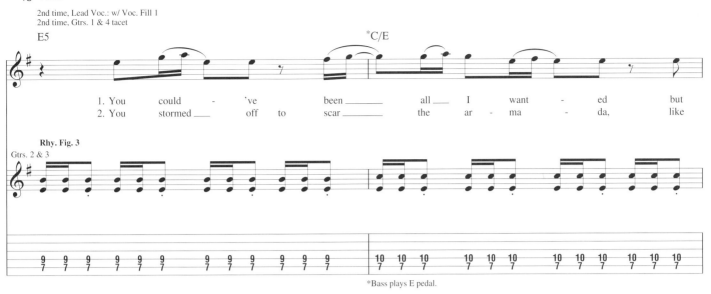

1. You could -'ve been _____ all _____ I want - ed but
2. You stormed _____ off to scar _____ the ar - ma - da, like

*Bass plays E pedal.

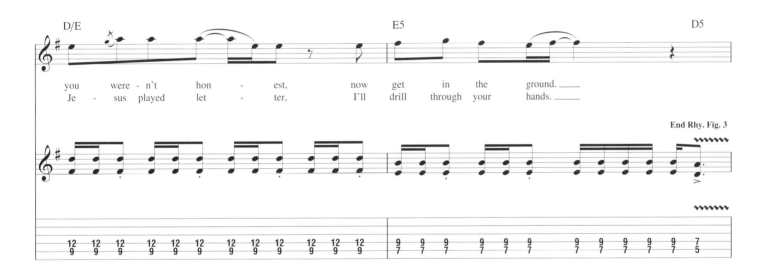

you were - n't hon - est, now get in the ground. _____
Je - sus played let - ter, I'll drill through your hands. _____

Gtrs. 2 & 3: w/ Rhy. Fig. 3 (3 times)

You choked _____ off the sur - est of fa - vors _____ but if you real - ly love _____ me you
The stone _____ for the curse _____ you have blamed _____ me. With love and de - vo - tion, I'll

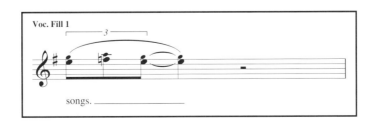

Voc. Fill 1

songs. _____

would-'ve en-dured my world. Well, if you're just as I pre-sumed; a
die as you sleep. But if you could just write me out to

Gtr. 4

whore in sheep's cloth-ing, fuck-ing up all I do. And it's all
nev-er-less won-der, hap-py will I be-come. Be true that

To Coda ⊕

here we stop then nev-er a-gain will you see this in your life.
this is no op-tion. So with sin, I con-demn you. De-mon play, de-mon out.

356

Chorus

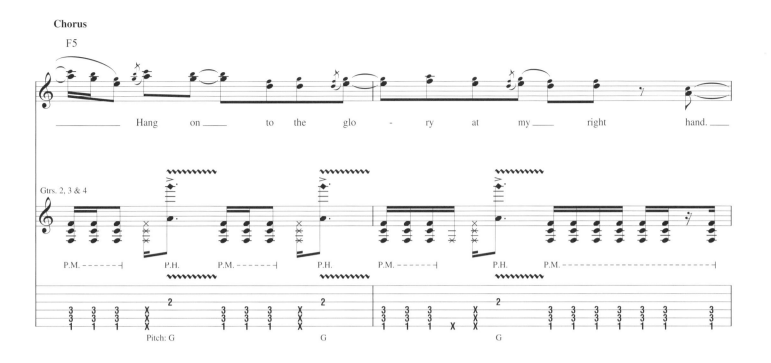

Hang on ___ to the glo - ry at my ___ right hand. ___

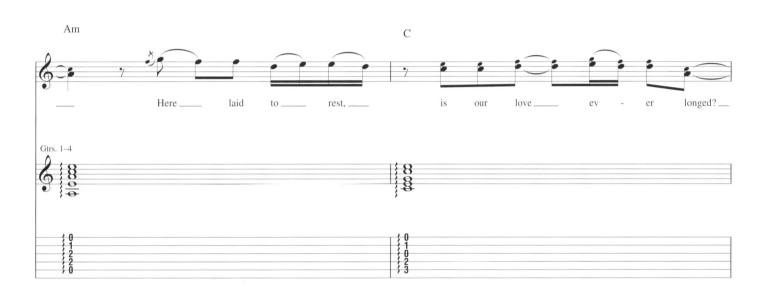

Here ___ laid to ___ rest, ___ is our love ___ ev - er longed? ___

Gtr. 1 tacet

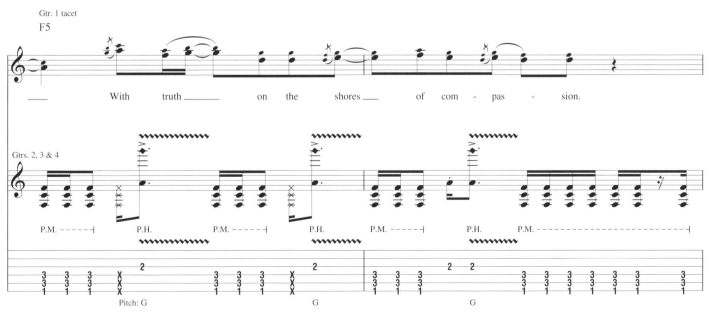

With truth ___ on the shores ___ of com - pas - sion.

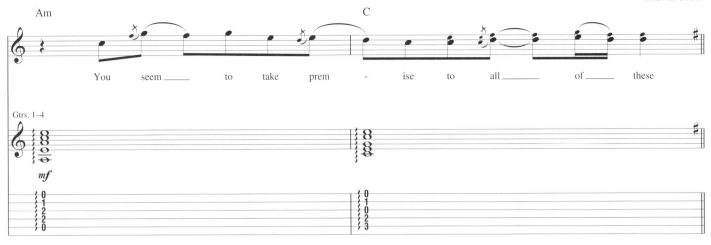

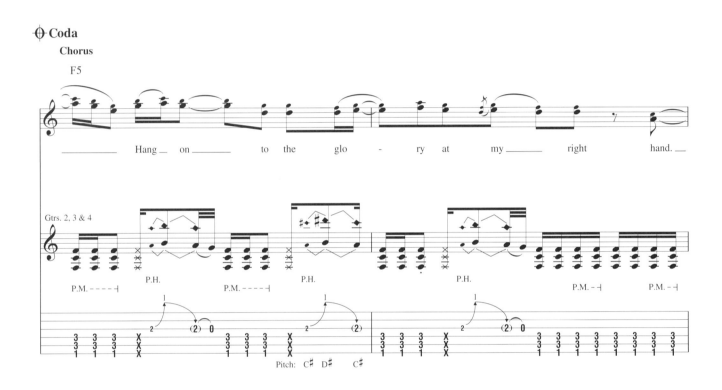

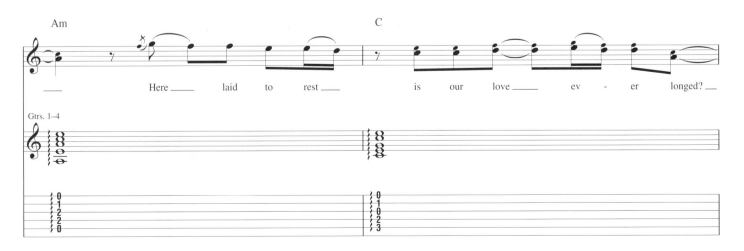

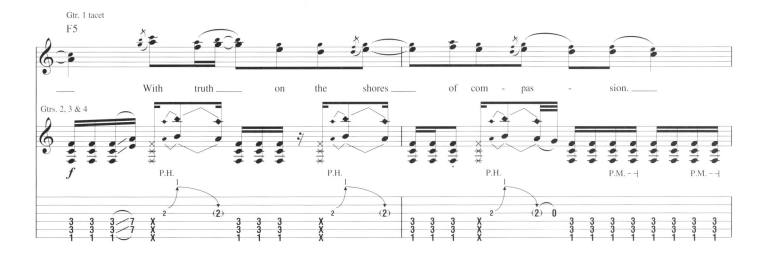

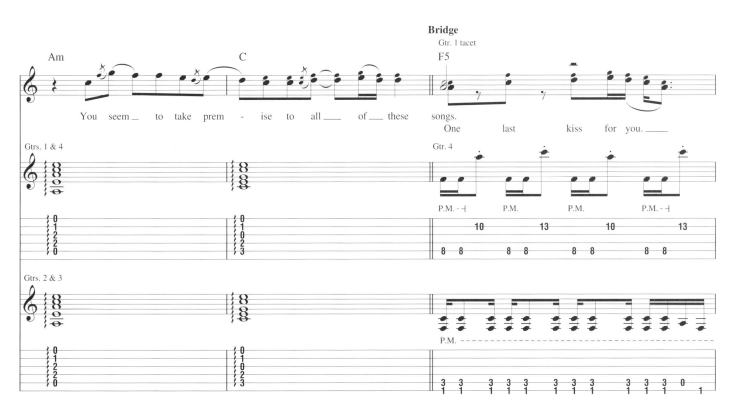

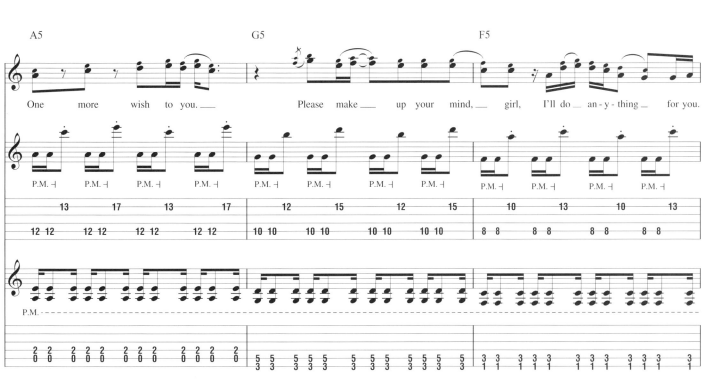

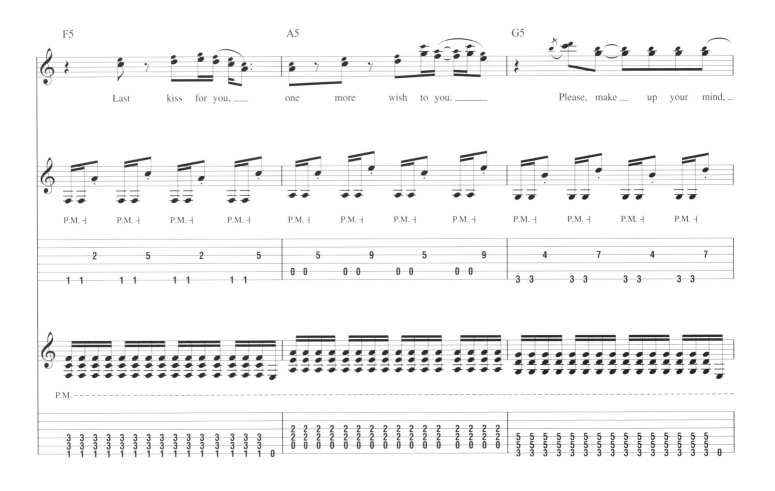

Last kiss for you, ___ one more wish to you. _____ Please, make ___ up your mind, ___

Guitar Solo

Gtrs. 2 & 3: w/ Rhy. Fig. 3 (5 times)

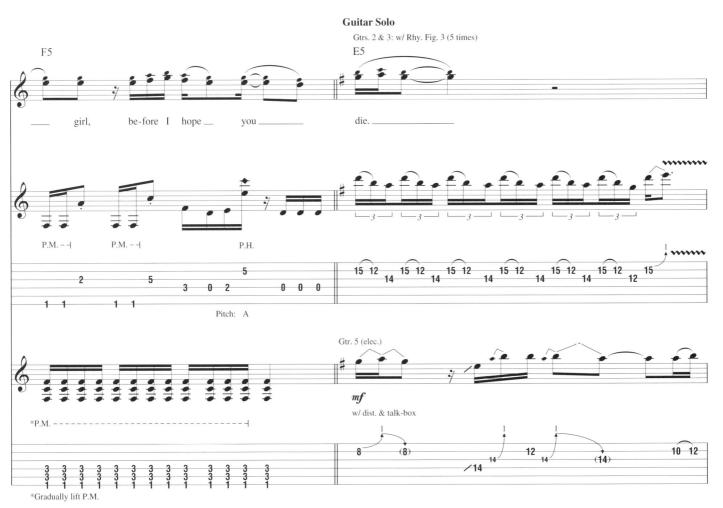

___ girl, be-fore I hope ___ you _____ die. _____

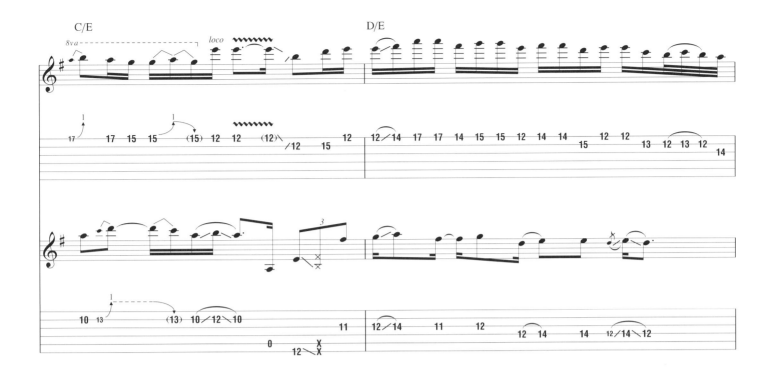

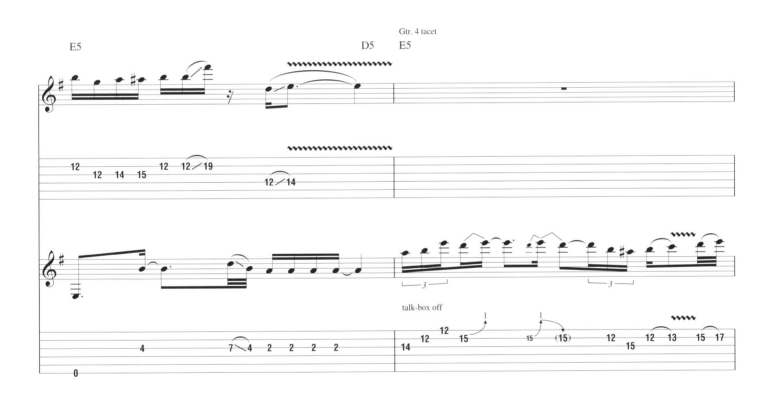

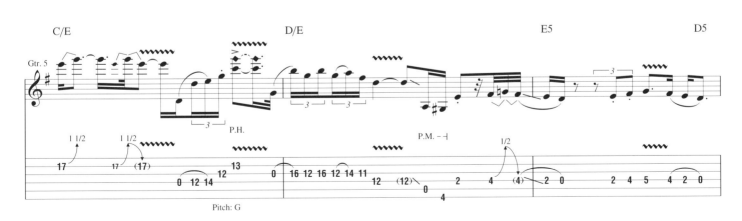

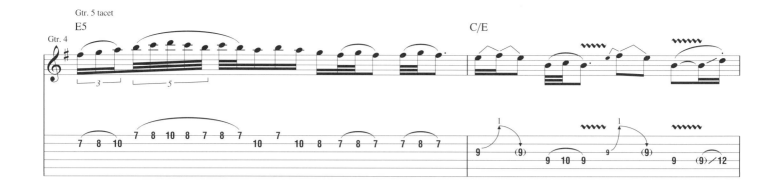

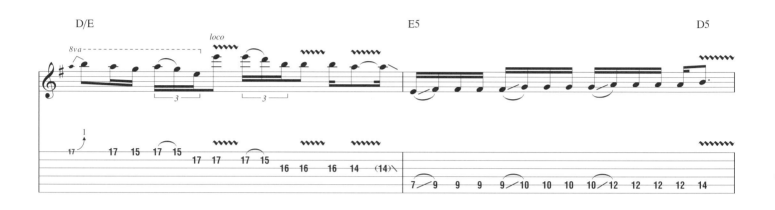

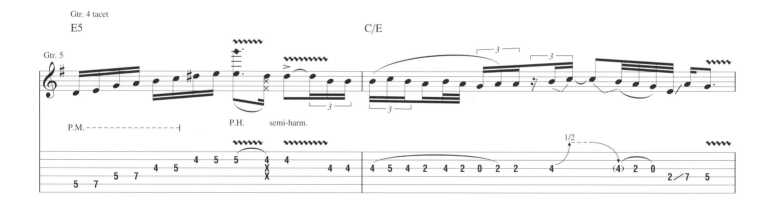

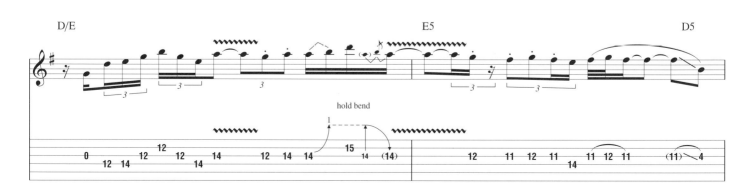

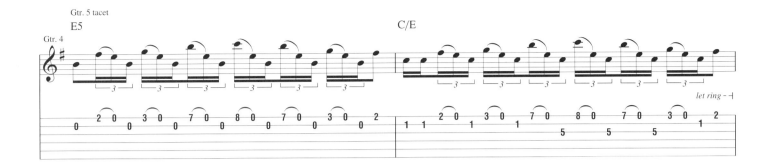

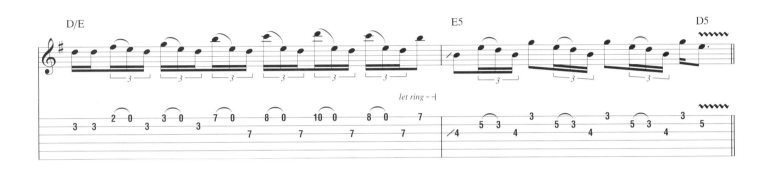

Outro

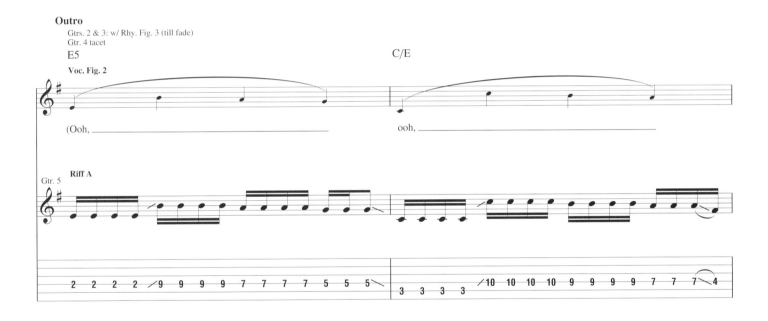

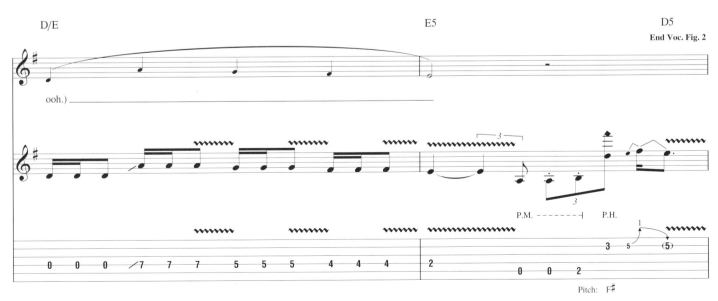

Bkgd. Voc.: w/ Voc. Fig. 2 (till fade)

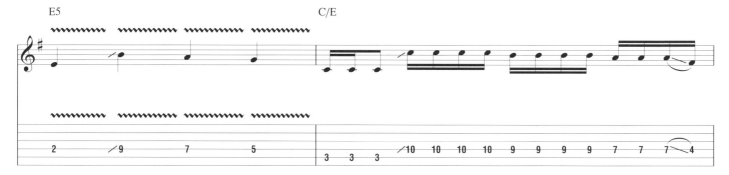

Gtr. 5: w/ Riff A (till fade)

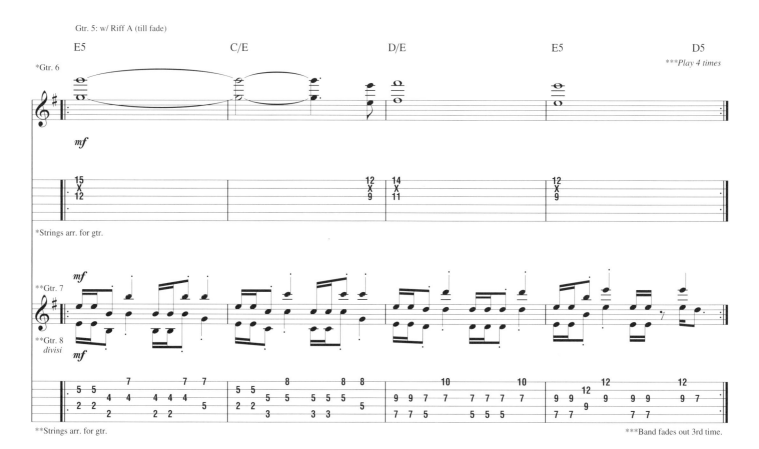

*Strings arr. for gtr.

**Strings arr. for gtr.

***Band fades out 3rd time.

Wild Thing

Words and Music by Chip Taylor

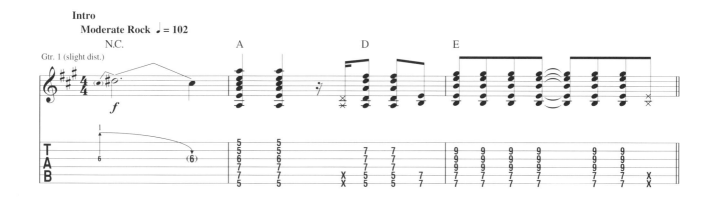

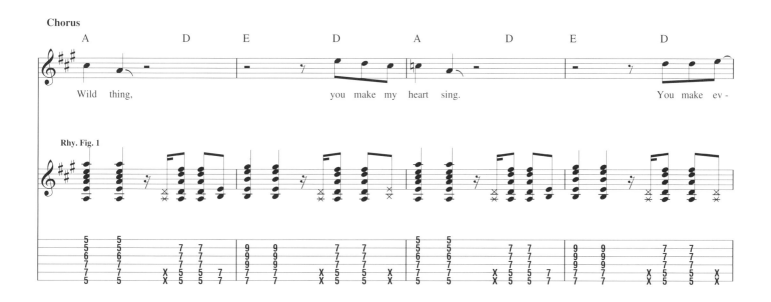

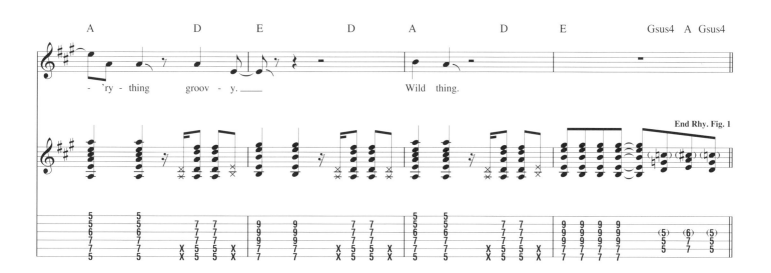

366

Woman

Words and Music by John Lennon

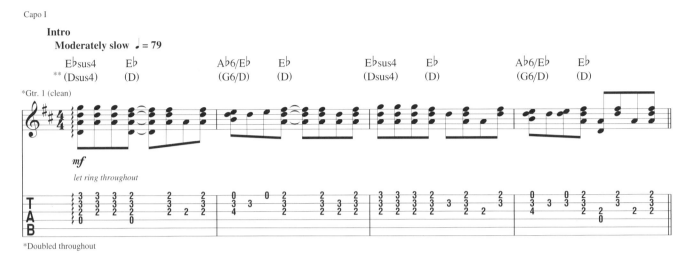

*Doubled throughout

**Symbols in parentheses represent chord names respective to capoed guitar.
Symbols above reflect actual sounding chords. Capoed fret is "0" in tab.

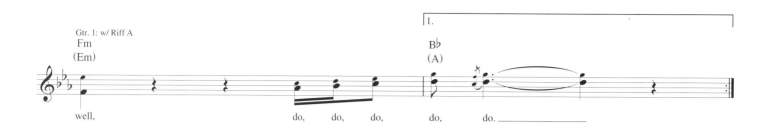

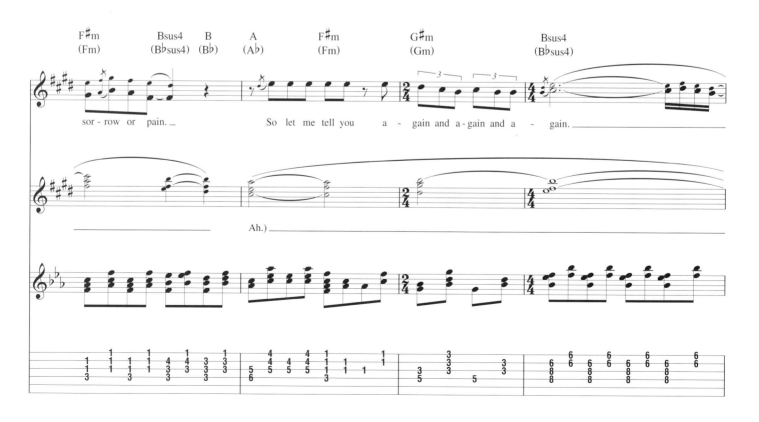

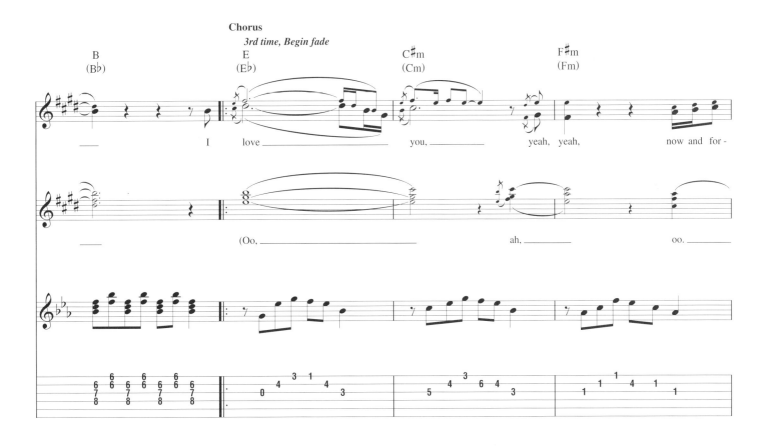

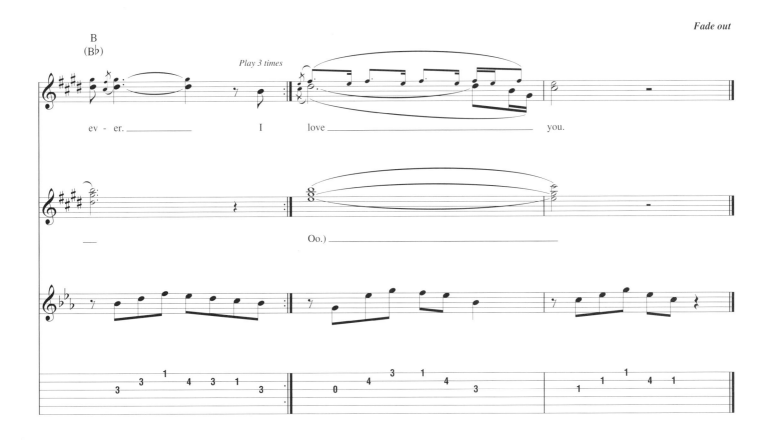

Wonderwall

Words and Music by Noel Gallagher

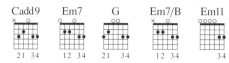

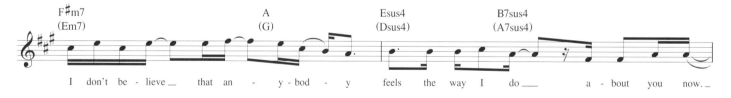

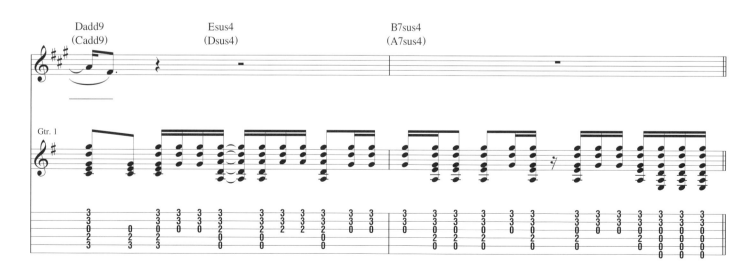

Verse

Gtr. 1: w/ Rhy. Fig. 1, 4 times, simile

F#m
(Em7)
A
(G)
Esus4
(Dsus4)
B7sus4
(A7sus4)

2. Back - beat, the word is on the street that the fire ___ in your heart is out. ___
3. To - day was gon - na be the day, but they'll nev - er throw it back to you. ___

F#m7
(Em7)
A
(G)
Esus4
(Dsus4)
B7sus4
(A7sus4)

I'm sure you've heard it all be - fore, but you nev - er real - ly had a doubt. __
By now you should have some - how re - al - ized what you're not to do. ___

F#m7
(Em7)
A
(G)
Esus4
(Dsus4)
B7sus4
(A7sus4)

I don't be - lieve ___ that an - y - bod - y feels the way I do ___ a - bout you now. ___

F#m7
(Em7)
A
(G)
Esus4
(Dsus4)
B7sus4
(A7sus4)

___
And all ____
And all ____

Pre-Chorus

*D
(C)
E
(D)
F#m7
(Em7)

___ the roads ___ we have ___ to walk ___ are wind - ing, and all ___
___ the roads ___ that lead ___ you there ___ were wind - ing, and all ___

Gtrs. 1 & 2 (clean)

mf

let ring throughout

* Chord symbols reflect overall harmony.

D
(C)
E
(D)
F#m7
(Em7)

___ the lights ___ that lead ___ us there ___ are blind - ing.
___ the lights ___ that light ___ the way ___ are blind - ing.

There are man-y things___ that I___ would like to say to you,___ but I don't know how.___

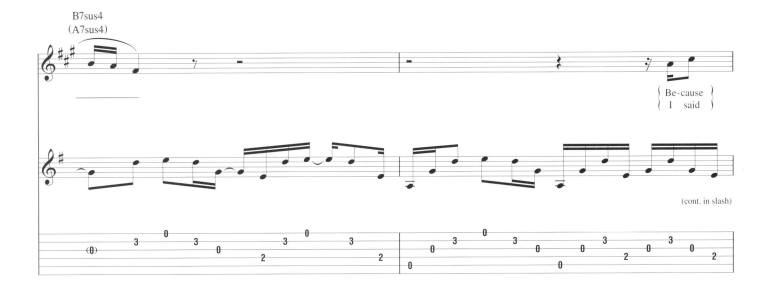

Be-cause
I said

(cont. in slash)

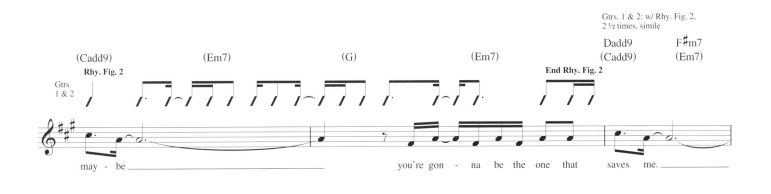

may - be ___ you're gon - na be the one that saves me. ___

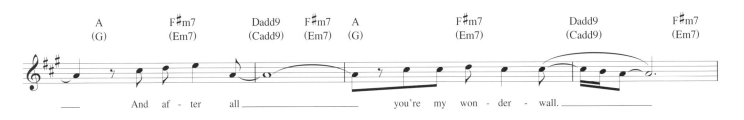

___ And af - ter all ___ you're my won - der - wall. ___

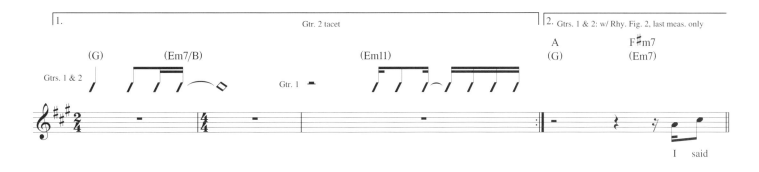

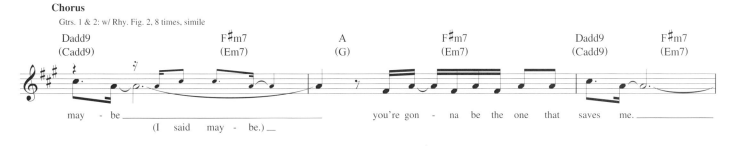

Chorus

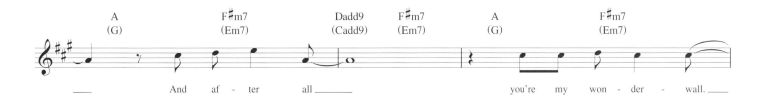

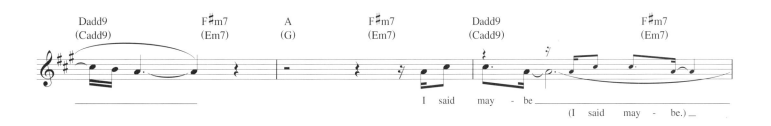

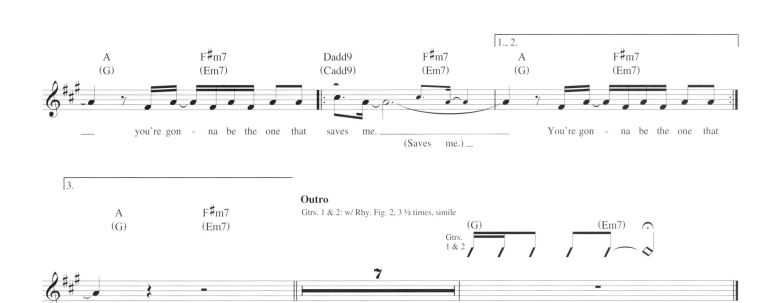

You've Got Another Thing Comin'

Words and Music by Glenn Tipton, Rob Halford and K.K. Downing

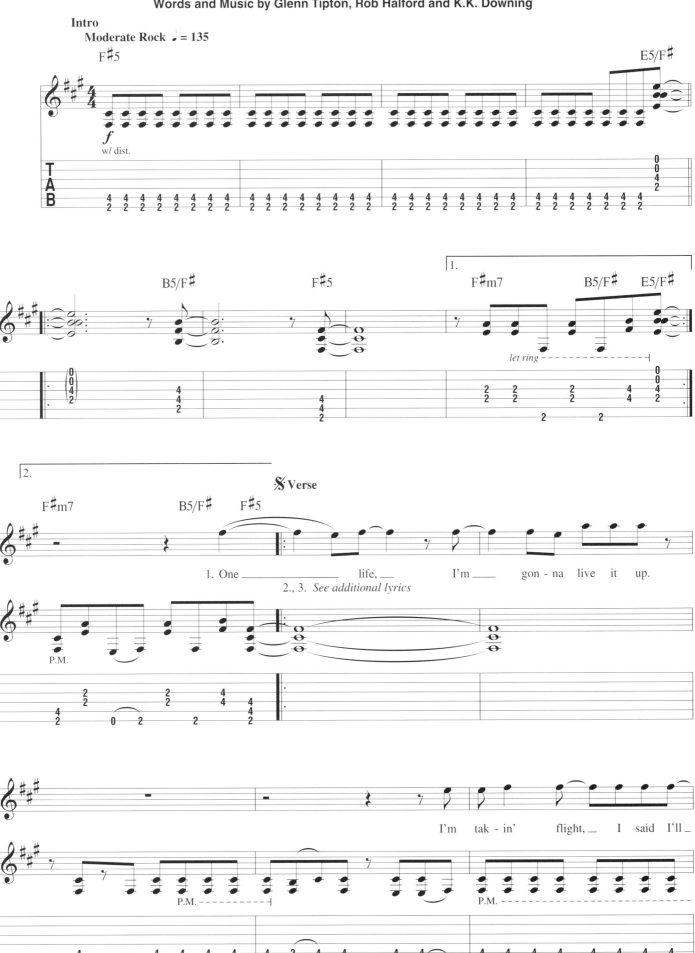

379

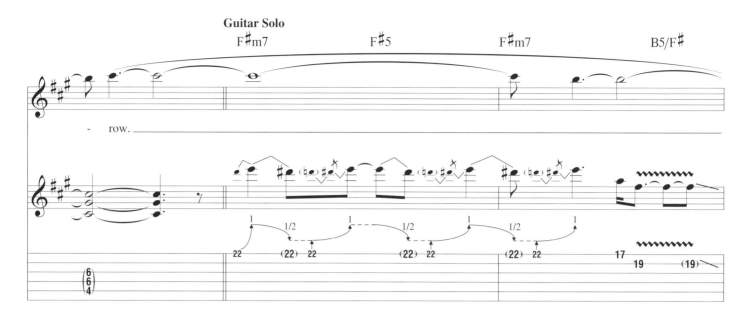

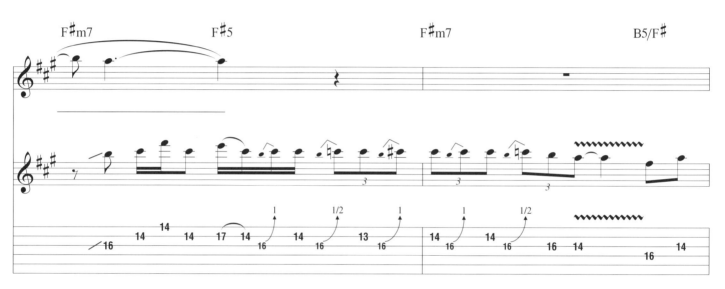

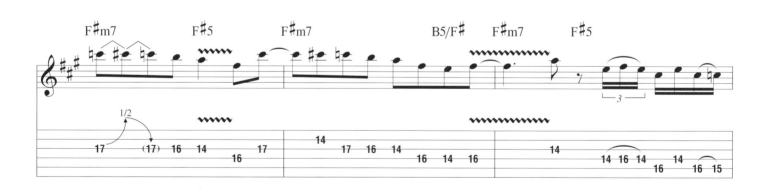

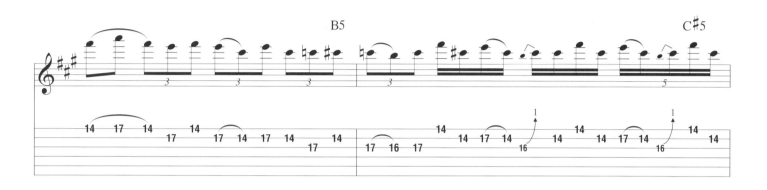

D.S. al Coda
(take 2nd ending)

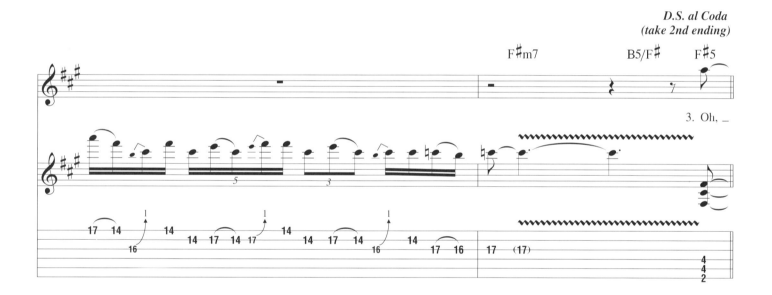

3. Oh, __

Coda

Interlude

You've got an - oth - er thing, ah. __

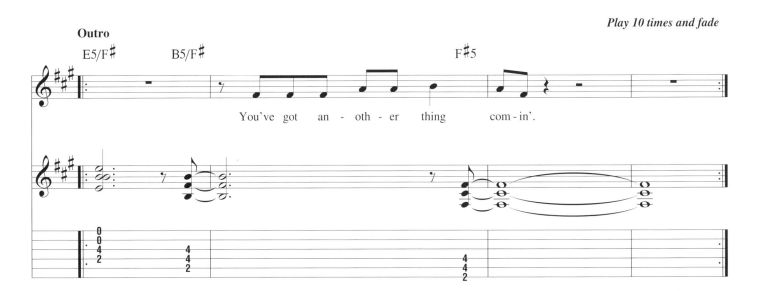

Play 10 times and fade

Outro

You've got an - oth - er thing com - in'.

Additional Lyrics

2. That's right, here's where the talking ends.
   Well listen, this night there'll be some action spent.
   Drive hard. Callin' all the shots.
   I got an ace card comin' down the rocks.

Pre-Chorus 2. If you think I'll sit around while you chip away my brain,
   Listen, I ain't foolin' and you'd better think again.
   Out there is a fortune waiting to be had.
   If you think I'll let it go you're mad.

3. Oh, so hot. No time to take a rest, yeah.
   Act tough, ain't room for second best.
   Real strong. Got me some security.
   Hey, I'm a big smash; I'm goin' for infinity, yeah.

GUITAR NOTATION LEGEND

Guitar music can be notated three different ways: on a *musical staff*, in *tablature*, and in *rhythm slashes*.

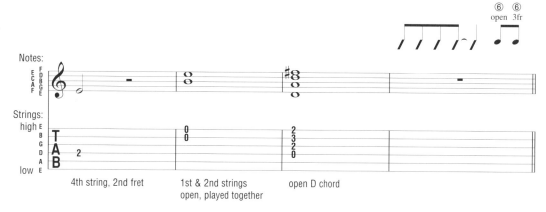

RHYTHM SLASHES are written above the staff. Strum chords in the rhythm indicated. Use the chord diagrams found at the top of the first page of the transcription for the appropriate chord voicings. Round noteheads indicate single notes.

THE MUSICAL STAFF shows pitches and rhythms and is divided by bar lines into measures. Pitches are named after the first seven letters of the alphabet.

TABLATURE graphically represents the guitar fingerboard. Each horizontal line represents a string, and each number represents a fret.

4th string, 2nd fret   1st & 2nd strings open, played together   open D chord

Definitions for Special Guitar Notation

HALF-STEP BEND: Strike the note and bend up 1/2 step.

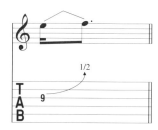

WHOLE-STEP BEND: Strike the note and bend up one step.

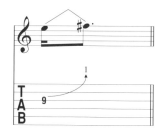

GRACE NOTE BEND: Strike the note and immediately bend up as indicated.

SLIGHT (MICROTONE) BEND: Strike the note and bend up 1/4 step.

BEND AND RELEASE: Strike the note and bend up as indicated, then release back to the original note. Only the first note is struck.

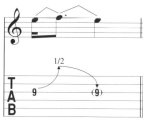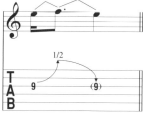

PRE-BEND: Bend the note as indicated, then strike it.

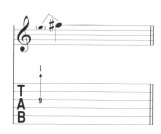

PRE-BEND AND RELEASE: Bend the note as indicated. Strike it and release the bend back to the original note.

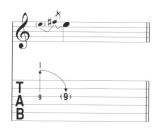

UNISON BEND: Strike the two notes simultaneously and bend the lower note up to the pitch of the higher.

VIBRATO: The string is vibrated by rapidly bending and releasing the note with the fretting hand.

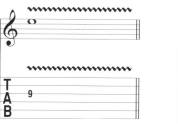

WIDE VIBRATO: The pitch is varied to a greater degree by vibrating with the fretting hand.

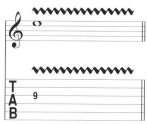

HAMMER-ON: Strike the first (lower) note with one finger, then sound the higher note (on the same string) with another finger by fretting it without picking.

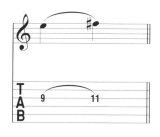

PULL-OFF: Place both fingers on the notes to be sounded. Strike the first note and without picking, pull the finger off to sound the second (lower) note.

LEGATO SLIDE: Strike the first note and then slide the same fret-hand finger up or down to the second note. The second note is not struck.

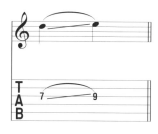

SHIFT SLIDE: Same as legato slide, except the second note is struck.

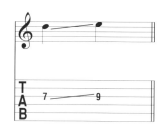

TRILL: Very rapidly alternate between the notes indicated by continuously hammering on and pulling off.

TAPPING: Hammer ("tap") the fret indicated with the pick-hand index or middle finger and pull off to the note fretted by the fret hand.

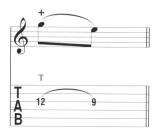

NATURAL HARMONIC: Strike the note while the fret-hand lightly touches the string directly over the fret indicated.

PINCH HARMONIC: The note is fretted normally and a harmonic is produced by adding the edge of the thumb or the tip of the index finger of the pick hand to the normal pick attack.

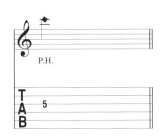

HARP HARMONIC: The note is fretted normally and a harmonic is produced by gently resting the pick hand's index finger directly above the indicated fret (in parentheses) while the pick hand's thumb or pick assists by plucking the appropriate string.

PICK SCRAPE: The edge of the pick is rubbed down (or up) the string, producing a scratchy sound.

MUFFLED STRINGS: A percussive sound is produced by laying the fret hand across the string(s) without depressing, and striking them with the pick hand.

PALM MUTING: The note is partially muted by the pick hand lightly touching the string(s) just before the bridge.

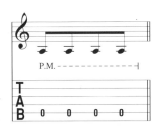

RAKE: Drag the pick across the strings indicated with a single motion.

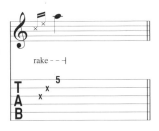

TREMOLO PICKING: The note is picked as rapidly and continuously as possible.

ARPEGGIATE: Play the notes of the chord indicated by quickly rolling them from bottom to top.

VIBRATO BAR DIVE AND RETURN: The pitch of the note or chord is dropped a specified number of steps (in rhythm), then returned to the original pitch.

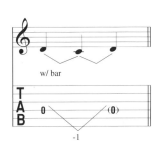

VIBRATO BAR SCOOP: Depress the bar just before striking the note, then quickly release the bar.

VIBRATO BAR DIP: Strike the note and then immediately drop a specified number of steps, then release back to the original pitch.

Additional Musical Definitions

(accent)	• Accentuate note (play it louder).	
(accent)	• Accentuate note with great intensity.	
(staccato)	• Play the note short.	
⊓	• Downstroke	
V	• Upstroke	
D.S. al Coda	• Go back to the sign (𝄋), then play until the measure marked "*To Coda*," then skip to the section labelled "Coda."	
D.C. al Fine	• Go back to the beginning of the song and play until the measure marked "*Fine*" (end).	

Rhy. Fig. • Label used to recall a recurring accompaniment pattern (usually chordal).

Riff • Label used to recall composed, melodic lines (usually single notes) which recur.

Fill • Label used to identify a brief melodic figure which is to be inserted into the arrangement.

Rhy. Fill • A chordal version of a Fill.

tacet • Instrument is silent (drops out).

• Repeat measures between signs.

• When a repeated section has different endings, play the first ending only the first time and the second ending only the second time.

NOTE: Tablature numbers in parentheses mean:
1. The note is being sustained over a system (note in standard notation is tied), or
2. The note is sustained, but a new articulation (such as a hammer-on, pull-off, slide or vibrato) begins, or
3. The note is a barely audible "ghost" note (note in standard notation is also in parentheses).